Building
Literacy in
Social Studies

Strategies for Improving Comprehension
and Critical Thinking

Donna Ogle
Ron Klemp
Bill McBride

ASCD

Association for Supervision and Curriculum Development
Alexandria, Virginia USA

Association for Supervision and Curriculum Development
1703 N. Beauregard St. • Alexandria, VA 22311-1714 USA
Phone: 800-933-2723 or 703-578-9600 • Fax: 703-575-5400
Web site: www.ascd.org • E-mail: member@ascd.org
Author guidelines: www.ascd.org/write

Gene R. Carter, *Executive Director;* Nancy Modrak, *Director of Publishing;* Julie Houtz, *Director of Book Editing & Production;* Deborah Siegel, *Project Manager;* Catherine Guyer, *Senior Graphic Designer;* Circle Graphics, *Typesetter;* Vivian Coss, *Production Specialist*

The image of Mohandas Gandhi on the cover appears with the permission of The Granger Collection, New York. The image of Martin Luther King Jr. on the cover appears with the permission of AP/Wide World Photos. The image of the Great Wall of China on page 87 appears with permission of AP/Wide World Photos.

All Web links in this book are correct as of the publication date below but may have become inactive or otherwise modified since that time. If you notice a deactivated or changed link, please e-mail books@ascd.org with the words "Link Update" in the subject line. In your message, please specify the Web link, the book title, and the page number on which the link appears.

PAPERBACK ISBN: 978-1-4166-0558-4   ASCD product #106010   s4/07
Also available as an e-book through ebrary, netLibrary, and many online booksellers (see Books in Print for the ISBNs).

Quantity discounts for the paperback edition only: 10–49 copies, 10%; 50+ copies, 15%; for 1,000 or more copies, call 800-933-2723, ext. 5634, or 703-575-5634. For desk copies: member@ascd.org.

Library of Congress Cataloging-in-Publication Data

Ogle, Donna.
  Building literacy in social studies : strategies for improving comprehension and critical thinking / Donna Ogle, Ron Klemp, and Bill McBride.
      p. cm.
  Includes bibliographical references and index.
  ISBN 978-1-4166-0558-4 (pbk. : alk. paper) 1. Content area reading. 2. Social sciences—Study and teaching (Middle school) 3. Social sciences—Study and teaching (Secondary) I. Klemp, Ronald M. II. McBride, Bill, 1953- III. Title.

  LB1050.455.O35 2007
  300.71'2—dc22

                                                                    2006039303

18 17 16 15 14 13 12 11 10 09 08 07   1 2 3 4 5 6 7 8 9 10 11 12

Building Literacy in Social Studies

Preface

I know of no safer depository of the ultimate powers of the society but the people themselves; and if we think them not enlightened enough to exercise their control with a wholesome discretion, the remedy is not to take it from them, but to inform their discretion by education.

Thomas Jefferson

Our students will soon be the citizens making decisions that will influence the direction of the world. The future is in their hands; their sensitivity to the variety of cultures and perspectives that influence the course of history will be critical as members of a global community. Yet, if current trends continue, few of our students will become active citizens in our democratic society. The percentage of eligible voters in the United States who take part in their civic responsibilities is embarrassingly low for such a wealthy country with universal public education. As astronaut John Glenn and Leslie Hergert note in Carl Glickman's book *Letters to the Next President: What We Can Do About the Real Crisis in Public Education* (2004):

> Today, American citizens are more educated than ever before—a larger percentage attend school longer—yet, civic involvement is on the wane. As adults' civic involvement has declined, so has that of the nation's

youth, and at even sharper rates of decline. Numerous studies have documented youth's low voter participation rate, negative opinion of elected officials, and general alienation from government and politics. Young people have learned apathy, not engagement. (p. 202)

Part of the responsibility placed on social studies teachers is to give students the skills and motivation to become informed citizens. Many students, however, care little about studying civics, government, or history. We are acutely aware that teachers are having a difficult time getting students to actively read and reflect on materials provided for the development of their knowledge about social studies themes and topics. This book will provide both the conceptual basis and the classroom strategies to help teachers actively engage their students in developing the skills needed to become informed citizens. As Grant Wiggins and Jay McTighe (2005) note, students need to be examining big ideas of "enduring understandings." Students need to be engaged in problems that matter to them and that have more than one solution or right answer. Thus it is vitally important that students learn to use a variety of sources to develop concepts about our society, government, and history. Students need to learn to work collaboratively and cooperatively on meaningful projects, regularly connecting what they are learning to their own communities and to world events. They need strategies to help them think critically about what they read, what they hear in and outside of school, and what they view in the media. Taking action is a natural impulse for adolescents that can be nurtured to help them become involved citizens.

Social studies teachers have unusual opportunities now to introduce students to a wide variety of materials in addition to textbooks. Computer technology and the Internet provide a wealth of visual and firsthand information for their use. Electronic resources available through the Library of Congress, for example, can invite reluctant learners into the reality of American history with photographs, posters, songs, and primary documents from the past. The availability of these primary source documents adds to the possibilities for teachers and students. With more materials available comes the opportunity to help students develop critical reading and thinking skills through document-based questions. By comparing interpretations and information in different materials, students can learn to look for accurate sources and develop understandings of different points of view.

Building Literacy in Social Studies is a sourcebook of research-based strategies for teachers and students. Chapters 1 through 5 provide research and strategies on the reading process, on fostering engaged learning, on vocabulary development for older students, on classroom organization, and on civic engagement. Each of these five chapters begins and ends with a fictitious scenario of a social studies teacher teaching today's students. At the beginning of each chapter, this teacher demonstrates ineffective strategies for helping students become engaged in learning. At the end of the chapter we bring the teacher back; however, this time he models some of the specific strategies discussed in the chapter. The addition of these scenarios enlivens the text and also shows readers how effective strategies can transform their classrooms.

The format of the book changes with Chapter 6. The last three chapters provide specific literacy strategies for students in the areas of textbook literacy, primary and secondary documents, and newspaper and magazine literacy. A number of practical and engaging strategies are provided in each of these areas. Each strategy presented includes the following four elements: (1) instructions that explain to the teacher how to model the strategy; (2) instructions that explain to the student how to perform the strategy; (3) a completed model or graphic organizer of the strategy; and (4) a blank model or graphic organizer for teacher and student use.

Alexis de Tocqueville noted that "there is nothing more arduous than the apprenticeship of liberty." Creating informed, engaged citizens is arduous work. To be critical thinkers, students must be critical readers. To be critical readers, they must first be literal readers. This book presents research-based tools to help students understand the varied materials that represent past and present events; analyze, synthesize, and evaluate these materials; and most important, reflect on and make informed decisions as active citizens in today's democracy.

PART

1

Reading Social Studies Texts

1

John Reaf watched the students crowding through the door of his U.S. History class, smiling at their faces, which reflected a variety of ethnic backgrounds. The first day of school—always a challenge. How to make a good impression yet still set proper boundaries? The veteran teacher felt ready, though. He had lined up the desks in neat rows and placed a new textbook on each desktop.

The noise of a desk scraping across the floor caught Mr. Reaf's attention. Two of the boys had shoved each other in the second row, trying to sit by a particular girl. Mr. Reaf smiled to himself. He'd set up a seating chart once he got to know them. Slowly the remaining students found seats, leaning across to each other, laughing quietly and casting their eyes up at him. None of the students opened the new textbooks.

Feeling a bit intimidated, Mr. Reaf looked down at his desk for his roll sheet. On top of it was the document that the social studies department chair had handed him that morning. He glanced at the title: National Council for the Social Studies, Disciplinary Standards, Teacher Expectations.

"Well," Mr. Reaf thought, "this could be helpful on the first day." He read quickly down the list of bulleted items:

• Enable learners to develop historical comprehension in order that they might reconstruct the literal meaning of a historical passage; identify the central question(s) addressed in historical narrative; draw upon data in historical maps, charts, and other graphic organizers; and draw upon visual, literary, or musical sources.

• Assist learners in acquiring knowledge of historical content in United States history in order to ask large and searching questions that compare patterns of continuity and change in the history and values of the many peoples who have contributed to the development of the continent of North America.

"Noble goals, high expectations," he thought. "Well, that's what we're supposed to set nowadays—high expectations." He looked out at the waiting faces.

"Good morning, class. My name is Mr. Reaf. I want to welcome you to your American History class. This is my 17th year as a teacher. Yes, that's right. I have taught longer than most of you have been alive. Over my career I have also taught English, P.E., science, and health, and coached a number of sports. As a coach I never tolerated any misbehavior on the field. I'm sure that will not be a problem here.

"Now, that being said, would you please open your books to the beginning of Chapter 1? Appropriately, Chapter 1 begins on page one. Please begin reading while I call the roll. At the end of roll, I'm going to ask you questions about the first two pages."

The students stared blankly at him. None of them opened their textbook.

"Open your books, please. The beginning of Chapter 1," he repeated.

All smiles disappeared. Several boys slouched in their seats. One or two of the girls began turning pages. He heard bubble-gum pop.

"No gum chewing, please. Swallow it or throw it away."

"First boundary set," he thought.

Mr. Reaf began calling the roll. Students answered as he called their names. Having marked only two students absent, he looked back up at the class. Most were staring into their books.

"OK, let's see what we learned." Mr. Reaf opened his teacher's edition to page one. He glanced at the questions in the margin.

"How long ago did the first Americans enter this continent? Anyone? Anyone?"

No answer. No hands were raised. Mr. Reaf glanced back down at his roll sheet.

"Mr. Hernandez. How about you? When did the first Americans enter this continent?"

Wide-eyed, Carlos Hernandez looked up at the teacher.

"¿Que?"

Eyebrows raised, Mr. Reaf asked, "Mr. Hernandez, do you speak English?"

"Of course, man. You think I'm stupid or something?"

"No, no. Not at all, Mr. Hernandez. Did you read page one?"

"Yes, but I don't understand what it's saying, man."

"Oh, my," thought Mr. Reaf. "Here we go again. How many of my students can't understand the textbook?" He and the boy stared blankly at each other. They sighed in unison.

* * * * * * *

Sound familiar? Many teachers today are finding more and more students unable to comprehend their textbooks. Whether they are nonnative-English speakers or just struggling readers, they are not able to read the curriculum materials. And because most social studies teachers have had little or no training in teaching reading, the inability of middle and high school students to get information from texts becomes a formidable problem.

The goal of social studies is to teach students to read and think critically so that they will become informed and engaged citizens. What, then, can social studies teachers do to help struggling readers in their classrooms? To answer this question, it is necessary to answer two prerequisite questions. First, why are social studies texts so difficult to comprehend? And second, what skills and strategies do students need to become expert readers of history? What exactly is it that Carlos Hernandez needs to be able to do?

The answers to these questions point to a host of strategies that social studies teachers can use to help *all* students glean more from informational texts. Each chapter in this book provides a variety of practical, research-based strategies to help students become engaged readers and civically responsible adults. But first, some background information may be helpful.

Why Are Social Studies Texts So Difficult to Read?

There are a host of reasons why students find social studies texts hard to understand. One of the chief reasons has as much to do with today's students as today's textbooks. Many students have a poor attitude about the subject of history. They feel that studying about "old events and dead people" has little relevance to their lives. Recent brain research has shown that a student's emotional attitude has a profound effect on engagement, learning, and retention (Jensen, 1998; Sousa, 2001; Sprenger, 1999). Consequently, when social studies is taught only in the context of past events and not related to today's issues, teachers fight an uphill battle for students' attention. When choosing textbooks, teachers should look for texts that make connections with present-day events and also include activities that actively engage adolescents.

No matter which textbooks teachers use, most likely the texts will be difficult for many readers to comprehend. The readability of social studies texts is affected by a number of factors:

• Students may have no prior knowledge about the concepts, such as foreign cultures, people, places, and previous eras. Prior knowledge is a key determinant of student engagement and comprehension. As Alexander and Murphy (1998) note, "Existing knowledge serves as the foundation of all future learning by guiding organization of representations, by serving as a basis of association with new information, and by coloring and filtering all new experiences" (p. 28).

• Social studies texts cover a large amount of information. A typical middle or high school textbook includes 800 to 1,200 pages of facts, anecdotes, statistics, questions, activities, and graphic images. Students have difficulty discerning which concepts to focus on and which are the most important to retain.

• Because of the large amount of information, teachers may feel pressured to cover material quickly and superficially, which hinders student engagement, comprehension, and retention.

• Social studies texts are filled with abstract "-isms" about economics, religion, government, and culture. A student who doesn't understand key concepts such as imperialism or Buddhism can't understand the main ideas of a chapter.

• Social studies texts also contain a great deal of academic vocabulary—content-specific terminology with meanings specific to history or government. For example, when students read in Section 10 of the

U.S. Constitution that a state may not make gold or silver *tender,* they may think that states can't make money that is *soft* or *easily crushed.* Students need time to learn the multiple meanings of terms. Through multiple exposures to words, they develop sensitivity to their meanings (Stahl & Fairbanks, 1986).

• Students who come from minority populations may feel disengaged from a country's history and politics. Within some texts, minority students may see their cultures described only in negative ways, such as African Americans pictured as slaves with no mention of the rich African culture that they possessed when they arrived in America.

• Social studies texts, tests, and standards often require students to analyze and synthesize much information—a skill that they may not have been explicitly taught and that assumes comprehension of the material.

• The ability to understand and summarize the literal narrative in social studies textbooks is related to a student's age and reading ability. Britt, Rouet, Georgi, and Perfetti (1994) found that students in 4th through 6th grades gave one of three types of summaries of their reading: a simple list of facts, a substory rather than the main idea, or a full recounting of the main events. Younger students more often recounted a list of facts or were sidetracked by a substory that had been included to enliven the text. However, older students with greater reading ability could provide a better representation of the text's narrative structure, both recounting the main events and showing the causal linkage of those events.

• Readers who are less able may also struggle with the wealth of visual information—such as maps, graphs, and charts—in social studies texts. Hegarty, Carpenter, and Just (1991) note that "when the text is accompanied by a diagram, the comprehension process is more involved because the information that readers have to integrate is presented in two different media. It takes added attention and flexibility to integrate information from the narrative, linear text with material presented in graphic forms" (p. 652).

With so many factors affecting the readability of social studies texts, teachers such as Mr. Reaf see a wide variation in the comprehension attained by their students. Struggling readers often simply don't get the literal meaning. Other students may be able to read fluently; however, they read the text as a set of facts rather than as a writer's reconstruction of a set of events. These "mock readers," as Wineburg (2001) calls them, read to gather information rather than reading critically as a historian.

Without literal comprehension, however, a student cannot attain even the level of mock reader. Let's discuss the differences between a struggling and a fluent reader first. Then we'll look at the characteristics of students who can get the literal meaning, but who ignore the "human subtext" of a writer's assumptions and biases.

Reading for Basic Comprehension

Fluent readers have acquired a variety of comprehension strategies that they bring to bear on any text. Fluent readers not only have these strategies, they also are aware of when to use them and which strategies to use. Fluent readers are in charge of the process, monitoring how they read and adjusting to ensure success (Alvermann, 2001; Duke & Pearson, 2002). Reading experts speak of the sequence of instruction in reading as a three-part process. A fluent reader applies reading strategies to a text before reading, during reading, and after reading.

Before fluent readers delve deeply into a text, they use a host of skills and strategies to promote comprehension. Using text features and graphics, fluent readers make predictions about the content and activate their background knowledge to impose meaning upon the print. The chart in Figure 1.1 compares fluent readers with struggling readers, such as Carlos, as they prepare to read.

Once fluent readers begin reading in earnest, they add another set of skills and strategies to promote comprehension. These readers continue to use text features and visual information to predict and connect to content, but now they begin monitoring their comprehension; determining key ideas; asking mental questions about the content; noting differences and similarities; visualizing people, places, and events; rereading what is unclear; and, often when reading school texts, taking notes to aid retention. Figure 1.2 compares the skills used by a fluent reader

---

Figure 1.1
Differences Between Struggling and Fluent Readers *Before* Reading

Struggling Reader

• Sees reading as a difficult task filled with failure and expects to gain little, if anything, from the task except frustration and embarrassment.

• Doesn't possess prior knowledge about the general topic or doesn't connect existing knowledge with the text.

• Doesn't try to understand the text until questioned after reading.

• Reads one word at a time or groups words together but not necessarily in meaningful phrases.

• Doesn't possess background knowledge of abstract terms often used in social studies texts that describe government, economics, culture, or religion, such as *colonialism* or *Buddhism.*

• Doesn't preview the text to note such features as headings, subheads, vocabulary words in bold type, information in the sidebars, pictures, maps, graphs, and charts.

• Begins reading without predicting what the text might be about, doesn't plan what to read in what order, and doesn't know on what part of the text to focus the most attention.

• Begins reading without a purpose other than decoding for meaning.

Fluent Reader

• Sees reading as an opportunity to gain knowledge about the world and to feel more self-secure in school and among peers.

• Possesses and activates relevant background knowledge from previous reading, viewing, or conversations about the topic.

• Uses strategies throughout the reading process to construct meaning.

• Groups words in meaningful phrases noting punctuation and transition words that show text structure.

• Possesses background knowledge of abstract terms often used in social studies texts from previous years of wide reading.

• Surveys textbook features to understand the context of the reading task and to begin setting purposes for reading.

• Predicts the text content by surveying the text features and then plans how and what to read in what order.

• Begins reading to answer questions about the writer's ideas, purposes, and biases.

Figure 1.2
Differences Between Struggling and Fluent Readers *During* Reading

Struggling Reader

• Possesses few, if any, decoding skills beyond basic phonemic awareness.

• Identifies words individually or in small clusters without using meaning to group words into larger comprehensible units.

• Skips unknown words and doesn't reread to decipher their meaning.

• Doesn't recognize that informational texts have different structures than narrative fiction and consequently doesn't use these structures to aid in comprehension.

• Doesn't stop to visualize descriptions of important people, places, and events to help "see" what the text is stating.

• Ignores maps, graphs, charts, and other important visual information.

• Possesses few, if any, "fix-up" strategies, such as using context clues, text structure, structural analysis, or visual information, to apply when comprehension is lost.

• Reads through text once, and if comprehension is lost, either continues "reading" or quits altogether.

• May retain only substories presented as colorful additions to enliven the text rather than core events (Britt et al., 1994).

• Doesn't understand the context of primary sources or the archaic language in which they are often written.

• Doesn't question the writer's assumptions or intentions, reading only to discern facts.

Fluent Reader

• Possesses and applies a variety of decoding skills, such as context clues and structural analysis (word parts and roots).

• Reads fluently by using punctuation and meaning to group words into larger phrases that make meaningful statements.

• Skips unknown words but monitors comprehension to see if the word's meaning is critical, and if it is, returns to the word to apply comprehension strategies.

• Recognizes the *signal words* that show various text structures, such as cause/effect, problem/solution, comparison/contrast, and sequence, and uses these to aid in meaning.

• Visualizes important descriptions and constantly tests these mental pictures against what the text is stating.

• Understands that visual information often restates the information in the text and uses this information to check for comprehension.

• Possesses a variety of "fix-up" strategies and applies them appropriately when comprehension breaks down.

• Monitors comprehension, recognizes where and when comprehension is lost, and rereads for clarification.

• Identifies and retains the core events of the text as separate from substories or anecdotes.

• Understands the context of primary sources and applies vocabulary and comprehension strategies to figure out archaic language.

• Continually questions the writer's ideas, assumptions, background, and biases.

during the reading process with those lacking in a struggling reader.

After finishing a text, fluent readers begin to reflect on what they have read. Fluent readers continue to monitor their comprehension to decide whether to reread parts that may still be confusing or unclear. With informational texts, they may begin to question the validity and reliability of main points or persuasive arguments. Fluent readers may question sources and do further research about the topic. Figure 1.3 compares the skills that fluent readers use after reading with those lacking in a struggling reader.

Obviously, when the entire reading process is considered, struggling readers may lack skills and strategies needed to make literal sense of texts. However, even if readers have acquired these skills and can read fluently, they still may not be able to read critically, especially with historical texts. Reading history as an expert means acting as an investigator who attempts to reconstruct the past from multiple documents, all of which have their own subtexts.

Reading as a Historian

Many social studies teachers are changing the focus of teaching history from a set of known facts to a process of investigation, modeled on how actual historians work. Students are learning that history is open to interpretation. Students are being taught to approach history like historians who analyze multiple primary and secondary sources and artifacts related to a single event, questioning earlier conclusions drawn from them. As Wineburg and Martin (2004) note in *Educational Leadership,* "The place to teach

---

Figure 1.3
Differences Between Struggling and Fluent Readers *After* Reading

Struggling Reader

• Doesn't reread any passages that are unclear.

• Doesn't analyze the author's viewpoints to see if the ideas are well supported.

• Doesn't reflect on the text to draw conclusions about the author's viewpoints.

• Sees the textbook as containing a sequence of accurate historical facts that must be memorized.

• Doesn't evaluate the author's views against other sources and personal viewpoints.

• Doesn't pay attention to sources of information and doesn't question the veracity of the information.

Fluent Reader

• Returns to the text to reread difficult passages or graphics and clarifies their meaning.

• Questions the viewpoints of the author regarding the support given through facts and evidence.

• Uses facts and opinions expressed by the author to draw conclusions about the author's views.

• Understands that historical facts are open to interpretation.

• Evaluates the author's views and compares them against other sources and personal viewpoints.

• Evaluates the sources cited by authors as to their reliability.

---

students to ask questions about truth and evidence in our digital age is the history and social studies classroom, and we should not delay" (p. 42).

Using multiple documents poses another set of challenges for readers, however. Some students are unable to use the organizational patterns of historical texts to promote comprehension. Textbooks may be mostly narrative, using a combination of structures: chronological, sequential, and cause-and-effect (Britt et al., 1994). The primary purpose of the textbook is to impart factual information. Primary and secondary sources, on the other hand, may have very different structures and purposes. These documents are often created in some rhetorical format, such as propaganda leaflets, political notices, essays, memoirs, journals, or cartoons. Texts such as these may not have main ideas explicitly stated, and the relationships between ideas may not be clearly expressed. Numerous studies by Armbruster (1996) have shown that comprehension weakens when main ideas are not clearly stated or when irrelevant details are included.

The writer's purpose can influence the organizational structure of a document. For example, a propaganda leaflet may use a compare/contrast structure to illustrate opposing viewpoints. Primary and secondary sources may vary from the sequential narrative form that students see in textbooks, instead using structures such as problem/solution, main idea with supporting details, or compare/contrast. When students do not recognize a text's structure, their comprehension is impaired. Reading researchers have shown that successful learners use text structures, or "frames," to guide their learning (Armbruster & Anderson, 1984; Buehl, 2001; Jones, Palincsar, Ogle,

& Carr, 1987). Students who identify basic text structures and graphically depict the relationships among ideas improve both comprehension and recall (Armbruster & Anderson, 1984; RAND Reading Study Group, 2003). For example, a fluent reader who recognizes a problem stated in a text will begin looking for a solution.

The use of a variety of documents, rather than one textbook, requires additional cognitive skills of the reader. As Britt and colleagues (1994) note, "Students must consider the conditions in which [the documents] were produced (by whom, when, for what audience). Thus, students have to be aware of the *source* information provided with the documents, in addition to their context" (p. 71). Also, rather than unquestioningly accepting facts, as students often do with their textbooks, readers of multiple documents often face different interpretations of the same event based on contradictory evidence. The documents themselves also have varying degrees of reference; for example, a secondary source may refer to a primary source. Hence, a student must be able to mentally organize a large amount of disparate and conflicting information and make literal sense out of it.

Sam Wineburg (2001) notes that true historians comprehend a *subtext* on the literal, inferred, and critical levels. These subtexts include what the writer is saying literally but also any possible biases and unconscious assumptions the writer has about the world. Historians "try to reconstruct authors' purposes, intentions, and goals" as well as understand authors' "assumptions, world view, and beliefs" (pp. 65–66). As noted, Wineburg calls readers who believe exactly what they read "mock" readers. "Actual" readers take a critical and skeptical stance toward the text.

Based on Wineburg's work at Stanford, Judy Lightfoot has constructed a chart detailing the characteristics of an expert reader of history versus a novice reader. With her kind permission, that chart is reprinted as Figure 1.4.

Hunting for Meaning

As we've shown, becoming a critical reader and thinker involves acquiring a number of skills and strategies. What, then, can social studies teachers do to help students

---

Figure 1.4
How Experts and Novices Tend to Read Historical Texts

Experts . . .	Novices . . .
Seek to *discover context and know content.*	Seek only to *know content.*
Ask what the text *does* (purpose).	Ask what the text *says* ("facts").
Understand the *subtexts* of the writer's language.	Understand the *literal meanings* of the writer's language.
See any text as a *construction* of a vision of the world.	See texts as a *description* of the world.
See texts as *made by persons with a view of events.*	See texts as *accounts of what really happened.*
Consider *textbooks less trustworthy* than other kinds of documents.	Consider *textbooks very trustworthy* sources.
Assume *bias* in texts.	Assume *neutrality, objectivity* in texts.
Consider word choice (connotation, denotation) and *tone.*	*Ignore word choice* and *tone.*
Read slowly, *simulating a social exchange between two readers,* "actual" and "mock."	Read to *gather lots of information.*
Resurrect texts, like a magician.	*Process* texts, like a computer.
Compare texts to judge different, perhaps divergent accounts of the same event or topic.	*Learn the "right answer."*
Get *interested* in *contradictions, ambiguity.*	*Resolve* or *ignore contradictions, ambiguity.*
Check *sources* of document.	Read the *document* only.
Read like *witnesses to living, evolving events.*	Read like *seekers of solid facts.*
Read like *lawyers making* a case.	Read like *jurors listening to* a case someone made.
Acknowledge *uncertainty and complexity* in the reading with qualifiers and concessions.	Communicate "*the truth*" of the reading, sounding as certain as possible.

Source: From Judy Lightfoot, "Outline of Sam Wineburg's Central Arguments in 'On the Reading of Historical Texts.'" Available: http://home.earthlink.net/~judylightfoot/Wineburg.html. Based on "On the Reading of Historical Texts: Notes on the Breach Between School and Academy," by Samuel Wineburg, *American Educational Research Journal,* Fall 1991, pp. 495–519.

---

comprehend the literal meaning and also read as an expert historian? The rest of this book is filled with strategies that can help students become better readers. One way to begin is with a Scavenger Hunt.

At the beginning of the year, Mr. Reaf might show his students how to survey the table of contents of their textbook by using a Scavenger Hunt. A Table of Contents Scavenger Hunt requires students to preview what they will cover during the course (see Figure 1.5 for an example). Later during the first quarter, Mr. Reaf can show his students how to survey the beginning of a chapter to identify key ideas and terms to be covered.

Doty, Cameron, and Barton (2003) state that "teaching reading in social studies is not so much about teaching students basic reading skills as it is about teaching students how to use reading as a tool of thinking and learning" (p. 1). Going back to the scenario that opened this chapter, with Mr. Reaf and Carlos Hernandez staring blankly at each other on the first day of school, perhaps the first change the teacher may want to make is to find a way to engage Carlos and his peers.

* * * * * * *

John Reaf watched the students crowding through the door of his U.S. History class, smiling at their faces, which reflected a variety of ethnic backgrounds. The first day of school—always a challenge. How to show students that they are expected to participate and at the same time make them feel successful? He looked out at the expectant faces as the last two students found seats.

"Good morning, class. My name is Mr. Reaf. I'll be your American history teacher. We're very fortunate to have brand new textbooks this year; but whenever you get anything new, I've found it's a good idea to look it over before you dive in. Do any of you play sports?"

A number of hands shot up in the air. Mr. Reaf chose a tall Hispanic boy sitting in the back corner. He walked back to the boy's desk, watching the boy's eyes widen as he approached him. Mr. Reaf reached out his hand.

"Hi, I'm Mr. Reaf."

The boy just stared for a moment. Then he shook the teacher's hand, smiling.

"It's Carlos, man."

"Thank you. Nice to meet you, Carlos."

A number of students laughed at Mr. Reaf's remark.

"Carlos, what sport do you play?"

Carlos smiled. "I'm one of the ends on the football team."

"Great," said Mr. Reaf. "Now, right before you take off from the scrimmage line, what do you do?"

Carlos thought for a second.

"Well, I look out at the defense."

"Why?" asked Mr. Reaf.

"To see what defense they are in and who's covering me."

"So, you survey the defense to decide how to attack it?"

"Right."

"Well, Carlos, and all of you sports fans out there, that is exactly what we should do with our new textbooks."

Mr. Reaf lifted up a copy of the new text from Carlos's desk.

"I'm sure some of you don't look forward to tackling this new book, but this year I want to show you some great plays, or strategies, that will not only help you read this book, but every textbook in every class."

The eyes of many students widened at this point.

Figure 1.5
Table of Contents Scavenger Hunt

1. How many chapters are in your textbook?
   There are 32 chapters in the book.

2. The chapters are organized into larger units. Write the titles of the units below.
   Unit 1: *Three Worlds Meet: Beginning–1763*
   Unit 2: *Creating a New Nation: 1763–1791*
   Unit 3: *The Early Republic: 1789–1844*
   Unit 4: *A Changing Nation: 1810–1860*
   Unit 5: *A Nation Divided and Rebuilt: 1846–1877*
   Unit 6: *America Transformed: 1860–1914*
   Unit 7: *Modern America Emerges: 1880–1920*
   Unit 8: *Depression, War, and Recovery: 1919–1960*
   Unit 9: *Tensions at Home and Abroad: 1954–Present*

3. Turn to Unit 1 on page viii. What two types of strategies are taught at the beginning of the book?
   Strategies for Studying History and Test-Taking Strategies and Practice

4. What handbook is provided at the beginning of the book, and why is this important?
   Geography Handbook. Because history is directly related to place.

5. Who do you think the "Three Worlds" are that will meet in Unit 1?
   Native Americans, Europeans, West Africans

6. Chapters contain special features that are printed in blue print. What three special features do you find in Chapter 1?
   Technology of the Time: The Mound Builders; Interactive Primary Source: The Iroquois Great Law of Peace; History Workshop: Create and Decode a Pictograph

7. In which chapter and time period of years will you learn about the 13 colonies?
   Chapter 3, between 1585 and 1732

8. Using the pictures in the margins of the page, in which unit does George Washington appear?
   Unit 2: Creating a New Nation: 1763–1791

9. In which chapter will you find the Declaration of Independence, and why is it called a "primary source"?
   Chapter 6; it is a primary source because it is an original document.

10. What two special handbooks do you see in Chapter 8?
    Constitution Handbook and Citizenship Handbook

11. In which chapters do you learn about the Civil War, and whose picture is presented?
    Chapter 16: 1861–1862 and Chapter 17: 1863–1865; Abraham Lincoln

12. Who is pictured in the chapter entitled "Changes in American Life"?
    Immigrants approaching Ellis Island

13. You will read about four different wars from Chapter 24 to the end of the book. List the chapters and the names of the wars.
    Chapter 24: World War I; Chapter 27: World War II; Chapter 28: The Cold War; Chapter 30: The Vietnam War

14. What might you learn about in the chapter entitled "The Civil Rights Era"?
    You will learn about the struggle to bring equality to African Americans.

15. Which special section in the back of the book interests you the most?
    [Answers will vary.] Historic Decisions of the Supreme Court; The War on Terrorism; Rand McNally World Atlas; or the Reference Section

Authors' note: Figure is based on Creating America: A History of the United States. © McDougal Littell, 2002.

"The first play I want to show you is one that Carlos has already told us is important—how to survey something new. OK, without getting out of your seats, you have six seconds to pick a partner within two feet of you."

No one moved. The class just stared at Mr. Reaf.

"Hey, four seconds left. Pick a partner!"

Everyone quickly chose the person sitting next to, in front of, or behind them. Mr. Reaf had learned to give students a choice whenever possible, especially at the beginning of an assignment. He knew that having a choice makes students feel empowered, gets them into the activity, and often bypasses that potential discipline problem when a student refuses to take part. He also wanted to see whom they wanted to work with and how they worked together. When he reorganized the classroom later, he'd want to know which few should be separated.

Mr. Reaf walked back to his desk and grabbed a stack of handouts.

"OK, this is a scavenger hunt. Who knows what that is?"

A small girl in the front raised her hand.

"Yes?"

"It's when you are given a list of things or clues and you have to find stuff."

"Excellent. I'm Mr. Reaf, by the way." Mr. Reaf held out his hand.

The students laughed as Andrea shook his hand and said her name.

"Just as Carlos surveys the opposing team, we are going to survey our new textbook."

"The whole book?" someone called out.

Mr. Reaf smiled.

"No, but good question. Today we're going to survey just the Table of Contents. I've made a list of questions that you should be able to answer just by looking at the Table of Contents. I promise that all the answers are in there. You can look together. I suggest that one of you read a question quietly to your partner, and then both of you look at the Table of Contents together. Just as Carlos's team believes in teamwork, I want you two to help each other. Show each other how you're finding the answers. We'll be helping each other learn all year long. Everyone understand?"

No one said anything, so Mr. Reaf began to pass out the two-page Scavenger Hunt sheet.

"Hey, this is long! It's got 15 questions."

Mr. Reaf kept passing out the papers, one to a pair.

"Yes, but there are two of you working together on it, so that works out to seven and a half questions per person, which really isn't so bad. OK, does each pair have one? Does any pair want to do the first question to model for everyone how easy it is?"

A boy in the far left row raised his hand. His partner groaned and hid his head on his desk. Mr. Reaf walked over to him and put out his hand.

"Hi, I'm Mr. Reaf."

Everyone laughed as the boy introduced himself as Thomas.

"OK, Thomas. Read the first question."

"How many chapters are in the book?"

"How will you find that out, Thomas? And remember, you can use only the Table of Contents."

"I'll turn to the end of the Table of Contents."

"Good. And the answer is . . . ?"

"Thirty-two."

"Excellent, Thomas. Now, you all have the first answer. Please go to work. I'll be walking around to explain any words or ideas you don't understand or to help you if you get stuck. If you need help, ask your partner first. If you're still stuck, then raise your hand, and I'll be there as fast as I can. Oh, and one last thing. You don't want another pair to hear your answers, so let's speak in what I call 'two-foot' voices. That means that if someone is two feet away from you, they can't understand what you're saying. OK, go!"

The students huddled together over their books as Mr. Reaf began to move around the room. Occasionally he stopped to hear a student read, making mental notes of who was struggling and who wasn't. After a few minutes, he looked over the class from the back of the room. Everyone was on task. Well, at least he had them working today. This seemed to be one of his biggest challenges with today's kids—keeping them engaged in any activity. He looked up at the class.

"OK, let's hear what you've found in your scavenger hunts."

2

Fostering Engaged Learning in Social Studies Classrooms

As his U.S. History class entered noisily, John Reaf stared down at his curriculum guide and shook his head. How had this class gotten so far behind? He had been pushing them as hard as he could—in fact, maybe too hard. Mr. Reaf could tell that a number of students seemed lost since the study of the U.S. Constitution.

Well, they'd just have to catch up. There was so much to cover. The social studies standards for his district required students to have a wealth of knowledge. And now the principal had made it clear that *all* teachers had to build in time to prepare students for the yearly standardized tests. God forbid their school should get a failing grade.

Mr. Reaf thumbed through Chapter 11. It was long—25 pages. He just couldn't take the time to let them plod through it. He'd have to start feeding them the information.

"OK, class, let me have your attention. Quiet down, please."

Slowly the private conversations ceased.

"Thank you. I've got good news and bad news. Which do you want to hear first?"

"The good news!" Ramona called out.

"The good news is that we have made it to Chapter 11 on slavery and the Southern rebellion."

No one reacted. Evidently this didn't matter much to the class.

"What's the bad news?" yelled Carlos.

"The bad news is that we are supposed to be on Chapter 13 on the Reconstruction. We're two chapters behind."

Again, no reaction.

"So," continued Mr. Reaf, "instead of you reading at your desks today, I'm going to cover most of Chapter 11 quickly in a lecture format. You'll need to take notes, so please get some paper out."

A chorus of groans went up.

"Come on, let's go. Would you rather I read the entire chapter aloud?"

"What difference does it make?" someone in the back corner mumbled.

Mr. Reaf ignored the comment.

"OK, everyone ready. Let's first talk about the plantation system and the Southern economy. The plantation system was built around one main cash crop—cotton. Thanks to a man named Eli Whitney, a machine was invented called the cotton gin."

Mr. Reaf turned and wrote *Eli Whitney* on the board. A few students copied the name down.

"This machine," continued Mr. Reaf, "was able to pull the seeds out of the short-fibered cotton grown in the South for the English textile mills. Cotton was now valuable and easily harvested; however, a lot of land was needed to grow it, and it required a large labor force to pick it. Consequently, Native Americans were driven from their land, and slaves were imported from Africa to farm the crop."

Mr. Reaf looked up. A number of boys in the back had laid their heads on their desks. He saw Mary Anne pass a note to Audrey. As he continued, he walked back and picked up the note from Audrey's desk and put it in his pocket.

"Now, you know the conditions for slavery were harsh. A woman named Harriet Beecher Stowe wrote about the cruel existence on many plantations in a book called *Uncle Tom's Cabin.* I'm sure you've all heard of this, so I'll skip it and move on to Nat Turner's Rebellion and the Monroe Doctrine. Who's heard of Nat Turner?"

No hands were raised.

"Well, you may find this interesting. Nat Turner was a slave who learned to read and write and also became a preacher."

As Mr. Reaf continued to lecture, more students simply laid their heads on their desks.

* * * * * * *

Most students like to be actively involved in learning—asking their own questions, creating their own projects, being the experts, and developing their own interpretations based on various data sources. Rather than seeing social studies as a place where they have to memorize important information, they want some opportunity to participate, to challenge ideas, to find their own voice, and to create something new and unique.

Social studies teachers like John Reaf struggle with issues of motivation and willingness of students to study the content that is important for them to learn. An issue central to this book is how to get students to engage with history. A second issue is how to ensure that they do more reading as part of that engagement. This goal becomes especially challenging when textbooks are written at a level beyond many of the students' abilities and in such a dense form that the books defeat many students before they begin.

Part of the solution comes by using the strategies described in Chapters 1 through 5 of this book. Another part of the solution comes by thinking beyond the chapter-by-chapter ritual of teaching and instead grounding instructional planning in what we know about the learning process. The "easy" approach of lecturing to students and distilling key ideas in text materials for them doesn't produce the necessary results. Moving outside the content frame a bit, research on academic learning (Bransford, Brown, & Cocking, 1999; Guthrie & Davis, 2003) has identified some important guidelines for teachers who want to reach and teach students effectively. Both researchers and practitioners have confirmed that students learn best when they can do the following:

- Connect the content under study with what they already know.
- Link the content to their own lives and contemporary issues.
- Engage actively in posing questions and coming to their own conclusions.
- Have multiple opportunities to study the same content to deepen understanding, and in the process build neural paths that deepen memory.
- Engage with peers in constructing ideas and points of view.
- Involve all their modes of learning—visual, kinesthetic, verbal, and social—as they construct new understandings.
- Call upon a repertoire of reading and study strategies.

These realities about academic learning suggest that teachers need to provide focused, in-depth learning opportunities for students that begin with their interests and knowledge. Teachers may need to set new priorities in their use of time and encourage students to engage more deeply in some topics or units. Students may need a wider array of learning opportunities—opportunities to manipulate artifacts and primary documents, to engage in concrete activities, to approach topics from varied perspectives, and then to think about and synthesize their

understandings in personal ways. Simply reading from a textbook is not sufficient for most students to build the level of knowledge needed for deep understanding; the "once over quickly" approach also fails to develop the depth of interest in topics that motivates students to look for connections between what they learn in social studies and what they experience in other arenas, both in and beyond school. The textbook can provide a foundation for students' more extensive exploration of ideas. When teachers help students engage in multiple types of learning activities, students are more likely to become grounded in the significance of their exploration.

Having a Voice

One of the easiest ways to involve students more fully in thinking about history is to make their ideas and thinking more central. Teachers who begin new topics of study by asking students what they already know about the topics using KWL+, for example (Carr & Ogle, 1987), show interest in students' ideas and experiences and respect for them. Students learn that their voices are honored. Listening to the students' ideas and connections also models the importance of linking new content to prior knowledge. Students may be familiar with the practice of making connections between the text and themselves, other texts, and the world, because this is a common reading comprehension strategy. It is a valuable way to extend understanding while reading fiction; it is equally important in the study of history.

Students also extend their connections and meaning when they are encouraged to discuss with other students their associations with the content. Teachers can productively use time by letting students engage in small- and whole-group discussions of their prior knowledge, activating their associations with and attitudes toward topics. The experience of learning together becomes a positive force, inviting students to want to learn more as part of the classroom's sharing and growing in learning.

Once students have activated their connections with the topic or unit, they need to feel confident in using text materials. Too many students fear the density and expository structures of the materials they need to read. Helping students overcome their resistance to informational texts is important. Students need strategies to help them read actively and critically. Therefore, after helping students connect to the topic, the next hurdle is helping students make connections with the texts themselves.

Questioning the Author

The strategy of Questioning the Author (Beck, McKeown, Hamilton, & Kucan, 1997) provides a good starting place to help students become more actively engaged as readers with a voice. Based on years of solid research with students reading social studies text materials, this strategy is straightforward. Essentially, by Questioning the Author, students assume a new role when reading; they become evaluators of the success of the author in making material comprehensible to them. Students discuss how successful they find the author in helping them understand and make sense of the ideas in the text. While they are reading each portion of text, students maintain a critical perspective and think of who has written the text and why. Rather than approach textbooks or other content materials as true and ready to be memorized, students learn to think beyond the text.

They learn to ask and answer questions such as the following:

- Who wrote this (what kind of person was the author)?
- Why was this information included?
- What point is the author trying to make?
- What else could have been said?
- Whose voice is missing?
- How could it be improved to help students like me understand?
- Are the visuals helpful? Is something else needed to make it clear?

Students learn to think of texts as being written by particular authors for particular purposes. They learn that sometimes the author's assumption about what a reader knows is inaccurate, and an author can leave out important connections and details. Some authors have a particular bias and focus on only some aspects of a topic. Some texts need maps and visuals to be comprehensible. Other texts need terms explained and points elaborated. When students realize the problems with text and learn how to overcome them, they can approach informational reading with more confidence. Often the problems in comprehension occur because of differences between the author and the actual readers, not just because of the student reading the material.

When teaching students to Question the Author, teachers should work with a small group of students at a time. As Mr. Reaf starts using this strategy to promote discussion of the text he has assigned, he decides to put one small group in the "fishbowl" so the rest of the class can observe them. He leads the querying of the text and models the process for all the students. He assigns a short portion of the text to be read and then engages the students in a discussion of this section. He starts by asking the questions that seem appropriate for that portion of text. "What was the author trying to say?" "How else could you have made this clear?" After some practice with this form of text dialogue, students read and discuss texts, section by section, in small groups. They use the group discussion for portions of the texts and extend the reading individually.

As students become more comfortable with querying the text, they assume a more equal position in relation to the author. What they need in order to understand becomes more clear; students also learn that they can rewrite or embellish a text to make it more friendly and comprehensible. This strategy has helped many teachers like Mr. Reaf identify problems with the texts they use and do more teaching at confusing points. The strategy also helps students with their writing. Once students gain confidence evaluating authors' success for them as learners, they also become more aware of the importance of thinking of the audience when they compose pieces or create projects.

Questioning the Author develops students' understanding that people construct text for particular audiences and purposes. This understanding allays their fear of text materials and frees them to engage in a dialogue with authors whose works they read. The strategy promotes the kind of questioning that all historians use when they approach documents in their own research and study. Questioning the Author helps develop the critical orientation to primary and secondary sources that historians need.

Using I-Charts for Inquiry

Another useful graphic organizer, the I-Chart (Hoffman, 1992), also helps students understand that authors vary in how they present information and interpret events. Hoffman developed the I-Chart when he became upset that his daughter was learning only one point of view about Christopher Columbus. Thinking about how teachers can help students learn that historians create interpretations and have biases, he conceived the I-Chart. Like Questioning the Author, this strategy helps students become more actively involved in using evidence to form conclusions and make judgments. The chart provides a framework that students can use to engage in inquiry, while asking and locating answers to key questions from multiple sources of information. The chart helps them compare and contrast information from these sources. Students (or the teacher) list key questions to be answered, the sources they will use, and what they learn from each source; then they formulate their own answers to their questions. The chart includes cells where students can note information that they find interesting but that does not answer specific questions. They also note new questions they have generated as a result of their extended exploration of the topic. Figure 2.1 is an example of an I-Chart.

An easy way to get students to realize the importance of using multiple sources of information is to introduce a controversial topic and provide a set of materials that represent differing points of view on that topic. When using this strategy and graphic organizer the first time, the teacher should help students frame some basic questions to guide their further study of the topic. In this way literal questions can be omitted, as uncontested information doesn't generate much interest. Questions should be ones for which students will find different interpretations in the materials they search.

One 7th grade teacher decided to introduce this strategy when students read

Figure 2.1
I-Chart

Topic	What We Know	Source 1	Source 2	Source 3	Summary

a short biography about Amelia Earhart (Blachowicz & Ogle, 2001). The biography implied that Earhart was lost over the South Pacific and her plane crashed into the ocean. To help students begin to understand how historians and chroniclers make inferences about events for which data are not available, she decided to have students read from two encyclopedia accounts of Earhart's life. These short texts had very different focuses and interpretations. One suggested that she had been captured by the Japanese and the other that she simply ran out of gas and was lost. The teacher started having the students think about these texts with a Venn diagram. She had pairs of students use the Venn diagram to put information that was the same in both articles in the center and the discrepant information in the outer areas of the circles. It was clear that these authoritative writers had different interpretations of the meaning of Earhart's last trip and what had happened to her. This piqued the curiosity of the students. How could authors write as if they knew the answer to her disappearance? What actually happened?

From this initial stimulation of inquiry, the teacher explained that she had some additional sources on Earhart. She asked what questions students most wanted to have answered. Because this was their introduction to the I-Chart inquiry strategy, she helped them frame key questions: What really happened to Amelia Earhart? What evidence do we have? What kinds of planes did she fly? She then gave students time to read and summarize other authors' interpretations of the significance and ending of Earhart's life. Students in the groups read different pieces of information, and one scribe made notes for each group. Then they discussed what they had learned together. Figure 2.2 is a representation of what one

group concluded. Clearly, the students had their own interpretations of the events; one group of girls thought that Amelia Earhart and Fred Noonan, her navigator, must have disappeared to a "fantasy" island!

Self-Selected Topics for Research

One simple way to engage students more personally in the study of history is to encourage them to approach it from the perspective of their own personal interests. One effective middle school teacher involves her students in the study of the 20th century by having each do an individual research study on a topic of his or her own choosing. The range of topics is impressive; for example, students have chosen to study popular music, guitars, Lucille Ball, bicycles, tennis, and the stock market. The assignment requires them to explore the development of their topic and to show how it reflects the 20th century.

By making connections to the larger social context, students are drawn into knowing more about how their topic reflects the larger whole. The students' reports are then shared orally as well as in written form with their whole class, so students develop a rich picture of American society in the last century. The teacher has also created a hallway time line showing each decade of the 20th century, with an icon representing each student's chosen topic placed on the appropriate decade. This personalization of the study of American history has ensured high levels of engagement and learning.

Using individual student choices is a central feature of the instruction that many teachers provide (Ogle & Blachowicz, 2002). It helps ensure that students take an active role in thinking about history and society. Even upper-elementary students often take

Figure 2.2
Group-Constructed I-Chart on the Disappearance of Amelia Earhart

Topic	What We Know	Source 1	Source 2	Source 3	Summary
Amelia Earhart		Amelia Earhart official Web site—www.ameliaearhart.com	Chicago Tribune newspaper article (1998)	Amelia Earhart by Chadwick (1987)	
What happened to her?	She disappeared in 1937.	A new search will begin spring 2005 in the ocean near Howland Island in the South Pacific.	They landed on Nikumarora Island; died of lack of water.	Due to clouds, unable to navigate and crashed into ocean.	No one is sure what happened to her or Noonan.
What evidence has been found?	Nothing remains.	Nothing about evidence; just lists theories, including crash on island; Japanese captured her; living as NJ housewife still.	Gillespie found plane fragment, shoe sole, and medicine bottle cap.	E. Long is still looking for the plane in the ocean.	No evidence is absolute yet; only fragments of hope!
What kind of airplane did she fly?	Old-fashioned planes	Twin-engine Lockheed aircraft	Lockheed L-10 Electra	Biplane; Kinner Canary; Fokker trimotor; Lockheed Vega	Several kinds—last was Lockheed WWII style
Interesting facts	First famous woman pilot; flew solo over Atlantic in 1932.	She was called "Lady Lindy" after Charles Lindbergh; she married George Putnam, and her stepson is still alive and lives in Florida.	U.S. Navy didn't see her but were watching; many don't believe it.	She was an adventurous child; her father was an alcoholic; she wore pants when women didn't.	She opened the way for other women pioneers; she was a modern woman!
New questions	Did she have a family?	Are they finding any new clues?	Can her plane still be in the ocean and found?	What happened to her husband?	Did she and Noonan have a special relationship? Did they escape together?

more responsibility and extend their learning when they have a choice of projects and research. Teachers who use the wide range of resources available on the Internet can help students pursue learning through their own interests.

For example, a team of 4th–5th grade teachers in a Technologically Rich Educational Environment in Glenview, Illinois, involve students in conducting individual research projects three times a year. The students are introduced to the research process and given clear guidelines on using the Internet, evaluating sources, combining multiple sources of information, and interviewing a knowledgeable person. They begin the year by doing reports on states within the United States of America. Students select the states they are most interested in, based on vacations, where grandparents live, places they want to visit, or those states highlighted in the news. Their second report of the year is on important conflicts. Again, students choose their own topics. One 5th grader had been to the Black Hills in South Dakota during the summer and visited the Crazy Horse Memorial. As a result of that experience, she decided that she wanted to know more about the conflict between Native Americans and the U.S. government. By providing choices, teachers help students see the reporting process as personal and engaging rather than as a formal requirement they might be asked to master—as is the case in many other schools.

Extended Unit Approach

Teachers can organize instructional units in several different ways to provide rich, extended learning opportunities. Some teachers create units around a central question and provide learning materials that offer an array of points of view and forms of presentation. This is often called an *inquiry approach.* By exploring important or essential questions, students understand that history is not just represented by one set of "facts" but that history is complex and is experienced and understood differently by those affected.

A second way teachers develop units is to identify *major issues or themes* and then build students' study around a variety of primary source artifacts and documents. This orientation is designed to make the learning of history as much like the work of real historians as possible. Students learn to examine primary source documents that can help in answering the big unit questions. Students engage in a specific form of inquiry based on the documents included in the materials for study. One version of this approach has been developed by teachers at Evanston Township High School in Illinois and is published as *Document-Based Questions in American History* (Brady & Roden, 2002). The whole American History course is built around big questions that can be addressed by studying the primary and secondary sources included in the materials.

A third approach is to use the textbook chapters and units as a framework for *in-depth exploration of topics.* An important aspect of this more elaborated approach to the topics is to ensure that both historical information and contemporary connections are emphasized. Rather than presenting historical eras, movements, or parts of the world as discrete, each unit is designed so that students address implications for current life. The focus may be as simple as "Studying Mesopotamia helps us understand modern-day Iraq and the reasons for war," or "Learning about the Westward Movement helps us understand current exploration of space," or "The election of 2004 in the United States can be connected to 'heartland conservatism' in America."

Teachers using this unit orientation collect supporting, correlate materials that help students deepen their study of the topics. Teachers often keep elaborating on and adding materials over the course of several years. As current events related to the topics occur, teachers quickly incorporate them into the unit.

Although teachers can help students make connections between the past and the present, the goals of instruction also need to be focused so students themselves learn to think of the links. Most students are very "now" oriented, and helping them build respect for how their lives have been shaped and molded by past events and movements needs to start with them. The past can be approached as a way of building understanding of themselves and current issues and life. As David Kobrin (1996) explains:

> Ultimately, it was the students who had to feel that this academic work mattered to them, that the classroom atmosphere we established and the learning we structured were valuable . . . we developed a repertoire of classroom activities to help kids discover their own reasons for being involved with history. Beginning here was always necessary. (p. 19)

Designing units that connect with the students and have clear purpose is important. Making the outcomes clear will increase students' engagement. They need to know the end-of-unit questions that they will be responsible for addressing. They also need to have options for sharing these syntheses—in written essays, in artistic representations, or as PowerPoint presentations or films. In designing units, teachers need to provide a range of materials. By highlighting a list of core vocabulary terms, teachers can give all students access to the ideas, including the English language learners whose academic vocabularies are least developed. Then teachers need to think of a sequence of activities to engage students initially as they enter the unit, to help them build their knowledge and understanding of different perspectives as they read and study, and finally to share their learning and celebrate their accomplishments.

See Appendix A for an example of a unit that incorporates many of these features.

Developing Reading Abilities While Learning History

Reading is central to the study of history. Therefore, one of the goals of good instruction is to ensure that students have access to ample materials that they can read and that they are expected to read regularly. Teachers need to be aware of students' reading abilities and ensure that materials are available at a range of levels of difficulty. Many publishers indicate the reading level of their materials; if this information is not given, then testing the materials by asking students to do short oral readings can provide a window on their difficulty. Students should be able to read 95 percent of the words accurately without hesitating when the text is at their "instructional level." Independent-level reading requires 98- to 99-percent automatic word recognition.

Creating Text Sets

Publishers offer a wide variety of short books at a wide range of reading levels. When preparing to teach a unit, teachers can create a text set of short books representing the range of reading abilities of their students. To get started, they can collect catalogues from publishers of short topical books and magazines and then ask for samples of the titles they think are appropriate. Conferences are convenient places to see materials displayed and to talk with representatives from the companies. Magazines are also available at a variety of reading levels and target particular topics. *Cobblestone, Scholastic, National Geographic, Newsweek, Time,* and *Weekly Reader* are good sources of materials that are attractive and accessible to students.

Roles for Textbooks

Textbooks have an important role to play in these units of inquiry and thematic study. They can provide an overview of a topic and show how particular events and people fit into the larger context. Sometimes students have a hard time seeing how primary sources and focused books connect; the textbook provides a starting point and a reference to which students can return to clarify issues that arise as they engage with the more extensive and focused resources.

Textbooks also serve an important function as a litmus test for ideas that are found in unedited sources, either on Internet sites or in primary source documents. For example, one 8th grader decided to conduct his research on the Ku Klux Klan totally via Internet resources. However, he selected sites without checking their sponsors and ended up with a very positively skewed report that began, "The KKK, one of the most important voluntary organizations in American history. . . ." When his teacher asked about the sources he used, they realized that he had ignored the Southern Poverty Law Center site (which was not graphically

engaging to him) and instead selected three Klan-sponsored sites. Had he cross-checked his sites with the textbook, he would have been alerted to the differences of interpretation, would have looked further before reaching conclusions, and would have produced a more balanced report.

Many students get involved in projects without much personal investment. That, in part, was what led to the report on the KKK described above. Helping students sort through the answers to the questions "So, why should I learn this?" and "What does this matter to me?" (Meier, 2002) can make a real difference in their long-term learning. Questions like "Why should I know about the KKK? Where are there signs of its activities in our area?" provide a more engaging purpose for learning than simply identifying one of the groups that persecuted African Americans after the Civil War. Inviting students into the joy of examining historical records and forming their own interpretations of what is significant sustains their engagement.

Learning means being motivated, looking for connections to oneself and the community, forming an understanding of issues in our culture, and exerting the effort needed to build new understandings. Providing students with an array of materials, both primary and secondary, helps them pursue their own questions about the topics or themes being studied. Teachers are creating these conditions for student engagement in the context of mandated standards and assessment, but the effort requires thoughtful planning and clear goal setting. A good guideline is this: *Always provide students more than one source and type of content material. Also, be sure that they can find themselves in some of the texts they read.*

Supporting Struggling Readers

These conditions for engaged learning are also supported by the research on reading—especially studies of students who struggle with reading. We lose students when we move too quickly through materials. Those who are not strong readers often fail to make the initial effort to open their books and read. Many teachers try to compensate by requiring students to be responsible only for material they present orally through lecture and discussion. This approach avoids the issue of students' unwillingness to read the texts, but it doesn't help them become better readers of social studies content, nor does it engage them with the flow of ideas and the ways history is communicated, either through textbook syntheses or from primary sources.

The more students read on the same topic, the more likely they are to move from novice to expert ways of thinking (Alexander, Kulikowich, & Schulze, 1994). Therefore, students need to be surrounded by *more* rather than less material on the topics being taught. They need to be enticed into reading and writing in as many ways as possible. Only by reading regularly will they develop fluency with the content, vocabulary, and style of academic writing. Teachers who present everything orally through supported lectures don't help students become independent learners. Taking time to find appropriate written materials teaches the students "how to fish" rather than just handing them a "fish."

Easy reading materials are the natural entry into a topic. So, too, are visuals that invite students to consider the topic under study. Many times a close examination of a photograph or painting can activate connections and questions (Buehl, 2001; Yell & Scheurman, 2004). These initial activities can then be followed by more elaborated texts at more difficult levels. With the availability on the Web of magazine articles, historical pictures, maps, and other documents, it is possible for teachers to give students accessible materials. Rather than avoid reading, teachers should scaffold reading experiences to develop students' reading abilities as their conceptual knowledge of social studies is developed. Roaming in a variety of materials provides those multiple encounters needed for learning. It also familiarizes students with the variety of ways authors structure information and blend visual and graphic information with text. With the increased emphasis on primary sources, students need as many opportunities to use a range of types of materials as teachers can provide. When students learn to look for specific text features characteristic of the genre of documents they are reading, they are much more likely to interpret the content appropriately.

Many students struggle to understand social studies content because they lack the vocabulary specific to social studies. Again, the amount of reading that students do is important. Students need many opportunities to see, hear, and use new terms to make them their own. When teachers give students several different texts on the same topic, students encounter the same content-specific terms frequently and thus build their familiarity with the key vocabulary. When teachers avoid giving struggling students texts to read, they exacerbate the learning problems that students face. When teachers share with struggling readers the advantages of reading multiple pieces of text on the same topic, students can become part of the solution. They can look for contemporary documents in magazines and newspapers that relate to the content; they can review magazine articles and other primary source materials that teachers locate, and evaluate their appropriateness for themselves and other students. Teachers who create bulletin boards with news articles related to the topic of study and give students extra credit for contributing to the class's learning help students see the relevance of what they are learning in social studies and history.

Ensuring More Reading

A simple way to increase the amount of reading that students do is to ask them to help create a resource file of articles connected to the topic under study. The teacher can label a basket in the classroom "Articles/information about _____" and give students extra points for bringing in articles, pictures, and graphics on the current topic. When students make a contribution to the file, they clip a 3-inch-by-5-inch card to the article indicating the source and their name. Early in the term, the teacher introduces the purpose of the file and how students can locate connected texts.

For example, Ms. Meyers, an 8th grade teacher, began the fall term with a unit on the right to vote, as it was an election year and she wanted her students to link voting to citizenship and also introduce the study of the Bill of Rights. The big question she posed to students to guide their learning was this: "Why do only about half of our citizens vote when the fight to get the vote for both minorities and women was a huge struggle in our history?" She explained that there would be a lot in the news about the election and students could help by bringing in good articles on the effort to get citizens to vote. She showed her class a current newspaper with two editorials on the push to get to new constituencies and register voters. She also held up an article from a news magazine on the issue of how far in advance of an election voters need to be registered. (She has in her classroom two levels of student news maga-

zines, so all students can find periodicals they are comfortable reading.)

Having made this link to the community, she introduced the students to *Cobblestone Magazine*'s March 2004 issue on voting in America and suggested that student magazines would be great sources for interesting articles. Finally, she turned to the computer and located the American Memory Web site (www.loc.gov). She explained that the Library of Congress has digitized most of the documents in this national resource, a collection of important historical documents. She had bookmarked a section on the struggle for women to gain the right to vote and showed the students some posters and songs used by anti-franchise groups. The students were amazed by the music that put down women's efforts. The teacher asked the students if they would like to have a copy of the song sheet, and their enthusiasm led her to suggest that searching for more documents like these could lead to great resources that the class would enjoy.

This search for articles that connect with the topic of study can be aided by asking colleagues to make contributions, too. Some teachers work together and keep folders in the teachers' work room for articles they locate. In this way, the efforts of individual teachers can be greatly augmented by sharing among the team. Some teachers are great at locating political cartoons and jokes—and hearing radio and TV programs that connect ideas and issues. Others know the music and video world better and can help connect with places where students might engage in media gathering. Still others read the newspapers avidly and can clip articles that build connections. Some teachers may be great with the arts and can direct a team to works of art, exhibits in the local area, and collections that can extend the study.

Soliciting the Help of Librarians and Media Specialists

Finally, librarians and media specialists are tremendous resources in building a rich array of materials for students to use. Both school and public librarians are trained to locate materials and know what is available in all formats. Working with them can greatly enrich support for students. They can collect materials, develop bibliographies, and create lists of appropriate Web sites. Some have developed more extensive sets of search steps so students can save hours trying to access materials that are useful to study areas that teachers have established. They can also help teachers access good sites for lesson plans and ways to connect with others who are engaged in similar units of study.

Librarians often are willing to come into classrooms and give book and magazine talks for the students. Some now are in charge of computers and can bookmark good sites for students at different levels of literacy development and interest. They also can teach students how to use the library resources and become part of the instructional team when students engage in research projects. If they have access to EBSCO or other magazine services, librarians are often willing to develop a set of materials at various readability levels to help all students access the ideas in printed forms.

When teachers collaborate with school librarians, the librarians can add the kinds of materials to their collections that are most useful in the classroom. In one Chicago school, the teachers bring information about students' reading levels with them when they have library sessions, so the librarian is able to guide individual students to the materials they are most likely to be able to use confidently.

Jigsaw Reading with Sets of Articles

The benefits of developing collections of articles and artifacts to support topics under study are many. A key benefit is that it makes possible the differentiation of the materials that students read by both their reading abilities and their interests. For example, Ms. Meyers realized that the students in her first-period class had widely different reading abilities. She decided to try letting students choose from three articles the one they would read and discuss in class. She found one article written at about a 6th grade reading level in *National Geographic World;* a second, more challenging article was by Gloria Steinem; and the third was an essay by a conservative journalist interpreting the failure of the United States to pass the Equal Rights Amendment.

Students previewed all three articles and then selected the one they felt they could read confidently. Then the students read the article, using their standard system of note taking and marking notes with a plus sign (+) for significant ideas, the letter *A* for ideas the reader agrees with, a *D* for ideas the reader disagrees with, and a question mark (?) for points for discussion. Working individually, the students then were to make sticky notes of the three ideas they thought most important as well as notes of points they agreed or disagreed with or questions they wanted the group to discuss. After reading on their own, students gathered with the others who had read the same article. The three groups met to discuss what they thought were the most important points. As students spoke, their sticky notes were added to a chart (a large page divided into four columns). The final step for each group was to create a graphic overview of their consensus about the important ideas from their article and explain it to the rest of the class.

The activity went very well. As Ms. Meyers moved from group to group during the discussion time, she could easily identify those students who fully understood the reading and those who needed the discussion time to clarify parts of the content. The submitted questions also gave her insights into students' lack of familiarity with the issues underlying the push for franchise. She recognized that some of the families of her students might be quite traditional, and others had mothers who were single heads of families. Listening permitted Ms. Meyers to learn a great deal about her students.

Benefits of Differentiating Materials

When teachers provide a set of text materials from which students can choose, they are recognizing students' individuality and levels of development. They also are creating the conditions under which students can become "experts" on aspects of the curriculum and take on the teaching role. The old adage "Those who teach learn!" proved true for Ms. Meyers's class.

Another important aspect of using a variety of materials is that it keeps students attuned to making connections between what they are studying in their textbook and the rest of the world around them as reflected in other types of texts. This transfer is at the heart of social studies education, yet too often teachers never get to the contemporary world or to the ways the study of history and social studies is alive all around us. Students who think of social studies as something they can see on TV, find more about on the Internet, read about in magazines and newspapers, and hear about in music and on the radio are more likely to engage in class.

It is also clear that students learn differently—some need visual displays and pictures to create images of what is being studied; others need personal stories and

lived experiences to bring history alive; and still others connect with the music and auditory links to historical events and periods. When teachers include a wide variety of materials and artifacts—photographs and pictures, primary source documents, videos, and interviews with community members—the likelihood that most students will learn is greatly increased.

Equally important for developing students' literacy is that a collection of articles and other texts makes it possible for teachers to find materials that are both inviting and at students' reading levels. By beginning with fairly easy materials, students are often later able to handle more difficult texts on the same topic, including the textbook if it happens to be challenging. If students can begin with short, fairly easy texts, they can develop a basic understanding of key ideas and also be introduced to some of the vocabulary. They can then try more difficult texts on the same topic. The textbook may be the second or third level of resource material that students gain confidence in reading.

Finally, such a collection helps teachers move beyond reliance on workbook pages and dittoed sheets for struggling readers. Authentic articles and texts create a much more inviting form of reading. The varied formats, visuals, and points of view personalize topics and provide support for new content. Because some students are visual learners, having a variety of presentations of information can increase the likelihood that all students will make connections to the new ideas and information.

Types of text materials to provide include the following:

• Short books and articles at a variety of reading levels (easy to hard)
• Visual/graphic materials (pictures, cartoons, maps, diagrams)

- Documents
- Stories or novels
- Newspaper and magazine articles representing varied points of view
- Vocabulary-focused pieces (history of terms, contemporary connections, etc.)
- Interviews (student-done, video, audio, printed)
- American Memory digital materials (available at www.loc.gov) and links to other Web sites

Planning for Engagement

This chapter has explored ways social studies classrooms can become places where students and teachers engage deeply in the study of issues important to us all. It takes careful planning to bring students to the place where they feel confident asking questions, identifying differing perspectives, and developing their own interpretations of data they gather. We have suggested ways to collect resources that are accessible to all students and that reflect their interests and their own cultures and ethnicities. With the increasing diversity of students, the materials teachers use take on more importance. Specific strategies—such as Questioning the Author, I-Charts, and Jigsaw Reading assignments—strengthen students' abilities to make personal choices, to work in teams, and to engage actively with the authors of materials they read. These strategies work effectively when teachers weave them together in thoughtful units of instruction.

* * * * * * *

As his U.S. History class entered the room noisily, Mr. Reaf asked the Number 3 person in each group of four to come forward to pick up the day's instructions for each group. [A description of this grouping strategy is provided in Chapter 4.]

"OK, class, let me have your attention. As you know, we've been looking into the effects of slavery on African Americans during the plantation years. Let's review for a second. Besides the information in the text, what else have we read and discussed? Would the Number 1 in each group raise your hand to answer, please?"

Ramona raised her hand.

"Yes, Ramona."

"We've read parts of the book that lady wrote about Uncle Tom and Eliza. How she described how horrible slavery was on some plantations and how people escaped through the Underground Railroad."

"Right. Who in Ramona's group can tell me the author?"

"Harriet Beecher Stowe!" Louise yelled.

"Excellent. OK, Number 1s, something else we've read."

"A speech by Frederick Douglass against slavery."

"Good, Maria. What else? Thomas?"

"A speech by Sojune Truth."

"Right, Thomas, and her first name is Sojourner. Excellent, class. Now today we're going to read one more primary source. This one is by a white Northerner named Levi Coffin. Levi was an abolitionist, a Quaker, who helped about 3,000 slaves escape on the Underground Railroad. There's some more information about him at the top of your handout. We're going to read Mr. Coffin's version of how he helped the real Eliza Harris, the one depicted in Stowe's fictional work, escape."

"Please remember that each time we read a primary source, we play our investigator game of Question the Author. We want to think about who this author is and why he or she wrote it. The Number 3 in each of your groups has a sheet with eight questions. Each group member will choose two questions to answer individually first. Then, once everyone has answered his or her two questions, your Number 3 will lead your group in a discussion. I'll be moving around the room giving out bonus points to groups in which I see everyone taking part. Let's look at our eight questions now. Be thinking about which questions you want to answer."

Mr. Reaf put up a transparency with the following eight questions:

1. Who was the author and what kind of person was he or she?
2. What information did the author choose to include?
3. What point do you think the author is trying to make?
4. What information or facts might have been left out?
5. How does this author's message compare to other accounts you've read?
6. What motives, or reasons, might the author have had to write this?
7. Whose voice or opinion is missing?
8. What connections can you make between this piece and events today?

"OK, does everyone understand?"
Carlos raised his hand.
"Yes, Carlos?"
"Are we going to read this silently? I don't get a lot of these words, man."
John Reaf glanced down at the textbook page, peppered with terms in boldface. He realized he'd need to start doing some vocabulary strategies with his students, but for now. . . .
"OK, why don't we have each group choose one person to read? Let's use our 'two-foot' voices in which I can understand what you're saying only if I'm within two feet of you and your partner. Are we good to go?"
"Cool," said Carlos.

Teaching Vocabulary to Older Students

John Reaf looked down at the Key Terms listed on the page of his teacher's edition of the textbook. The first word was *Antifederalist*. "Well," he said to himself, "let's see what they know."

"Ramona, what does the word *Antifederalist* mean?"

Ramona turned away from the girl she had been whispering to. She stared at the teacher blankly.

"Ramona?"

"Yes?"

"The word *Antifederalist*. What does it mean?"

"I don't know."

Mr. Reaf let out a breath. "Jeffrey, please pass Ramona a dictionary. Ramona, look the word up and read us the definition."

The dictionary was passed down the row like a relay baton. Ramona groaned as she took the thick book in her hands.

"This thing's heavy!" she whined.

"Words carry a lot of weight, Ramona. Just look up *Antifederalist,* please. We're waiting."

The other students shuffled in their seats. Mr. Reaf remembered the workshop in August in which he had learned that average "wait time" for a student response was often only a second or two before the teacher called on someone else or gave the answer. He had decided that this year he would wait a bit longer. Ramona was idly turning pages in the book.

"Well, Ramona?"

"I can't find it," she answered sharply.

"Why?" answered the teacher.

"I don't know how to spell it."

A couple of boys in the back row started giggling.

"Can anyone spell *Antifederalist?*"

The class quieted immediately.

"Ramona, it's *a-n-t-i-f-e-* . . ."

"Wait a minute!" she exclaimed. "You go too fast, man."

Mr. Reaf got up from his desk and walked to the front of the room to the blackboard. He wrote the word in large letters.

"There, Ramona. Now, read us the definition please."

Ramona turned pages, looking repeatedly up at the blackboard. Finally she seemed to have found it.

"Ramona?"

"Which one?" she replied.

"I believe there is only one Ramona in here," replied Mr. Reaf, growing impatient.

"I mean which definition?" she replied. "It's got a whole bunch of numbered things after it. Which number do you want me to read?"

"Just read the first one, please."

Ramona stared silently at the page.

"Out loud, please. Just sound it out."

Hesitantly, Ramona began to read, struggling through the words. Two students buried their heads in their arms on their desks.

"An opponent of the rat—i—fi—ca—tion of the U.S. Constitution."

"Good. Now tell me again what the word means, Ramona."

She looked up at Mr. Reaf, an expression of frustration and bewilderment on her face.

"I don't know, so stop asking me. I don't understand this stupid book."

She pushed the dictionary away from her.

Mr. Reaf looked at her. He looked up at the clock on the wall. Ten minutes, and he hadn't even gotten one word defined. It was going to be a long year.

* * * * * *

How Do We "Know" a Word?

Ramona is struggling to learn a new key word, and John Reaf's strategy for teaching this word doesn't seem to be very successful. What could Mr. Reaf, or any teacher, do to help Ramona know the word *Antifederalist?* To answer this question, we first need to consider what it means to "know a word."

Vocabulary experts speak of the process of knowing a word as a continuum. Initially we have very little knowledge about a new word. Over time, as we encounter the word in reading, in discussion, and in the media, we begin to possess a deeper understanding of its meanings. For example, think about the words *match* and *metaxylem*. Many of us have seldom, if ever, encountered the word *metaxylem,* and we know little, if anything, about it. Some of us may recognize that it has something to do with science, but we still don't know its definition. William Nagy (1988) refers to these initial stages of learning a word as "partial word knowledge."

At the other end of the continuum is the word *match.* We've had a lifetime of encounters with this word in its many forms; consequently, we have a wealth of knowledge regarding the multiple denotations and connotations of it. Whenever we see or hear the word, we bring up this prior knowledge to apply to the context in which *match* is being used—whether it's something to start a fire, a game or competition, or two things that are alike. Nagy would call this "full concept knowledge."

The more frequently we encounter a term, the deeper the level of knowledge we acquire about the word. How, then, do teachers help students like Ramona have frequent and successful encounters with new words? The first recommendation is to avoid time-consuming strategies that provide only limited success with learning new words. Mr. Reaf demonstrated two such unsuccessful strategies with Ramona by asking her to "look it up" and "sound it out."

Inappropriate Vocabulary Strategies

Looking Words Up in the Dictionary

Dictionaries are excellent reference tools, and all students should be trained in how to use them. However, as a tool for learning new words, a dictionary is very inadequate. Research has shown that relying solely on definitional approaches to teach new words provides little improvement in word knowledge (Baumann, Kame'enui, & Ash, 2003; McKeown, 1993; Nagy, 1988; Stahl & Fairbanks, 1986). The problems with teaching words only by using dictionaries are many.

First, brain research has shown that emotion plays a critical factor in learning (Jensen, 1998; Sousa, 2001; Sprenger, 1999). Ramona's reaction to the heavy dictionary is not uncommon. Students know when their chance of success is limited. Ramona cannot spell the word, so she does not know how to look it up. Already she feels defeated in front of her peers. Once she finds the word, she has no idea which of the multiple definitions is the "correct" one. In our example, Mr. Reaf makes the task even more difficult by not providing any context. He simply calls out the word. In situations such as this, many students will simply choose the first or shortest definition.

Once students choose a definition, they face additional problems. As Nagy (1988) points out, definitions do not always contain adequate information for students to understand the word. For example, the word *metazoal* is defined as "of or relating to the metazoans." The definition of the word *metaxylem* is "the part of the primary xylem that differentiates after the protoxylem and that is distinguished typically by broader tracheids and vessels with pitted or reticulate walls" (*Webster's Ninth New Collegiate Dictionary*, 1983). Did you get that?

Word knowledge is based on a wealth of prior knowledge acquired over time and reinforced with repeated exposures to, and use of, new terms. The only prior knowledge many of us may be able to apply to the definition of *metaxylem* is based on the word *vessels,* which suggests one of three different contexts—the human body, containers, or ships at sea. Again, that's not very helpful.

Isolated Phonics Instruction

Because Mr. Reaf has had no formal training in reading, he might try the only other strategy he knows to help Ramona decode the word *Antifederalist.* He might ask Ramona to "sound out" the word when she doesn't recognize it, thinking that sounding it out might provide meaning. This phonics approach to reading works with most students in the very early grades, but sounding out words will provide only limited help to older readers. Why does this strategy work better with younger readers than older students?

George Bernard Shaw once stated that the word *ghoti* is actually the word *fish.* Shaw said that if you took the *gh* from the word *enough,* you got the "f" sound. If you took the *o* from the word *women,* you got the short "i" sound. And if you took the *ti* from any word that ends in –*tion,* such as *nation,* you got the "sh" sound, thus *fish.* Shaw's point is that the letter-sound relationships in the English language are not very systematic. Unlike a language such as Spanish, in which the government systematized all letter-sound relationships, English does not allow one to always rely on "sounding a word out" to pronounce it correctly. In the early grades, the vocabulary of texts is controlled so that letter-sound relationships are easily taught. In the later grades, as texts become more sophisticated, letter-sound relationships are not so reliably systematic.

Even if one can correctly pronounce a word, the correct pronunciation does not necessarily produce meaning. Phonics instruction focuses on the correspondence between letters and sounds. If Ramona can phonetically decode the word *antifederalist* but has never heard of it, then saying or hearing it still does not register any meaning for her.

Phonics would be helpful to Ramona if she used it in the context of syllabication—that is, to break a word into its parts (affixes and roots). However, as Ivey and Baker (2004) state, "No existing evidence suggests that phonemic awareness training or isolated phonics instruction helps older struggling readers become more competent at reading" (p. 36). Ivey and Baker also point out that there is no evidence that focusing on phonics instruction with older struggling students makes them want to read more, which *is* one of the most effective ways to improve a student's vocabulary. With older students, phonemic awareness and phonics instruction are helpful when taught in the context of an intensive intervention program, especially if students have materials that they *can* read and *want* to read.

Appropriate Vocabulary Strategies

Independent Reading

One of the most successful strategies a teacher or parent can implement to increase a student's vocabulary is providing time to read. Most of the words we learn we do not learn through direct instruction. Nagy, Anderson, and Herman (1987) estimate that a student can learn about 3,000 new words a year; 25 to 50 percent of these words are learned incidentally. We learn words incidentally in many ways—through speech, through the media, through the computer, and through reading. Of all the incidental ways to encounter words, however, having students read materials that they care about and that they can read is the most powerful. There is a definite positive relationship between the time children spend reading for fun and their reading achievement (Greaney, 1980; NAEP, 1996; Taylor, Frye, & Maruyama, 1990). Other researchers such as Cunningham and Stanovich (1998) and Nagy and colleagues (1987) insist that wide reading is a major contributor to differences in children's vocabularies. As Nagy (1988) states, "Increasing the volume of students' reading is the single most important thing a teacher can do to promote large-scale vocabulary growth" (p. 32).

Hayes and Ahrens (1988) have done extensive research into the relationships between reading and vocabulary development. The researchers used a standard frequency count of 86,741 different word forms in English. For example, the word *the* is ranked number 1 because it occurs with the greatest frequency; the word *pass* is ranked number 1,000, and the word *vibrate* is ranked number 5,000. The less frequently a word appears in communication, the "rarer" it is.

Hence, the more rare words used, the more difficult the text is to comprehend.

Hayes and Ahrens (1988) found that the average rank of words in a children's book was 627; the average rank of words in a popular magazine was 1,399, and the average rank of words in a newspaper was 1,690. In contrast, the average rank of words used in popular prime-time adult television shows was only 490, and the average rank of words used by college graduates when speaking informally to friends or spouses was 496. In other words, "Children's books have 50 percent more rare words in them than does adult prime-time television and the conversation of college graduates. Popular magazines have roughly three times as many opportunities for new word learning as does prime-time television and adult conversation." In separate studies, the researchers also found that reading volume contributed significantly to vocabulary knowledge and general knowledge about the world for all children, not just the "smart kids." In other words, when it comes to learning words, talking is not a substitute for getting kids to read.

To promote vocabulary development in the social studies classroom through reading, teachers must provide two critical factors: time and appropriate materials. Even though teachers feel pressured by such issues as covering standards and preparing for standardized tests, they still need to find time for students to read enjoyable materials. Many students, after graduating from high school, rarely pick up a book again. Beginning in the 4th grade when content area reading begins in earnest, many students find that school materials become more and more boring and difficult. By 10th grade many adolescents spend their days reading algebra, Shakespeare, biology, the Constitution, and similar materials. And being adolescents, the last thing they want to do is read something else after school. The result is that schools may help create negative emotional associations with reading itself. Studies have indicated that as many as 60 percent of high school graduates never complete a single book, and the remaining 40 percent read about one book a year (Woiwode, 1992).

How, then, can teachers promote reading in their classrooms? Teachers need to set aside time for students to read. Some teachers set aside time at the beginning of the class as "bell work"; others require students to read during the last 10 minutes of class while the teacher collects work or holds individual conferences. Still other teachers set aside parts of days, such as 20 minutes on Monday and Friday, and others make free reading a mandatory part of study hall. Small amounts of reading time add up very quickly. The chart in Figure 3.1, based on the research of Anderson, Wilson, and Fielding (1988), shows the variation in reading time among a group of 258 fifth graders.

Once time is set aside, students need appropriate materials. Classrooms need to be filled with a plethora of materials covering a wide variety of interests, formats, genres, and reading levels. For example, John Reaf can create nine baskets of materials, one for each group of four students. Within each basket there might be magazines, newspapers, historical novels written at a variety of reading levels, "hi-lo" materials (short books of high interest to teenagers and low vocabulary demands), classic comic books, and challenging works, such as John Steinbeck's *The Grapes of Wrath* or Upton Sinclair's *The Jungle*. Mr. Reaf can also encourage students to add materials to the baskets once he has reviewed them.

Figure 3.1
Variation in Amount of Independent Reading

Percentile	Independent Reading Minutes per Day	Words Read per Year
2	0.0	0
10	0.1	8,000
20	0.7	21,000
30	1.3	106,000
40	3.2	200,000
50	4.6	282,000
60	6.5	432,000
70	9.6	622,000
80	14.2	1,146,000
90	21.1	1,823,000
98	65.0	4,358,000

Source: Table 3 from Anderson, Richard C., Wilson, Paul T., & Fielding, Linda G. (1988, Summer). Growth in reading and how children spend their time outside of school. *Reading Research Quarterly, 23*(3), 285–303. Reprinted with permission of Richard C. Anderson and the International Reading Association. All rights reserved.

A number of publishers provide materials of great interest to adolescents. Teachers can personally review them by stopping by publishers' exhibits at reading conferences. Another source for materials is the Young Adults' Choices booklists compiled by the International Reading Association. These are available at www.reading.org under the section titled Focus on Adolescent Literacy. Also, the National Council for the Social Studies provides a compilation of appropriate independent reading materials at www.socialstudies.org.

Mr. Reaf can use a Book Pass early in the year to allow students to choose a number of titles they want to read. In a Book Pass, students pass around reading selections, previewing the summary on the back cover or inside flap, checking for readability, and then marking each title on their personal chart as to whether they "Want to Read," "Might Want to Read," or "Don't Want to Read." In this way students have committed to specific titles once reading time arrives. (A blank Book Pass form is included in Appendix B.)

Mr. Reaf would explain to students how free reading builds vocabulary and ask them to pick something that is fun and easy to read. This comment about "fun and easy to read" is especially important to struggling readers who often, out of embarrassment, will choose something difficult and "fake read" it in front of their peers. The reading of textbooks or doing homework for other subjects is not allowed during free reading time. Finally, as a model, Mr. Reaf needs to read something he enjoys during this period. Not a bad way to spend part of the day, when you think about it!

Activating Prior Knowledge

Researchers and psycholinguists in the 1970s and '80s began to understand the importance of prior knowledge in making meaning. They realized that comprehension is more than simply decoding the graphic and sound symbols on a page. Comprehension involves an interaction between textual information and a reader's schemata, or how the reader has constructed reality (Adams & Collins, 1979; Anderson & Pearson, 1984; Smith, 1994).

Brain-based research in the 1990s has supported this view of comprehension as a process of connecting new information to what is already known. The brain "looks" for similar information already stored to make sense of incoming data (Jensen, 1998; Sousa, 2001; Sprenger, 1999).

Activities that help students connect what they know to what they are about to learn positively affects comprehension. Connections can be of two types—personal and in context. For example, a teacher starting a chapter on the Bill of Rights can first ask students what "rights" they think they should have as teenagers. Students understand "rights" as privileges granted by an authority. This is a personal connection.

Teachers might also make connections in context. This means that they explicitly relate, or say aloud to students, how what they are about to read directly relates to what they have just covered. As Linda Darling-Hammond (2000) has stated, by not assuming students are making such connections, "powerful teachers build explicitly on their students' prior knowledge and experience."

John Reaf can use a number of activities to help students make connections with what they know and what they are about to read. One such activity is Concept Definition (or Semantic) Mapping (Heimlich & Pittelman, 1986; Johnson & Pearson, 1984). Studies by Johnson, Toms-Bronowski, and Pittelman (1982) and Toms-Bronowski (1983) found that intermediate students who were taught key target words with semantic mapping did better than students who learned the words through context.

Mr. Reaf begins by identifying a key academic vocabulary word that is central to understanding the reading selection and that most of his students have some familiarity with. He passes out a Concept Definition Map with only the key word (in this case, the word *democracy*) filled in. (A blank copy of a Concept Definition Map is provided in Appendix B.) Rather than asking students to look the word up in a dictionary or their textbook, Mr. Reaf asks each group of four students to define the key term. If necessary, he uses the word in a sentence with good context clues so that the students can make guesses as to the word's meaning. He selects a particular member of each group to write their definitions on the board. He then asks each group to synthesize all the definitions into one and asks for each group's definition. The class votes on the best definition. The completed example in Figure 3.2 shows that the class chose "government by the people with elected officials" as the definition for *democracy.*

Mr. Reaf now asks each group to come up with at least three characteristics, synonyms, or properties of the key word. Following the same procedure as before, he records the characteristics each group has brainstormed. He then asks groups to come up with real-world examples of democracies. Finally, he asks each group to come up with contrasting forms of government or non-examples.

Concept mapping lends itself particularly well to teaching abstract terms, or those "-isms" found throughout social studies texts. By the time the activity is finished, students have used oral language to share how they relate a key term to the real world, thereby teaching one another and saving the teacher valuable time later in the lesson.

One of the outcomes of using concept mapping is having students discover similarities and differences between ideas (Marzano, Pickering, & Pollock, 2001). A graphic organizer called a Y-Chart is a very effective tool for this purpose. Easier to use than a Venn Diagram, the Y-Chart allows students to take notes as they read; study their notes to determine how two terms, events, or persons are alike; and then separate out the differences.

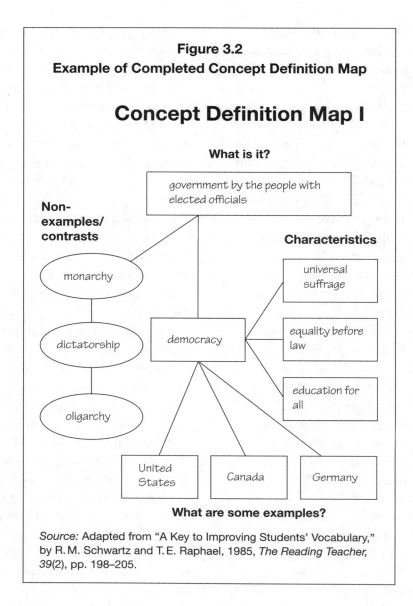

Figure 3.2
Example of Completed Concept Definition Map

Concept Definition Map I

What is it?

government by the people with elected officials

Non-examples/contrasts

monarchy

dictatorship

oligarchy

democracy

Characteristics

universal suffrage

equality before law

education for all

United States

Canada

Germany

What are some examples?

Source: Adapted from "A Key to Improving Students' Vocabulary," by R. M. Schwartz and T. E. Raphael, 1985, *The Reading Teacher, 39*(2), pp. 198–205.

Figure 3.3 shows how one student used a Y-Chart to note the differences and similarities between Stephen Douglas and Abraham Lincoln at the time of the Lincoln/Douglas debates. (A blank copy of a Y-Chart is provided in Appendix B.) The student draws a line through any similarities in the top parts of the Y and copies those items in the bottom section, leaving the differences on the top and the similarities at the bottom. The chart works equally well for examining the types of abstract terms often used in social studies, such as *socialism* and *communism*.

Another vocabulary activity that helps students connect prior knowledge to concepts and historical events is one recommended by Janet Allen and known as Predicting ABCs (Allen, 1999). This activity requires students to come up with terms they expect to find before reading about a specific topic.

Mr. Reaf begins by passing out the Predicting ABCs graphic organizer (a blank

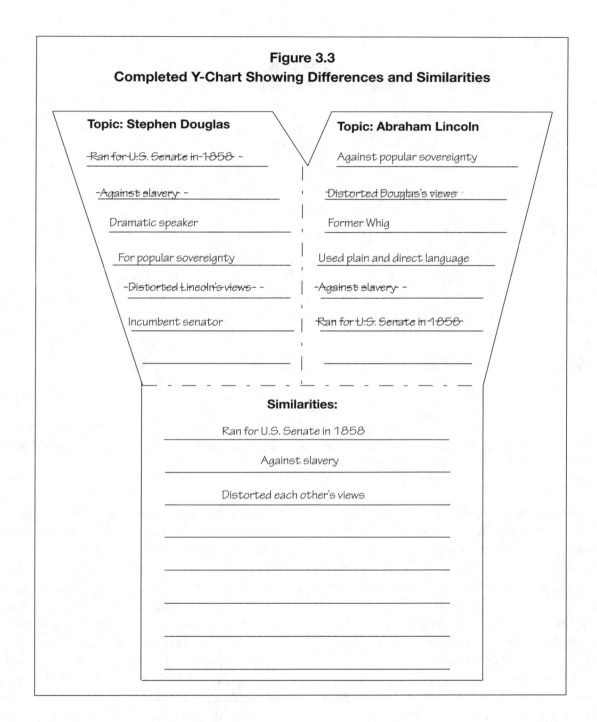

Figure 3.3
Completed Y-Chart Showing Differences and Similarities

Topic: Stephen Douglas

~~Ran for U.S. Senate in 1858~~

~~Against slavery~~

Dramatic speaker

For popular sovereignty

~~Distorted Lincoln's views~~

Incumbent senator

Topic: Abraham Lincoln

Against popular sovereignty

~~Distorted Douglas's views~~

Former Whig

Used plain and direct language

~~Against slavery~~

~~Ran for U.S. Senate in 1858~~

Similarities:

Ran for U.S. Senate in 1858

Against slavery

Distorted each other's views

copy of this graphic organizer is provided in Appendix B). He tells students that they'll be using their Think-Write-Pair-Share strategy. Students first individually list as many terms associated with the topic as possible in five minutes. For example, if the students were about to start a chapter on the Civil War, Mr. Reaf would model the activity by writing "Grant" in the G-H block and "Lee" in the K–L block on a transparency of the graphic. Figure 3.4 shows how a student might complete the chart.

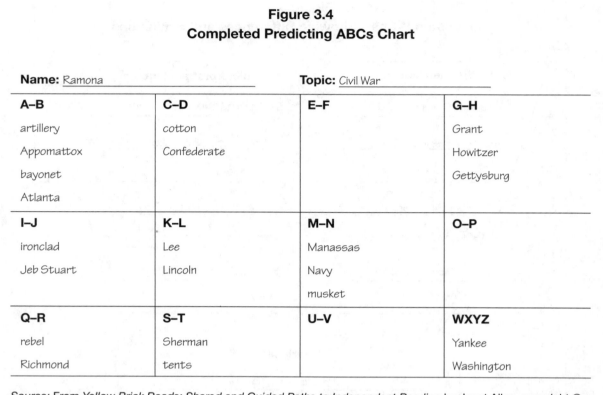

Figure 3.4
Completed Predicting ABCs Chart

Name: Ramona   **Topic:** Civil War

A–B	C–D	E–F	G–H
artillery	cotton		Grant
Appomattox	Confederate		Howitzer
bayonet			Gettysburg
Atlanta			
I–J	**K–L**	**M–N**	**O–P**
ironclad	Lee	Manassas	
Jeb Stuart	Lincoln	Navy	
		musket	
Q–R	**S–T**	**U–V**	**WXYZ**
rebel	Sherman		Yankee
Richmond	tents		Washington

Source: From *Yellow Brick Roads: Shared and Guided Paths to Independent Reading* by Janet Allen, copyright © 2000, reprinted with permission of Stenhouse Publishers.

After students have worked individually for about five to eight minutes, Mr. Reaf asks them to turn to their side partner and combine their lists. Partners should explain to each other what each term means. Then he asks students to move into their groups of four. He might ask all the Number 2s in the groups to be the recorders as groups combine their two lists into one.

At this point Mr. Reaf is ready for his students to begin teaching each other. He might ask all Number 4s to stand up and each share a word from the S–T box. If students don't have a word in that box, they may say "pass." After a student states a word, Mr. Reaf writes it on the master transparency and instructs all students to add the word to their lists if it isn't already there.

He then asks an essential question: "Why is this word important?" As students share the significance of their word, they also share background knowledge that will help all class members as they read the text. Students must encounter words many times and in many contexts in order to know and use them. With this activity, Mr. Reaf is beginning this process before students have even opened their texts, while at the same time ascertaining what they already know.

Once all the terms are listed and explained and students have filled out their graphic organizers, Mr. Reaf instructs the class to add terms to their charts as they begin reading the chapter. Students should be sure that all boldface terms in the book are added. If necessary, students can also copy definitions of terms that are hard for them to remember on the back of the graphic. At the end of the chapter, Mr. Reaf will pass out a blank copy of a graphic organizer called Summarizing ABCs and have each group of four students compete to see which group can remember the most terms from their reading and discussions. (A blank copy of this graphic organizer is provided in Appendix B.)

Teaching Context Clues

A reader who can use context clues as an aid in comprehension is using the words and phrases around the unknown word to infer meaning. Only a limited number of studies have been done regarding the efficacy of teaching context clues; however, work by Buikema and Graves (1993); Jenkins, Matlock, and Slocum (1989); and Patberg, Graves, and Stibbe (1984) shows that instruction in using context clues does improve students' ability to infer meaning.

A number of factors determine how helpful context clues can be: the proximity of the clues to the unknown word, the reader's prior knowledge, whether the unknown word is an abstract concept or something concrete, the number of unknown words, and the explicitness of the clues (Baumann, Kame'enui, & Ash, 2003; this source provides an extremely thorough review of the research regarding vocabulary).

Janet Allen (1999) refers to the explicitness of clues as either "lean" or "rich." Lean clues provide little specific information in defining a word. For example, note that in the following sentence, the word *inebriant* could mean a number of things, such as soda, cocktail, fruit juice, spring water, or type of coffee:

> This drink is an *inebriant.*

In contrast, a rich context clue provides very specific information about a word's meaning.

The following sentence makes clear that *inebriant* must mean an intoxicant or alcoholic drink:

> This drink is an *inebriant,* or a drink with alcohol that makes you drunk.

Rich context clues often use signal words to show the reader there is a definition or to illustrate the relationship between an unknown word and the rest of the sentence. The "inebriant" example has two signals—the comma followed by the word *or.* These signals tell the reader that a definition follows. Fluent readers use signal words and punctuation to figure out context clues. Figure 3.5 lists some of the major types of context clues and signal words that identify them.

When teachers like Mr. Reaf see sentences that have difficult terms but also have rich context clues with signal words, they have an opportunity to model how to use context to derive meaning. Modeling context clues and pointing out signal words is especially helpful for struggling readers and English language learners. For example, imagine that Mr. Reaf comes across the following sentence in his social studies text:

> The British soldiers were indefatigable; however, their enemy tired quickly.

Mr. Reaf realizes his students may not know the word *indefatigable,* but he also sees a semicolon and the signal word *however,* followed by a comma. He might say the following to his students.

"Class, I see a tough word in the second sentence in the first paragraph. Would everyone look at the second sentence, please? Do you see the word *indefatigable?*

"I want to show you how I figure that word out. First, I remember that sometimes there are clues in a sentence as to the meaning

Figure 3.5
Context Signal Words

Type of Clue	Signal Words and Phrases
Example	like, for instance, this, such as, these, for example, other, includes, especially, in this model, as you can see here
Definition or restatement	or, which is, in other words, also known as, sometimes called, that is, also called, also referred to as, that is to say
Cause and effect	therefore, as a result, consequently, because, hence, so, since, for this reason, it follows that, and then, whenever
Comparison	like, as, resembling, related to, similar to, also, take after, be akin to
Contrast	but, on the other hand, however, in contrast, unlike, although, rather than, yet
Chronological order/sequence	first, then, now, lastly, in 1776, afterward, in conclusion, finally, thirdly

of an unknown word. These clues are often shown by punctuation and signal words. OK, I see a semicolon, which tells me something is about to happen in the sentence. The semicolon is followed by the word *however* and a comma. Let's look at our chart of signal words on the wall. Does anyone see a signal word that is in this sentence? What kind of signal word is *however?*"

A student raises her hand and calls out, "Contrast."

"Correct. Now if the word *however* is a contrast clue, then the opposite of something is stated after it. In this case it would be the opposite of the unknown word *indefatigable*. So, let's read what comes after the word *however*. After the word *however*, the rest of the sentence says that the enemy got tired very quickly. Well, the opposite of getting tired quickly is having lots of energy and not getting tired. So the British soldiers must have been strong and not gotten tired, which must be the meaning of *indefatigable*."

At this point Mr. Reaf might also ask his class if they see or hear a smaller root or

base word within the unknown word—in this case, *fatigue*—which affords him the opportunity to teach word parts, or structural analysis.

Structural Analysis

Structural analysis (or *morphemic analysis,* as it is also called) is a strategy of figuring out a word's meaning by breaking it up into meaningful parts. Structural analysis involves five components: affixes (prefixes and suffixes), inflections (plurals, comparatives, possessives, and verb tenses), compound words, contractions, and roots. Research on the efficacy of teaching these components is varied. However, in one of the more sound studies, Graves and Hammond (1980) found that 7th graders who were taught prefixes not only outperformed the group taught definitions only, but also outperformed the control group on a set of "transfer words," which were difficult words containing the prefixes previously taught. In another study, Nagy, Diakidoy, and Anderson (1993) evaluated the knowledge of suffixes of 4th through 7th graders and concluded that knowing those endings was a "distinct component of skilled reading" (p. 168).

The question then becomes, "Which word parts to teach?" As inflections and contractions are often taught in the language arts class, it may make more sense for social studies teachers to focus on compound words, affixes, and roots.

Compound words, such as *battleship,* are easily taught during class. Whenever one appears in the text, it takes only a moment to point it out and ask students to identify the parts and give the word's meaning. Affixes and roots occur in large numbers, so it is helpful to have a system for choosing which parts to teach. Regarding affixes, White, Sowell, and Yanagihara (1989) found that only 20 specific prefixes are found in 97 percent of all words that contain prefixes. Because the number is so low, it makes sense for teachers to ensure that students know the meanings of these prefixes as well as the most common suffixes. Based on the work of White and colleagues (1989), the charts in Figures 3.6 and 3.7 present the most commonly occurring prefixes and suffixes in printed school English. Students should know either the function or meaning of these affixes. Figure 3.7 includes a column with the heading "Change in Function" because, unlike the addition of a prefix, the addition of a suffix often changes the function of a word in a sentence. One activity to teach these word parts is the Word Part Generator, which is discussed later in this chapter.

Similar to prefixes and suffixes, there are a large number of roots, especially Greek and Latin roots, in the English language. Roots are the basic part of a word family, such as the Latin root *aud,* which means "to hear." A number of words are derived from this root, for example, *audience, audio, audible,* *auditorium, audiotape, audition,* and *audiovisual.* Reading experts have suggested that subject area teachers teach the roots that appear most often in their content materials. Consequently, Appendix B includes a chart containing 50 roots often found in historical texts. Each root's meaning and examples of derivations are also given. For example, the chart includes the Latin root *poli,* which means "city." Members of this root's word family include *police, politics, politician,* and *metropolitan.*

Another effective strategy for teaching both affixes and roots is to have students generate both real and nonsense words with the word parts. Students generate nonsense words to make the activity more personal and fun. This activity works well with both affixes and roots. Mr. Reaf can pass out copies of the Word Part Generator, a graphic organizer like that shown in Figure 3.8, and have groups brainstorm words. (A blank copy of this chart is provided in Appendix B.)

Which Words to Teach?

Deciding which words to teach is a critical part of vocabulary instruction. To choose critical vocabulary, Mr. Reaf must first determine the essential ideas he wants students to retain in a chapter. The tendency is to teach too much information, so he should consider what students need to know for high-stakes tests as well as cultural literacy. Once he has identified the essential ideas, he should consider which terms in the text must be understood to comprehend these big ideas. Mr. Reaf must also consider any "academic vocabulary"—the specialized terms and phrases endemic to specific content areas. Two excellent sources of these terms and strategies to teach them can be found in Robert Marzano and Debra

Figure 3.6
Common Prefixes

Prefix	Meaning	Examples
un-	not	unequal, unfair, unpopular
re-	again	replace, recount, revote
il-, im-, in-, ir-	not	illegal, improper, inequality, irregular
dis-	not	disarm, disloyal, distrust
en-, em-	to put *or* to go into *or* to cause to be	ennoble, enact, empower, embattle
non-	not	nonviolent, nonpartisan, nonissue
in-, im-	in	inrush, impoverish
over-	above *or* beyond *or* too much	overpower, overturn, overpay
mis-	bad *or* wrongly	mismanage, miscount, mistreat
sub-	below *or* less *or* secondary	subset, subway, substandard
pre-	before	preview, pretest, prehistoric
inter-	between *or* among *or* within	interstate, interchange, international
fore-	earlier *or* near the front	foresee, foretell, forerunner
de-	the opposite of *or* remove *or* out of	dethrone, depopulate, deconstruct
trans-	across *or* on the other side	transport, transcontinental, transplant
super-	above *or* over *or* better *or* greater than	superpower, supercomputer, superhuman
semi-	half *or* partly *or* happening twice	semiannually, semicircle, semifinal
anti-	against	antisocial, antitrade, antiaircraft
mid-	middle	midyear, midnight, midpoint
under-	below *or* less	underpaid, underage, underdog

Pickering's *Building Academic Vocabulary: Teacher's Manual* and the accompanying student notebook (Marzano & Pickering, 2005).

Once he has selected key terms, how should Mr. Reaf go about teaching them so that students actually understand them rather than just memorizing definitions that they will later forget? Beck, McKeown, and Kucan (2002) recommend looking at the definitions of words in three tiers. For example, let's look at the definition of the word *speculation:*

speculation—the buying and selling of stock in the hope of making a profit.

The First Tier consists of basic sight words and other simple words that rarely require instruction except for students learning English. The First Tier words in this definition are words such as *and, of,* and *hope.* The more First Tier words in a definition, the greater the chance that students will be able to comprehend it.

Figure 3.7
Common Suffixes

Suffix	Meaning	Change in Function	Examples
-s, -es	inflectional ending	singular to plural	vote/votes, church/churches
-ed	inflectional ending	present to past tense	play/played
-ing	inflectional ending	active verb ending	watch/watching
-ly	inflectional ending	adjective to adverb	quiet/quietly
-er, -or	one who performs an action	verb to noun	teach/teacher, invent/inventor
-ion, -tion, -ation, -ition	tells the state of something *or* an action or process	verb to noun	elect/election, reconstruct/reconstruction
-able, -ible	able to be *or* inclined to be	verb to adjective	elect/electable, combust/combustible
-al, -ial	relating to something	noun to adjective	politics/political
-y	inflectional ending	noun to adjective	creep/creepy
-ness	tells the state or quality of something	adjective to noun	great/greatness, sad/sadness
-ity, -ty	tells the state or quality of something	adjective to noun	equal/equality, diverse/diversity
-ment	action *or* process *or* result of action	verb or adjective to noun	movement, contentment
-ic	related to something	noun to adjective	history/historic, hero/heroic
-ous, -eous, -ious	possessing *or* full of	noun to adjective	joy/joyous, space/spacious
-en	to become	noun or adjective to verb	quick/quicken, strength/strengthen
-er	to compare two things	adjective to adjective	tall/taller
-ive, -ative, -tive	describe how something is	noun to adjective	offense/offensive, progress/progressive
-ful	full of *or* having	noun to adjective	truth/truthful
-less	without *or* lacking	noun to adjective	power/powerless
-est	having the most of a quality	adjective to adjective	great/greatest, brave/bravest

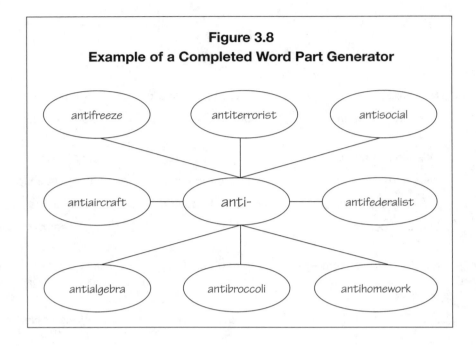

Figure 3.8
Example of a Completed Word Part Generator

antifreeze

antiterrorist

antisocial

antiaircraft

anti-

antifederalist

antialgebra

antibroccoli

antihomework

The Second Tier consists of critical foundation words that are useful and found across a great range of domains. Such words are used in the media and can be easily connected to other concepts. If students cannot understand the Second Tier words in the definition, they cannot understand the key term. For example, Mr. Reaf realizes that his students must understand *stocks* and *profit* to understand the key term and to function well in the real world. That is, he needs to teach the definitions of these words also.

The Third Tier is the actual key term in the text, or in this case, *speculation.* To optimize the chances of student success, Mr. Reaf should also select two or three terms covered in the previous section of the text. Brain-based research shows that main concepts must be retaught and reviewed if students are to retain them. Mr. Reaf's struggling students will also appreciate seeing terms they recognize, allowing them to participate successfully at some point in the

activity. In contrast, staring at a list of completely unknown words provides little incentive to take part in class.

After Mr. Reaf has selected his key words, he can use an activity that promotes student choice, activation of prior knowledge, and active verbal engagement, such as Vocabulary Knowledge Rating (Blachowicz, 1986). To begin this activity, Mr. Reaf passes out blank copies of the Vocabulary Knowledge Rating Chart and places a transparency of the chart on his overhead (see Figure 3.9; a blank copy of this graphic organizer is provided in Appendix B). He writes in the 10 words he selected and asks his students to copy the words on their sheets. Note that in Figure 3.9, the starred words (*) are from the previous section of the text.

Mr. Reaf then asks his students to make a check mark in one of the three columns for each word. If they "Know It" and can define the word, they make a check mark in that column. If they have seen or heard the word

Figure 3.9
Example of Vocabulary Knowledge Rating Chart

Name: Ramona   **Topic:** The Constitution

Term	Know It	Not Sure	Don't Know It	Definition
antifederalist				
slavery*				
trade*				
Great Compromise*				
federalism*				
ratify				
Bill of Rights				
republic				
rebellion				
amendment				

Source: Figure from Blachowicz, Camille L. Z. (1986, April). Making connections: Alternatives to the vocabulary notebook. *Journal of Reading, 29*(7), 643–649. Reprinted with permission of Camille L. Z. Blachowicz and the International Reading Association. All rights reserved.

but aren't sure they could define it, then they make a check mark in the "Not Sure" column; and if they "Don't Know" the word at all, they make a check mark in that column. Based on this information, Mr. Reaf will be able to teach a rather robust vocabulary lesson. (At the end of this chapter, Mr. Reaf will demonstrate how to complete the activity with his students.)

A Plethora of Practice, An Abundance of Activities

The strategies just described provide a variety of activities for practice and reinforcement in learning new words. As Nagy (1988) notes,

If students are to achieve both the depth and breadth of vocabulary knowledge that they will need to become proficient adult readers, they must have many encounters with large numbers of words—encounters that help them relate the word to their own prior knowledge and experiences and that give them practice in using their growing knowledge of these words to make inferences. (p. 32)

A student's vocabulary growth depends on multiple exposures to new words in a variety of contexts.

A student's encounter with new words cannot be relegated to just dry "skill and drill" sheets, however. If a primary goal of vocabulary development is to turn students into lovers of words, then teachers need to provide fun and engaging activities. Fortunately, the Internet is a great source for interesting and instructional vocabulary activities. Many sites provide complete vocabulary lessons and word games at no charge. For example, at www.puzzlemaker.com teachers can turn vocabulary lists into crossword puzzles and word searches. (A list of additional Internet sites that provide interesting activities and games for vocabulary development can be found in Appendix B.)

To Synopsize, to Capsulize, to Summarize

Social studies teachers can use many strategies to help their students develop better vocabularies. Providing a variety of enjoyable reading materials and the time to read them will increase students' word knowledge. Associating unknown terms with known concepts will help students retain new words. Teaching students signal words will help them recognize context clues. And having students learn affixes and Greek and Latin roots will help them structurally analyze words for meaning.

Learning new words requires integration, repetition, and meaningful use (Nagy, 1988). New terms need to be integrated with what students already know; new terms need to be taught and retaught in multiple contexts; and students need to use new terms in ways that are meaningful to them. It's important to note that in every activity described in this chapter, the teacher always turns to the students first to define a word before going to

a text. It's also important to note that every activity creates a structure for students to teach each other by orally sharing what they know about words.

Finally, learning words should also be fun. Good readers are also word lovers. They find amusement in puns and jokes. They enjoy searching for just the right word to describe something. They relish a passage that captures a person or place. They do crossword puzzles and word searches, and they play Scrabble and other word games. One of the most powerful strategies that social studies teachers can use is simply to model their own love and enjoyment of words.

* * * * * * *

John Reaf looked down at the Key Terms listed on the page of his teacher's edition of the textbook. The first word was *Antifederalist*. "Well," he said to himself, "that's a word they'll need to know."

"OK, class, if I can have everyone's attention. Today we're going to move on to Section 3 in Chapter 8 on Ratifying the Constitution. You remember that yesterday we talked about some of the struggles the early federal government was going through—issues like slavery, the Great Compromise, how much to limit government power. Before we start reading, though, I want to make sure we understand some key terms. OK, please move into your groups of four."

The students moved their desks at right angles to each other.

"Here's what I'd like you to do. Number 4s in each group, you'll be the director this time. Call out each word on the list and have each member of the group state what he or she thinks the word means. Remember that when we do this we try to answer two questions. First, what does the word mean? And second, how did you figure the word out?

"I'll be moving around the room to help you if you get stuck. Any questions? OK, go!"

The groups went quickly to work. Mr. Reaf moved around the room, passing out Participation Points for students who were working well or just needed some positive reinforcement. Once the groups had finished, he asked the students to return their desks to the straight rows.

"Now, would all Number 3s stand up?"

Nine students stood up by their desks.

"Number 3s, if you think your group knew the first word, remain standing. The rest can sit down."

"OK," continued Mr. Reaf as he turned to one of the students still standing. "Ramona, can you say the first word?"

Ramona looked up at the overhead screen.

"Antifederalist," she said loudly.

"Ramona, before you tell us what you think the word means, please tell us how you figured it out."

"Well," began Ramona. "We learned that the thing in front, *anti-*, means 'against.'"

"Does anyone remember the name for what comes in front?" interrupted Mr. Reaf.

"The bumper!" Carlos yelled from his seat.

Mr. Reaf laughed with the students.

"Mr. Hernandez, I thank you for reminding me that a good teacher is always explicit, or says exactly what he or she means. So, Carlos, what is the name for the word part in the front of this word?"

Carlos shifted in his seat.

"It's pre- something."

"Right. Here's a clue. If it ain't broke, don't. . . ."

"Fix it!" yelled Carlos. "It's a prefix."

"Excellent. Class, in unison. Let's all say the word *prefix* three times.

"OK, back to you, Ramona."

"It's about time," she said, feigning disapproval.

"What else did you know about this word's different parts?"

"Well, it ends in *-ist,* which means it's a person."

"Right," said Mr. Reaf. "Can a Number 2 tell me what the ending word part is called?"

A student in the back corner yelled out, "Suffix."

"Thank you, Sheila. Now, can a Number 3 give me some more examples of words that end in *-ist* and are people?"

Lorenzo raised his hand and called out, "Scientist, dentist, and terrorist."

"Good. So up to this point, Ramona, what did you know?"

"I knew it was someone against something."

"Excellent. Now, how did you figure out the middle part?"

"Well, I remembered the word *federal* from the chapter before. I couldn't remember its exact meaning, though. Then I thought about my dad always complaining about having to pay federal and state taxes. So, I figured federal must mean the big government in Washington."

"Bravo!" yelled Mr. Reaf, causing a few students to jump. "OK, Carlos, repeat for everyone the strategy that Ramona used to figure out *Antifederalist*."

Carlos shifted in his seat. "First she figured out the *anti-* at the beginning. That would be the prefix. Then she figured out the *-ist* at the end. Then she got tired of hearing her dad gripe about paying taxes."

Mr. Reaf joined the class in laughter.

"Very good, Carlos. OK, Ramona, can you give me a definition of the word?"

"Well," Ramona pondered. "I know it's someone who's against big government in Washington."

"Ramona, I think you're right, but I think we need more specific information; so we're not going to fill in the definition on our sheet just yet. Sometimes at this point we fill in the definition section on your chart, but this time let's wait to get some more information from the textbook."

"Mr. Reaf?"

He looked up to see Maria's hand raised. "Yes, Maria?"

"Why do you make us work in groups?"

Mr. Reaf smiled. He loved those "non sequitur moments" in teaching.

"Well, Maria, would you rather always work alone, or have help?"

Maria smiled. "I'll take the help, Mr. Reaf."

Organizing a Classroom for Democratic Engagement

Mr. Reaf reached down to adjust one of the pieces of masking tape on the floor. He smiled to himself as he inched the leg of the desk exactly into the right angle formed by the two pieces of tape. This may have been his best idea yet for controlling students. He told them on Day 1 that the legs of their desks should *always* be exactly within the "picture frame" formed by the right-angled pieces of masking tape that marked the positions for each leg. Now, that should keep them in their place!

The bell rang, and the first-period students straggled into the room. Mr. Reaf told them they should read the next chapter for 20 minutes and then he would "pepper" them with questions. There would be *no talking*. He set his timer for 20 minutes, waited to hear the seconds clicking away, and then sat down to grade papers.

A number of students jumped at the loud ring 20 minutes later. Mr. Reaf looked up at the class. Most were staring blankly back at him, except for one boy in the back corner who was sound asleep. When a neighboring student realized that Mr. Reaf had spotted the snoozer, he gave his friend a nudge. The boy looked up sleepily.

"OK, class, who can tell me who the Federalists were?"

Hands shot up from students sitting front and center.

"Yes, Juanita?"

Juanita cleared her throat. "They were people who supported the Constitution."

"Very good, Juanita! Well, then, what exactly is Federalism?"

Again, hands shot up from front and center.

"Yes, Matt?"

Matt lowered his hand, smiling. "Federalism is a system of government in which power is shared between the states and the federal government."

"Very good, Matt!"

"Now, *this* is teaching history," Mr. Reaf thought to himself. "OK, let's venture out into the hinterlands." He looked over to the far row by the windows. Samuel was staring outside.

"Samuel!"

The boy jumped, then turned to face the teacher.

"What exactly was in the *Federalist Papers?*" Mr. Reaf asked.

Samuel stared down at his book.

"Advertisements?" he offered.

Two students in the first row giggled.

"No, Samuel! It wasn't that kind of paper," Mr. Reaf answered sternly. He moved to the student behind Samuel.

"Tamara, name one of the most famous Federalists."

Tamara stared blankly. "Bill Clinton?"

"No!" Mr. Reaf said in disbelief. "Did you read the chapter? What have you been doing?"

Tamara lowered her head and began turning pages in her book. OK, he'd try one of the boys in the back.

"Carlos, how were the Antifederalists different?"

"They weren't uncles!" he shot back.

The room erupted in laughter.

"Quiet, quiet. Right now!" called out Mr. Reaf. He sensed that he might lose control of the class.

"OK, everyone turn to the end of this section and answer all the questions."

Groans erupted.

"Come on," Mr. Reaf chimed in. "Get to work."

Tamara buried her head in her arms on her desk.

* * * * * *

Obviously, Mr. Reaf is having a tough time trying to engage his students in a discussion of the Constitution. The irony is that Mr. Reaf loves his subject. He wants to instill in his students the literacy and decision-making skills they need to participate actively in a democratic society. In fact, the National Council for the Social Studies states that "exemplary social studies programs develop social and civic participation skills that prepare students to work effectively in diverse groups to address problems by discussing alternative strategies, making decisions, and taking action; to pursue social and civic agendas through persuasion, negotiation, and compromise; and to participate actively in civic affairs" (National Council for the Social Studies, 1997). Yet, in reality, many of Mr. Reaf's students don't seem to want to learn or even to behave.

Classrooms should serve students as models of democracy. Despite the fact that teachers control classrooms, the goal of the democratic classroom is to guide students in the accomplishment of the democratic process. In effect, teachers guide students in a fashion similar to the way that mayors, governors, and other elected officials guide their constituencies. Classrooms can be thought of as communities that are governed but are designed to engage all students in a democratic process of learning to further the common good. In practice, however, as Mr. Reaf's class illustrates, classroom management issues may make it difficult to achieve this goal.

Issues of Classroom Management and Discipline

In conversations with secondary teachers, it is rarely long before the issues of classroom management and discipline arise. Teachers often cite incidents of misbehavior and antisocial actions that obstruct the learning efforts of others. In a recent survey, 21 percent of teachers in large urban schools, when questioned about disruptive students, reported that they lost on average approximately 24 hours a week of instructional time; and they included statements about the commensurate anxiety that accompanies the constant disruption and conflict (Walker, Ramsey, & Gresham, 2003).

The reasons for misbehavior are many. We can all remember the awkwardness of being a teenager and dealing with the psychological, emotional, social, intellectual, and physical stresses of adolescence. Even changes in mood can add to the unpredictability of an adolescent (Milgram, 1992). The three-year "tour of duty" of the middle grades followed by high school can be a dramatic time for young people—and for the adults who oversee their development.

Classroom disruptions occur for a number of other reasons, such as the following:

• Struggling students are academically unable to engage in classroom activities. Students who are unable to read difficult texts may become disruptive because they would rather appear "bad" than "stupid."

• Brain-based learning research shows that old-style classroom methodologies, such as lecture or read-and-recite methods, contribute to student misbehavior. As David Sousa (2001) points out, today's children have become accustomed to rapidly changing sensory and emotional stimuli, resulting in a decrease in their attention spans. Their brains "respond more than ever to the unique and different—what is called *novelty*" (p. 28).

• Disruptions may be an outgrowth of the changing nature of the population of the United States. With little or no training, teachers and administrators are expected to accommodate a wide range of languages, cultural beliefs and practices, and communication and learning styles.

• Socioeconomic status may also affect student behavior. For example, students who grow up in poverty, dealing daily with health and welfare issues, and who attend deteriorating facilities with inadequate materials, may lose their sense of possibility.

• Finally, some students live in home environments where the only model of management is coercive in nature. Self-management is neither modeled nor taught. Consequently, these students may replicate their home management style in aggressive forms, such as intimidation or bullying.

For some adolescents, social and psychological factors contribute to a cycle of failure that often leads to dropping out (Haley & Watson, 2000).

Teachers' Management Styles

In response to the issues they face, teachers may not be well trained in classroom management techniques. Based on their own educational experiences, many will primarily adopt one of two management models: custodial or humanistic (Feddema, personal communication, 1998). In the custodial model, maintaining order is the priority. The underlying view of students in this perspective is that most are irresponsible, untrustworthy, and lack control. A signature to this view is the cliché "Never smile before Christmas!" The pedagogy in such a classroom centers on a high level of teacher control. Student behavior must be dictated, with little attention to the thoughts, feelings, or preferences of the students (Burden, 2003). Teachers with a custodial view often resort to coercive methods of discipline. However, as Mr. Reaf discovered with Carlos, using coercive management tactics with some students only creates more problems. When a teacher uses coercion with a student who experiences such interactions every day from peers or parents, the teacher is using the very weapon the student knows and handles best. Such techniques often create more disruption. As an ancient proverb states, "When you starve with a tiger, the tiger eats last."

In contrast, the humanistic view holds that students are trustworthy, able to be self-disciplined, and can make appropriate choices when given the opportunity. Understandably, this view reflects the potential for a more student-centered classroom characterized by high levels of student engagement and accountability. A humanistic management style is not a laissez-faire situation in which students get to choose whether or not to work. In fact, this environment can result in more student motivation and productivity.

Teachers often physically arrange their classrooms based on their inherent management perspective. For example, a teacher with a custodial view, such as Mr. Reaf, may seat students in straight rows so that he can oversee the entire room from one place.

In this configuration, at least three dynamics are at work. Students who are in close proximity to the teacher capture most of the teacher's attention. These students are generally attentive and on task. On the fringes, students may give tacit attention and tacit resistance. These areas are "pockets of intermittent attention" because the students may be out of the teacher's range of delivery, or they may be lacking command of the content. Often these students may be off task, although they appear to be working. Finally, the outer group is usually out of the teacher delivery zone completely, attending to the clock or to one another rather than to instruction.

Many teachers report that, when they were students, their classrooms resembled a model of organization like Mr. Reaf's, in which they sat in straight rows while the teacher lectured to them, read to them, or assigned independent seatwork. This didactic and long-held model of secondary pedagogy is very much alive today.

Pedagogically, this approach has its limitations. As Mr. Reaf discovered in his own classroom, there may be fewer opportunities for students to engage with one another in critical thinking, fewer opportunities for peer modeling, and a loss of any sense of the classroom being a community of learners. Formats for discussion may be limited. In a model typically described as "recitation," the teacher may engage in whole-group explanation and then stop to throw a question out for bid. After a brief silence, one or more of the attentive students may offer a response. Discussion may be limited to literal answers for the teacher rather than higher-level and engaging dialogues among students.

At-risk students in such classes have ample reason to either hide out or act out, because their chances for academic success are limited. Classroom organization can be particularly significant for struggling students because they begin a downward spiral academically that may lead to avoidance or antisocial behaviors that exacerbate their lack of performance. These students begin to resist instruction, and in so doing, obstruct the learning of others.

In contrast, in classrooms where student engagement is fostered, student achievement can increase. The creation of a positive social climate in classrooms may increase students' efficacy for relating effectively with their teacher and also may be related positively to students' perceptions of academic efficacy. Johnson, Johnson, & Holubec (1994) have stated that viewing classrooms in terms of "interaction patterns" can help maximize the opportunities for students to interact in productive ways. Other practices that may develop students' efficacy and social responsibility include task structures in which all students are included, the allowing of friends to interact, and a classroom environment that encourages a wide range of norms and values (Patrick, Hicks, & Ryan, 1997).

Teachers have also found that creating an interactive environment fosters achievement. In the ASCD *Education Update* of August 2004, Janice Daubenmier and Debby Kent, two former 8th grade teachers, note that "when students have to talk about the content with others, when they must explain it, they learn what they know as well as what they need to gain more knowledge of" (Checkley, 2004, p. 6). Furthermore, in the NEA document *Thought and Action* (Limbach & Waugh, 2005), an article titled "Questioning the Lecture Format" suggests that "students learn best in a supportive environment. Building a class community that emphasizes important concepts and builds background knowledge happens only in a comfortable classroom environment. Critical thinking in the classroom requires interpersonal relationships that support the participation of all." Finally, James Gee (1996) makes the analogy that literacy and the social dimension of learning are linked much like the squares of a chess-board, and if you remove either the white or the black, you no longer have a chessboard. Thus the social dimension of the classroom and the cognitive experiences of students' interactions with text and with learning are inextricably linked.

How, then, do social studies teachers change a custodial classroom with seats arranged in straight rows into a humanistic environment that fosters the democratic engagement called for in the social studies standards? One solution is a methodology called the Cooperative Literacy approach (Klemp, 2002; Klemp, Hon, & Shorr, 1993).

Cooperative Literacy

The Cooperative Literacy approach calls for organizing classrooms into mutually interdependent, noncompetitive learning teams of four to five students over an extended period. This approach allows teachers to transform classrooms into communities that provide for distributed authority, heightened accountability, and supported literacy instruction. Teachers can effectively balance whole-group, individual, and small-group instruction and seize opportunities to bring all students into the center of the "action zone" in each class.

PODS

Students are placed heterogeneously into four- or five-member groups known as PODS (Performance Organizational Design System). The term *team* is not used because this organizational strategy is noncompetitive. PODs can remain intact for four to six weeks. Grouping strategies may be dependent on the specific needs of a particular class, but a random selection is suggested. Student self-selection is discouraged, as students with similar behavior patterns may group themselves and become disruptive. Grouping strategies may consider such factors as ethnicity, reading ability, or gender. A teacher spending considerable time on, for example, the Civil War might make up I.D. cards or name cards that are pertinent to the content. There might be four Lincoln cards, four Grant cards, four Davis cards, and four Lee cards. Students are handed one of these cards as they enter the classroom. When students are called "to POD," students with the same cards group together in the seats assigned to each POD.

In a classroom of 36 students, the teacher would have 9 PODs of 4 students each. PODs sit with two students side by side and two more directly behind them in tandem. Occasionally a POD of five occurs. Space is allotted between each group so that the room appears to have nine islands. The spacing allows for the teacher's monitoring of groups through a Power Walk, which is discussed later. Rooms with tables instead of desks may be adjusted accordingly.

Each seat in the POD has a number (see Figure 4.1). The numbering scheme has both a logistical and an instructional purpose. Logistically, the use of the numbers gives the teacher a visual cue as to which POD member has which function, depending on a specific activity. In this new conceptualization of the classroom from 36 individual students to 9 PODs, the opportunities for distributed authority are many. For example, the teacher might ask all of the Number 2s in each POD to come forward to pick up materials for their group. Or students may be dismissed by POD. If the teacher notices some litter on the floor, he or she may ask the POD to pick it up as opposed to singling out one student. The teacher may also arbitrarily call on a number to explain the directions of an activity to their POD. From the student's point

of view, his or her role as a member of the classroom has changed from an individual to part of a community.

From an instructional standpoint, the teacher can now direct an activity, but the students manage its completion. Ideally, teachers begin the class in this configuration to "orient" the students to the day's lesson through a review or warm-up activity that focuses them on the topic at hand. When all students are facing the teacher, they can work individually or in pairs. When students are told to have a Face Off each group of four students turns their desks to face one another, to work as a group.

Numbered positions allow the teacher to specify certain roles, such as Questioner, Observer, Recorder, and Reporter. Activities are set up so that students can discuss one another's ideas, perspectives, and interpretations. Learning activities that encourage students to move from egocentric to sociocentric functions create better understanding on the part of all involved (Fabes, Carlo, Kupanoff, & Laible, 1999).

Each week a POD member is assigned to manage the Point Sheet (see Figure 4.2). The Point Sheet is a kind of rubric that states criteria on which the group evaluates itself. Criteria might be such items as absences, tardies, being prepared for class with materials, being on task, having homework completed, and exhibiting expected behavior. Teachers can modify the Point Sheet criteria to suit the demands of their content. On a daily basis, the teacher selects the categories on the Point Sheet on which to assess the PODs. Each week, each POD selects a POD Coordinator to record points at the teacher's discretion on the category or categories set by the teacher. For instance, if bringing materials to class is a selected issue, then the teacher would ask each

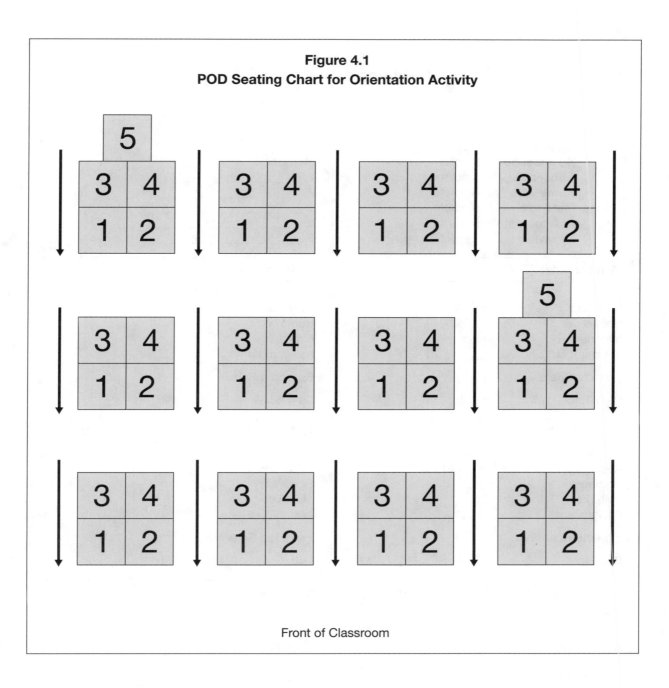

Figure 4.1
POD Seating Chart for Orientation Activity

Front of Classroom

Coordinator to evaluate his or her POD on their compliance.

The POD Point Sheet, aside from providing a guide, or script, for the PODs to follow, becomes an assessment (or self-assessment) tool. In this sense, the PODs manage and assess themselves, even though the teacher directs the placing of points. It is essential to note that the teacher directs the coordinators to write the points rather than leaving that to the students. As the class becomes more adept at this protocol, it might be possible for the teacher to release the issuing of points to the students. Until then, the POD Coordinators for the week write on the sheet the number of points as they are directed to do by the teacher.

Figure 4.2
POD Point Sheet

		POD # _____ POD Name _____
On time	5 points	
No absence	5 points	**Members:**
1 absence	3 points	1. _____
Homework	5 points	2. _____
Materials	5 points	3. _____
Assignment	5 points	4. _____
Behavior	5 points	5. _____

Monday date:	Points	Thursday date:	Points
Arrival		Arrival	
Absences		Absences	
Homework		Homework	
Materials		Materials	
Assignment		Assignment	
Expected Behavior		Expected Behavior	
Daily Total	_____	Daily Total	_____

Tuesday date:	Points	Friday date:	Points
Arrival		Arrival	
Absences		Absences	
Homework		Homework	
Materials		Materials	
Assignment		Assignment	
Expected Behavior		Expected Behavior	
Daily Total	_____	Daily Total	_____

Wednesday date:	Points	Bonus!	Points
Arrival		Sharing Information	
Absences			
Homework		Encouraging	
Materials			
Assignment		Listening	
Expected Behavior		Participating	
Daily Total	_____	WEEKLY TOTAL:	_____

In the example shown in Figure 4.2, the "Assignment" category relates to the period when students are engaged in a class activity that is either whole-group, individual, or "in POD." Points are issued by the teacher based on the POD's success in managing time on task, and the coordinator writes them onto the sheet as directed, allowing the teacher to provide immediate feedback. It should be noted that points are not given to create competition between PODs. Rather, the purpose of the points is to provide the opportunity for corrective feedback from the teacher for students. The rubric for the "Expected Behavior" category can be found in the lower-right-hand corner of Figure 4.2 which is labeled "Bonus!" This rubric covers behaviors that relate to the type of activity assigned. For example, if the PODs are engaged in a cooperative activity, the teacher would tell the POD Coordinators to list *sharing information, encouraging, listening,* and *participating* under the "Expected Behavior" category.

The Power Walk

Once an assignment has been given and students have moved from a whole-class organization to "in POD," the teacher circulates around the room in what is known as a Power Walk. (This name reflects the intention to empower the students by giving ongoing feedback on the criteria and expected behavior.) If PODs have lost points in the first assessment—say, for example, two students did not do homework—then the Power Walk affords an opportunity for the POD to generate more points. The teacher, acting as a facilitator, monitors each POD's work and awards performance points for good behavior and productivity. During the Power Walk, points are never deducted, but students who go off task may cause their POD to earn fewer points. This approach

helps create positive interdependence among students.

Positive Interdependence

When individuals display positive interdependence, members of a group realize that each must contribute for the sake of the others. Even the most recalcitrant students understand this concept. For example, students in musical groups, students who play sports, and even students in gangs all realize that they must contribute for the sake of others. However, adolescents must be taught how to mediate. When members of a POD don't know how to solve a particular problem, they may become hostile to the student who seems to be bringing the group down.

The Class Processing Worksheet (Figure 4.3) provides a format for an intervention by the teacher when group interactions stop being productive. Students answer the questions individually in a directed lesson format. Students should be specific in their answers. "Do my work" is too general an answer for Question 5, which asks, "What are examples of requests your teacher makes of you?" Instead, the teacher should ask students to repeat exactly what their behavioral expectations and assignments are. This strategy is an excellent way of finding out how well communication is taking place between teacher and students. Any experienced teacher knows that there can be a great deal of difference between what the teacher says and what the students hear.

Question 6 allows students to express their attitudes. After students have circled a word, they make a journal entry on the back of the Processing Worksheet. To initiate this, the teacher asks students to write the day's date and then complete the following phrase: "I am _____ because. . . ." These journal entries may provide crucial information for the

Figure 4.3
Class Processing Worksheet

The purpose of this worksheet is to determine if members of the class are behaving in a manner appropriate for learning. You will answer the following questions on your own. When time is called, a class discussion will be held to consider your answers.

1. Write your first and last name._____

2. What is the title of this class?_____

3. In your opinion, how would you describe the behavior of this class?

4. What are some actions you need to take to make sure that you can learn in this classroom?

5. What are examples of requests your teacher makes of you?

6. Which of the following words best describe you? Draw a circle around all the words that describe you.

happy   boring   studious   conscientious   caring

indifferent   concerned   worried   lost   misunderstood

curious   eager   positive   negative   humorous

7. What can you do to make this class better for you?

teacher when problems arise as to why a particular student is behaving a certain way.

Once students have completed the Processing Worksheet, their responses are polled and discussed. The teacher should give particular attention to Question 7, which asks what each student can do to make the class better.

After a week, the teacher can redistribute these same Processing Worksheets, asking students to re-evaluate the class. This revisiting implies a personal contract that students are making. In the event that a "contract" is broken, the teacher now has a paper trail as to how and why problems may have developed.

The POD Assessment Inventory (Figure 4.4) provides a less-formal group self-assessment. Many teachers use this self-assessment when PODs have performed well, so they can reflect on their good behaviors. The inventory can be used as often as once a week. Each member of a POD completes a form that asks them to rate the following:

- Their own performance
- The group's performance
- How they feel they were successful
- Ways in which they could improve before the next assessment
- What they learned from the exercise

Often it can be helpful for students to reflect on how they performed on an assessment. Students need to reflect on such questions as "Did I do my best?" "What did others do to succeed?" "Am I up to the task?" By publicly sharing their strategies, they can set a tone for improvement and receive validation from POD members using the POD Assessment Inventory. When students begin to reflect on their own efficacy and can share ideas about how better to prepare, they have a new opportunity to improve.

The Mediation Conference

As discussed earlier in this chapter, adolescence inevitably involves conflicts, no matter how much planning and organization the teacher provides. When difficult or disruptive situations arise with a student, teachers should plan an individual mediation conference with that student.

The mediation conference provides an opportunity for the teacher and student to explore the behavioral aspects of the problem. This dialogue-based strategy guides the student's thinking to help him or her solve the observed problem. This approach avoids an adversarial relationship. As Jere Brophy (1998) notes:

> Students will not respond to your motivational attempts if they are fearful, resentful, or too otherwise focused on negative emotions. To create conditions that favor your motivational efforts, you will need to establish and maintain your classroom as a learning community— a place where students primarily learn, and succeed in doing so through collaboration with you and their classmates. (p. 21)

The teacher brings the most recent version of the student's Class Processing Worksheet (see Figure 4.3) to the conference. A third-party mediator, either another teacher or an administrator, may also attend. In some instances, a parent may be asked to be part of the process. The teacher begins by noting that the student's POD points have been diminishing and explains that this conference is to figure out why and solve any problems. The group reviews the student's responses to the Class Processing Worksheet, asking the student to elaborate on

Figure 4.4
POD Assessment Inventory

Name:_____

When working with a group, or POD, it is important to be aware of how your efforts paid off. This form is intended to help the POD examine its assessment performance. **Discuss the questions and then each POD member will complete the form.**

1. Circle the number that best corresponds to how you would rate your individual performance on the assessment.

Needs to Improve		Average		Great!
1	2	3	4	5

2. Circle the number that best corresponds to how you would rate your POD's performance on the assessment.

Needs to Improve		Average		Great!
1	2	3	4	5

3. What were some of the ways in which your POD was successful with the assessment?

4. What are some of the ways in which your POD could improve on the assessment?

5. If you could redo the assessment, what would be some different strategies you would use to improve?

6. What did you learn from this exercise? (Use back if necessary.)

answers. Questions 3 and 4 help set the tone for the conference in that they validate the student's perceptions of the class and then ask the student to name specific actions that would help learning take place.

The mediation process then proceeds as an interview, with the teacher transcribing the student's responses onto the Mediation Interview Worksheet (Figure 4.5). The Mediation Interview Worksheet provides a script for this interview, but teachers can paraphrase the language so that students comprehend what is being asked. The focus of the interview is always on the student. Students are first asked to describe the conflict as if they were watching it on television. The metaphor of the video helps create dissociation from the described behaviors as students view themselves in the classroom.

The third question is the pivotal point in the interview. After a behavior is described, the teacher asks the student, "What makes that OK to do?" The question challenges the motivation behind the behavior rather than just the action. If the teacher has worked hard to keep the relationship objective, and the focus stays on the student and is not confrontational, students will likely respond that it is "not OK." The importance of this challenge to any misbehavior is the students' acknowledgment that their actions will not make them more successful in class, as described earlier on the Class Processing Worksheet. Growth occurs when students see the incongruity of their stated successful behaviors and their actual misbehavior. This protocol is designed to objectify the encounter so that the teacher is not an adversary. The teacher can help students see, however, that continued misbehavior will have long-term effects on their ability to perform successfully.

The mediation conference ends with the teacher asking the student to strategize about how the behavior can cease or be controlled. In response, a student may ask to be moved to another POD, or to be given more help in reading an assignment.

Once an agreement is made, the teacher and student set a sign-off date when the two will check on their progress. This sign-off may be as simple as a moment of positive feedback during the teacher's Power Walk a day or week later. In this way, the teacher is modeling problem-solving skills of how adults participate in a democratic society.

Cooperative Literacy and Learning

According to an old saying, "The systems you have in place are perfect for the results you are getting." Teachers who recognize that their classroom management beliefs and systems are not promoting active democratic participation should try new methods. The Cooperative Literacy model described in this chapter offers one such system to help turn classrooms into learning communities. Students who first work independently and then transition into a Face Off become a consensus group. Students become engaged because of their accountability to the larger group. The perspective of control shifts from that of a custodial teacher to that of a humanitarian facilitator. Increased oral communication derived from focused peer interaction also promotes literacy development. For some students, their ability to enhance their literacy skills in diverse situations may well depend upon the relationships established between the teacher and the students, as well as those among the students themselves (Au, 1993). Transforming a classroom into a learning community can happen, even with Mr. Reaf.

* * * * * * *

Figure 4.5
Mediation Interview Worksheet

Student's Name: _____ Teacher: _____ Date: _____

1. Description of conflict: (in the student's own words, while the teacher records)

2. For a starter: "What would we see you doing in class if we were watching you on television?"

3. Justification: "What makes your behavior OK?" (In the student's mind, how is the action justified?)

4. Alternatives: What are some occasions that the student can remember when this conflict did not exist?

5. Analysis: What other aspects of the class contribute to the problems, such as other students, or misunderstandings of the assignment or rules, or failure to pay attention?

6. Roles: What can the teacher do to assist the student in helping the situation to improve?

7. Strategies: Specific actions will make the situation better. What, in the student's own words, will he or she do differently?

8. Results: After talking about these strategies, what results might occur from them?

9. Follow up: When will the teacher and student reconvene to discuss progress?

Progress Conference: Date _____

(Additional comments, if any, on back)

Mr. Reaf realized that a few desks were scattered about the room as his first-period students scrambled in just before the tardy bell.

"OK, everyone, we'll be working in PODs today, so make sure your desks are set up properly and you leave room for me to walk between your groups."

Tamara moved a desk over to fill the group of four she was working with during the coverage of today's lesson—Chapter 3 on Ratifying the Constitution. Mr. Reaf waited for everyone to settle down.

"Would the Number 3 person in each POD continue to check attendance?"

The door flew open as Samantha came running in after the late bell.

"And be sure to mark any tardies."

Mr. Reaf gave Samantha his "not-so-evil" eye and smiled.

"Way to go, Sam!" said Thomas sarcastically as Samantha took her seat beside him. "You owe us a point."

Sam made a face at her partner.

"OK, let's do a quick review and orientation. You remember that it's around 1777 and the delegates have been hashing out some big issues for our country. One is to figure out how many people from each state will be in the national legislature. Any Number 2s out there remember what this compromise was called? POD members, you can help your Number 2."

Samuel's hand shot up from his spot in the front-right POD.

"Yes, Samuel?"

"The Great Compromise?"

"Excellent, Samuel. Let's begin our orientation for Chapter 3 on Ratifying the Constitution. First, does anyone know what *ratifying* means? I'll need a Number 1 to give us an answer. Any POD member can help."

The students quickly turned to put their heads together. A hand went up in the POD in the back corner of the room.

"Yes, Marie?"

"Does it mean to say something is OK?"

"Yes. Can someone say it differently?"

Juan's hand shot up.

"Juan?"

"It means when a group formally agrees on something."

"Excellent. You're both right. Now, you can imagine if these guys are building the framework for a new country, there is going to be some disagreement. For our orientation activity we're going to do an Anticipation Guide, or, as we like to call it, Agree/Disagree [see Figure 4.6]. Would a Number 4 in each POD come forward and pick up four of these handouts for your group?"

Nine students jumped up and retrieved their group's handouts and passed them out. Once they had settled back down, Mr. Reaf continued.

"I've written three statements that I want you to think about. We'll do our Think, Write, Pair, Square strategy on this. You know the drill, but I'll go over it quickly. First, think about each statement individually and mark whether you agree or disagree with it. Be sure to mark your answer in the Before Reading space. Remember that we'll mark the After Reading space once we read the text to see if our opinions have changed. I'll give you four minutes.

"When I say 'Stop and Pair,' turn to your partner and discuss your answers. I'll give you four minutes for that also. If you disagree with each other, find out why. When I say 'Stop and Square,' move your desks *quietly* to your Face-Off positions and share your answers. If there is disagreement, find out why. I'll give you five minutes.

"By the end of five minutes, your group has to choose whether it will agree or disagree with each statement. You can vote. If you have a deadlock—in other words, if the

---

Figure 4.6
Anticipation Guide (Agree/Disagree)

Agree/Disagree

Statement	Before Reading	After Reading
1. Individual states should have more power than the federal government in Washington, D.C.	_____	_____
2. The legislative branch, or the people representing the states, should have more power than the president.	_____	_____
3. When one person is placed in a high position, there is a good chance he or she will abuse his or her power and become a tyrant.	_____	_____

---

vote is two to two—then your group will have to explain the opposing viewpoints. Everyone clear? OK, I'll read the statements aloud one time and then you can begin."

Mr. Reaf read aloud the following three statements from the Anticipation Guide:

1. Individual states should have more power than the federal government in Washington, D.C.
2. The legislative branch, or the people representing the states, should have more power than the president.
3. When one person is placed in a high position, there is a good chance he or she will abuse his or her power and become a tyrant.

For the next 15 minutes, the class followed their instructions. The noise increased as the groups moved from pairs to Face-Off squares, but as Mr. Reaf did his Power Walk, he could tell that everyone was on task. Samantha made a point of vehemently expressing her view when he stopped at her POD. Mr. Reaf made a point of letting her know he was giving her group Participation Points.

After the Face-Off time had passed, Mr. Reaf called the class to order.

"OK, let's look at the first statement. If your group agreed with this statement, then the Number 3s in that group stand up."

Four students groaned and rose to their feet.

"Tanya, beginning with you, why did your group agree?"

Tanya proceeded to give her explanation. Mr. Reaf asked the other three students who were standing to express their group's opinions as well.

"Good. Agreeable 3s may sit down. Now, let's hear from our Disagreeable 2s. If your group disagreed with Statement 1 and you're a Number 2, stand up and tell us why."

The 2s rose and expressed their opinions. Mr. Reaf continued this procedure with the other two Anticipation Guide statements. Class members got into some spirited discussions, especially about whether a person with great power would become a tyrant or not. They talked about everyone from Saddam Hussein to Gandhi. Mr. Reaf looked at his watch. He still had 10 minutes left in the period.

"Class, tomorrow we'll see how these guys in the 1780s dealt with the same issues you've dealt with today. Since we still have a few minutes, this might be a good time to do one of our Group Processing Inventories. We haven't done one for a couple of weeks now. Would all Number 4s please come up and get inventories for your group? Please take the remaining time to fill it out honestly. Remember, putting your name on the form is optional. When the bell rings, Number 4s please collect the inventories and set them here on my desk. Would you also please bring up your POD's Point Sheet and put it in the appropriate folder on the table? We'll wait until tomorrow to deal with those disagreeable Antifederalists."

"Mr. Reaf?" asked Carlos.

"Yes, Carlos?"

"Why are we learning this stuff?"

John smiled. "Because, Carlos, I want you to get involved in something."

"Yeah? What's that something?" asked Carlos.

"Something called democracy."

5

Promoting Civic Engagement

Mr. Reaf stood behind his desk, staring down at the title of the chapter—"The Living Constitution." "Well," he thought, "'living'" remains to be seen. We'll see how much of it survives this class.

"Class, would you please open your texts to page 248? We're going to begin the chapter on the Constitution. Now, you hear a lot about constitutions in the press today. Whenever a country attempts to establish a democratic form of government, the first step is to write a constitution. This is what has been attempted in countries in Eastern Europe after they were free from communism. It's also what has been attempted in Iraq. Can anyone tell me what our Constitution does?"

Mr. Reaf stared into a sea of blank faces.

"Louise, what does our Constitution do?"

Louise shifted in her seat.

"I don't know," she muttered. "It's like, you know, uh, it's like the thing that tells us what to do."

"OK, good," Mr. Reaf nodded.

"Who can add to that?"

Again, no response.

"Well, let's start reading the document, and you'll see just what it does. We'll start reading aloud with Sara in the first seat of row 1. Sara, read a paragraph and then the second person, Leon, will read the next, and so on. OK, go ahead, Sara."

Sara stared down at her book. She read aloud, "Article 1. The Legislature," then stopped.

"Sara?"

"Well, you said to read one paragraph," she said, a bit frustrated.

"Well, you read one heading, not one paragraph," responded Mr. Reaf patiently. "Please continue."

"Section 1. Congress. All legislative powers herein granted shall be vested in a Congress of the United States, which shall consist of a Senate and a House of Representatives."

As Sara read, a number of students in the far rows lowered their heads onto their desks.

"Good, Sara. Leon, please continue."

Leon looked down at his book. He began falteringly.

"Section 2. The House of Representatives. 1. Elections. The House of Representatives shall be composed of members chosen every second year by the people of the several states, and the electors in each state shall have the qualifications re—re—qui—site—"

"Requisite," Mr. Reaf corrected.

"Yeah, whatever," replied Leon. He stopped reading.

Mr. Reaf finished the sentence.

"OK, the word *electors* is in bold print. Who can tell me what this word means?"

No response.

"Well, here's a hint. How many of you are over 18? Raise your hands."

Twenty-four of 32 hands went up.

"Those with your hands up are now electors. So what does it mean?"

"People who can vote?" offered Sheila.

"Exactly! So, how many of you voted in the election we had last month? Raise your hands."

Six hands went up.

"What!" exclaimed Mr. Reaf. "Only six of you? Why didn't the rest of you vote? Don't you know how important it is? People in other countries would give anything to be able to vote for elected officials."

"Then tell them to come vote here," mumbled Carlos.

Mr. Reaf stared in disbelief. He walked around the front of the desk to face his class.

"Carlos, you don't mean that. Voting is our civic duty. You must know how wonderful it is to have the right to choose our own government."

Carlos laughed. "Whose government? Those people don't represent me."

A number of students called out in agreement.

"Why would I care what politicians think?" continued Carlos. "They just want what little money we got. I ain't got no time to follow politics, anyway."

"But, Carlos, if you don't voice your opinion, someone else will do it for you, whether you agree with them or not."

"Come on, Mr. Reaf, who's gonna listen to me? Really."

Mr. Reaf looked at his class. No one challenged Carlos's views. They stared at him blankly. How could he get his students to care about democracy?

* * * * * * *

Engaging the Disengaged

Mr. Reaf's encounter with his students while studying the Constitution is not abnormal. Recent studies aimed at measuring the civic engagement of the DotNet generation, those students between the ages of 15 and 26, reveal some discouraging statistics. For example, Kurtz, Rosenthal, and Zukin (2003) found the following:

- Fewer than half of the DotNets think that communicating with elected officials or volunteering or donating money to help others is a quality of a good citizen.
- Only 66 percent of the DotNets say that voting is a necessary quality for being a good citizen, compared with 83 percent of those over age 26.
- Only half of the DotNets reported that they voted in the most recent elections or that they follow politics, compared with three-quarters of those over age 26.
- Among DotNets, 8 out of 10 know that the cartoon Simpsons live in Springfield, and the great majority know the most recent winner of *American Idol.* But fewer than half know the party of their state's governor, and only 40 percent can say which party controls Congress.
- The gap between the civic attitudes, knowledge, and participation of the new generation of DotNets and the older generations is substantially greater than the gaps between previous generations. It suggests that the DotNets will never be as engaged in democracy as their elders, even as they age.

Until the 2004 presidential election, "the electoral participation of Americans under the age of 25 [had] declined since 1972, when 18-to-21-year-olds were first permitted to vote. The size of the decline in presidential-election years [was] between 13 and 15 percentage points" (Levine & Lopez, 2002, p. 1). The November 2004 election was an exception. The Center for Information & Research on Civic Learning & Engagement (CIRCLE, 2005) estimates that in 2004 the turnout of 18- to 24-year-old voters was approximately 42.3 percent, up from 36.5 percent in 2000.

"Young people between the ages of 25 and 29 voted at a higher rate, 58.8% in 2004 vs. 53.1% in 2000. [However,] exit polls also indicate that 18–24 year olds' share of the total vote stayed about the same as in 2000, at around 9%" (pp. 1–2). Such statistics lead us to ask this question: What does civic education propose to accomplish?

According to the National Council for the Social Studies (1997), civic education consists of three major components: "first, the development of knowledge and understanding about our democratic institutions and principles and their history; second, the development of the intellectual and participatory skills necessary for competent participation in the democratic process; and third, the development of an appreciation for democratic values and principles that result in the civic dispositions essential for a vital civic life."

This chapter looks at the role that schools can play in fostering a desire among youth to become involved in civic activities, in helping teachers get students like Carlos engaged in civic programs, especially voting and volunteering. But first, let's look at the unique position that schools occupy in helping our youth become involved in a democratic society.

The Role of Schools in Civic Education

Throughout U.S. history, the role of providing civic education has fallen primarily on schools and specifically on social studies teachers. From the onset of public education in the United States, a major purpose of schooling has been to foster learning about and participation in the nation's democratic system of government. In 1835, Alexis de Tocqueville noted in his famous work

Democracy in America that "it cannot be doubted that in the United States the instruction of the people powerfully contributes to the support of the democratic republic." There are good reasons why the skills, beliefs, and values of democracy are best transmitted in the schools. The Campaign for the Civic Mission of Schools (2004) notes the following reasons why schools are important venues for civic education:

• It is crucial for the future health of American democracy that all young people, including those [from groups] who are usually marginalized, be knowledgeable, engaged in their communities and in politics, and committed to the public good.
• Encouraging the development of civic skills and attitudes among young people has been an important goal of education and was the primary impetus for originally establishing public schools.
• Schools are the only institutions with the capacity and mandate to reach virtually every young person in the United States. Of all institutions, schools are the most systematically and directly responsible for imparting citizen norms.
• Schools are best equipped to address the cognitive aspects of good citizenship—civic and political knowledge and related skills such as critical thinking and deliberation.
• Schools are communities in which young people learn to interact, argue, and work together with others, an important foundation for future citizenship.
• Many nonschool institutions that used to provide venues for young people to participate in civic and political affairs (such as political parties, unions, nonprofit associations, and activist religious denominations) have lost the capacity or will to engage young people.

• Forty state constitutions mention the importance of civic literacy among citizens, and 13 of them state that a central purpose of their educational system is to promote good citizenship, democracy, and free government.

The National Council for the Social Studies (2005) also acknowledges the place civic education holds in its programs:

> Civic efficacy—the readiness and willingness to assume citizenship responsibilities—is rooted in social studies knowledge and skills, along with related values (such as concern for the common good) and attitudes (such as an orientation toward participation in civic affairs). The nation depends on a well-informed and civic-minded citizenry to sustain its democratic traditions, especially now as it adjusts to its own heterogeneous society and its shifting roles in an increasingly interdependent and changing world.

A number of schools have accepted the challenge of engaging their youth in civic activities. The following is a brief description of the programs and progress of a select few.

Model School Programs

Schools have found many ways to help students connect what they are learning in school with their communities and the world in which they live. These concrete experiences help students apply what they learn about social studies and make their learning important and stimulating. Community experiences—both service learning and community study—build deep connections for students and increase their desire to become more involved. Both real and simulated experiences in taking on roles in government and taking action on social issues help students develop a deep understanding of civic responsibility and participatory government.

One clear way schools can connect with the larger community is during times of crisis. When tragedies strike, either locally or beyond the community, students can be involved in providing relief. For example, the tsunami that struck East Asia in December 2004 resulted in an outpouring of support for the victims. Elementary schools across the United States responded with fundraisers and collections of school materials. Middle and high schools did the same. When teachers support students' moral impulses to make a contribution to the world, they help to scaffold students' sense of civic participation. Many schools develop regular yearly activities that involve children's contributions to others, whether through Thanksgiving food drives or more ongoing involvement.

Service Learning

Service learning programs provide a concrete way for students to participate in their local communities. Many local, state, and national programs help structure such experiences (see www.ServiceLearn.com). One format popular in many states is to require a certain number of hours of service learning as part of secondary graduation requirements (Wysocki, 1999). Schools provide an array of options for such participation; for example, in some programs students can work in food pantries, help with environmental clean-up projects, volunteer in senior citizen programs, and assist with voter registration efforts. As they participate, students learn more about their own community and experience the personal satisfaction that can lead to a lifestyle that includes service.

Community Study and Recognition

The Pennsylvania State Department of Instruction provides guidelines for an interdisciplinary curriculum project that builds middle grade students' understanding of the roles that citizens play in democratic communities. In the project, each student selects one community member as the focus of his or her research. Because students have very different experiences with people who are making a difference—from daycare workers and maintenance personnel to the mayors and business leaders—generally a wide spectrum of the community is represented. The students learn skills of interviewing and then conduct interviews of the community members. They also do research in local archives with the help of the community librarians so they can depict the context of the person's life accurately. Finally, each student prepares a report and visual display highlighting that person's contribution within the context of social and political events. These large triptych display boards are shared at a community celebration that brings together the students and the adult community.

As a result of this project, the students gain a great deal of understanding about the myriad ways that often-unrecognized citizens contribute to community life. The adults gain, too, as they meet young people in positive contexts and dispel some of the negative stereotypes associated with adolescents. Teachers like the project because it provides a motivating context for students to develop language arts skills in interviewing, writing biographies, and creating visual displays. Social studies skills are developed as students research the social and political context of the community for their biographies.

Celebrating the contributions of community members develops middle graders' pride and awareness of citizenship.

High school students also gain when they can connect their school experiences with their lives as citizens. Several models of these kinds of programs have been developed (Wysocki, 1999). Evanston Township High School in suburban Chicago has found its program to be a key to helping students link their school and out-of-school experiences.

High School Senior Studies Program

Evanston high school's service learning program has evolved as a response to students' senior-year burn-out (Cooper, Allen, & Newman, 2003). Faculty members were aware that school sometimes loses its appeal for high school seniors. Therefore, they developed what has become a very popular Senior Studies program. This course combines history and English with community service. It is a daily, team-taught course with both departments' faculty members involved. During the first semester, students work together (in groups of five or six) on a community service project focused around the basic thematic units—community history, education, crime and punishment, writing, community activism, and individual expression/exposure to the arts.

During the second semester, each student conducts an individual project. These projects follow one of several paths: career exploration, traditional academic research, artistic expression, or community service. At the end of each semester, students present the results of their projects in a public forum to classmates, parents, community members, and the press. The local newspapers publish articles about student activities. The success of the project is clear;

more than twice as many students apply for the program as can enroll. Many students who are in the program regularly describe it as the high point in their schooling. They learn to work on real problems, connect with community leaders, and are able to make a difference.

In the fall, the course begins with an orientation unit designed to foster positive group dynamics and identity. Students learn about problem solving, about their own personalities as well as the diversity of others' personalities, and how to create a successful team effort. They also learn to take risks, a focus that faculty members have found is essential so students will commit to the challenges of group projects.

This orientation to the seminar is followed by a three-week education unit. In the unit, students examine critical issues of education. The connection to the community is made as they visit other schools, observe classes, and interview teachers and students. They also learn about schools worldwide with very different educational systems. A culmination of this unit is that students work in groups of three to design their ideal charter school and sell it to other students, staff members, and community guests. During a subsequent unit on crime and punishment, students visit the county jail and learn about the treatment of citizens in the criminal justice system. These experiences introduce students to the seminar's focus on collaborative examination of aspects of the real community and set the stage for their action.

Later in the semester, students work in groups of five or six on a community service project. These projects involve issues that range from local to international in focus. Each team determines the problem that it wants to address, and students spend time researching and interviewing leaders in the area who are already addressing that issue. Then the students develop a plan that involves them as part of the solution. After taking action, all teams report on the results of their efforts to their classmates and community leaders at the end of the semester.

Recent team projects have included the following:

• *Building community awareness of the impact of domestic violence.* One group created fliers with information about domestic violence, sold purple bracelets and safety pins signifying solidarity with victims, and raised money for a shelter for battered women.

• *Helping the community save elm trees.* Evanston elms have been hard hit by Dutch elm disease, with more than 800 trees lost in one year alone. One group of students chose this community issue as their problem. After learning from another community group, To Rescue Evanston Elms, the students developed their own plan of action. They raised awareness of the disease in the community by setting up information tables outside a local supermarket and by the commuter train station. They designed their own program to raise funds and collected enough money to pay for the expensive inoculation of several elm trees along a parkway in the city.

• *Addressing the need for adoptive parents for African American children.* The group addressing this issue learned that there were three times more African American children at a local adoption agency than actually get adopted. They gathered community opinions about adoption; explored the statistics; interviewed families and staff about adoption, especially interracial adoption; and uncovered additional information about why these children were not as readily adopted as others. The students participated in

agency meetings and interviews with prospective parents. One of their products was the creation of a movie, which they donated to the adoption agency for its use.

• *Helping relief efforts for AIDS orphans in Zambia.* The group studying this issue decided to raise awareness of the enormity of the AIDS crisis in Africa. They created and distributed fliers that highlighted the devastating facts about the crisis. They met with local youth groups to share the information they had gathered. They also raised money to build a school and help educate a Zambian child.

Each year students choose local and international issues like these for their community service projects. In the process, they learn more about their community; but most important, they learn that they can be effective community activists and problem solvers. Making this connection between school and community also reinforces the purposes of their entire education.

Projects Structured Around Governmental Bodies

Students can also build an understanding of civic life by being part of projects that permit them to take on roles of local, state, national, and international governmental bodies. Some of these projects are sponsored by civic organizations and others are under the aegis of universities. The resources provided in Appendix C can help locate organizations that engage students in community and government affairs within a particular geographic area.

YMCA Youth in Government

The YMCA's Youth in Government program is designed to introduce students to the real functioning of local, state, and national government. The program was initiated in 1936 by the New York State YMCA and has now spread to 37 states. About 25,000 teenagers participate annually in Youth in Government programs. The programs provide opportunities for adolescents to take on the roles of government officials and participate in simulated experience of all phases and procedures of actual government bodies. Students, under the guidance of either youth programs or their civics and history teachers, study the government roles; learn about real issues; prepare projects, bills, or court cases, depending on the area of government; and then participate at the actual government setting.

The state-level programs provide thousands of young people the opportunity to learn about how government functions. The Michigan YMCA Youth in Government program, for example, annually involves more than 1,500 high school students in a simulation of all phases and positions of the state government. Students take on the roles of state legislators, lobbyists, committee chairs, and lawyers. The process begins at the local school level with intensive study and research. Then students from across the state convene for the annual fall conference at the state Capitol. In this setting, students run for offices, and some are elected to leadership positions in the House, Senate, and executive branch. They work with their fellow officials to draft and introduce bills, debate, and vote on legislation. These activities simulate the full workings of the state government.

Illinois holds its annual three-day youth government conference in March in the state capital of Springfield. Students in schools across the state work throughout the year to prepare for the event. Some have high school government teachers as sponsors; others

work through local Y projects. Students select a branch of government in which they want to participate. At Stevenson High School, in Lincolnshire, for example, those choosing the legislative branch identify areas of real need that can be remediated at the state level. Then, working in teams of three or four with a faculty advisor, they engage in extensive research, develop bills, and test and refine them at two local prelegislative sessions. The culmination of their efforts comes as the students engage with all the other student participants in the Capitol House and Senate chambers, present their bills, and debate legislation. Other students who choose the judicial branch prepare by researching and studying cases. They then participate as lawyers appealing cases they have prepared and as Supreme Court justices hearing oral arguments and rendering decisions.

These state programs make deep impressions on the students and bring life to the study of the words *representative government* and *civic society.* Under the National YMCA umbrella, states and local communities have developed variants that fit their own situations. Many of these programs can be reviewed via the project Web sites. The National YMCA also sponsors the National Youth Governors Conference in Washington, D.C., and the Youth Conference on National Affairs.

Model United Nations Program

It is no surprise that many international leaders, including former United Nations Secretary-General Kofi Annan, have participated in the Model United Nations (U.N.) program. While participating in the college-level Model U.N., Annan developed his abilities to lead the anti-apartheid movement, growing intellectually and defining his values. The Model United Nations program continues to provide a context for thousands of students each year to make connections between their academic learning and the solution of real-world issues.

World Studies courses help students see their lives and the United States from a broader perspective. However, participating in the Model United Nations makes the experience real, according to high school students (interview with Amanda Kaiser, student at North Side Prep in Chicago, February 11, 2005). Students across the United States and worldwide become active participants in discussing and attempting to resolve current international issues through the Model U.N. program. The program provides authentic simulations of the U.N. General Assembly and other U.N. bodies. Students learn with their peers as they negotiate and take part in "international" diplomacy, discussing real issues facing the international community. As student delegates to the Model U.N., they represent one country and serve on a committee or commission. Preparation includes researching the country, understanding the issues from that country's perspective, and preparing position papers that will be brought before the organization.

Some Model U.N. activities take place in individual schools, but many are statewide and regional. As of 2004, conferences were held in 46 states (Rodriguez, 2004). These Model U.N. conferences occur at a wide variety of venues, from high schools to universities to community sites. Recently national conferences also have been held in New York City under the aegis of the United Nations itself. One advantage of the conferences is that students get to know peers from other schools, other states, and even, in some cases, other countries.

The United Nations Association of the United States of America (UNA-USA) has more than 175 chapters and divisions. Chapters are based in schools where teachers either sponsor and lead U.N. clubs or teach regular courses on the functioning of the United Nations. These chapters prepare for and participate in Model U.N. events that usually take place at universities over three- or four-day periods midyear.

Each school selects one country it will represent from a list of countries provided by the Model U.N. organizers. Usually the schools that register first have the best selection. The UNA-USA suggests that in selecting a country to represent, the following criteria are important.

1. What would your group like to learn from this experience? Which countries would be most useful in helping to satisfy this learning experience?
2. How do these countries fit into the existing course of study for members of the group?
3. How much of a challenge does each of the countries pose for the group?
4. How familiar are the students in the group with countries or regions you have chosen?
5. Are there enough participants in the group to represent the countries you have chosen to represent at the Model U.N. conference you will attend?

Once students have chosen the country or countries they will represent, they need to build a deep understanding of the country and its issues. In their course or club, students spend significant amounts of time learning what it means to be a member nation of the United Nations, doing research, and planning for participation in U.N. committees. They also learn how to function under parliamentary rules, something quite new for most high school students.

Learning about the countries and issues that they deal with in the U.N. requires a significant amount of research. The United Nations Cyberschoolbus Web site provides a list of sources that students can use in their research (www.un.org/Pubs/CyberSchoolBus/index.html). With the wealth of information available, students learn to hone their research skills and think critically about the data they review. They also know they have to read what authorities have to say on their issue both pro and con, as their position papers will then become part of the discussion and debate that takes place in their committee meetings and at the Model U.N. General Assembly.

Schools can learn more about participating by logging on to the Cyberschoolbus Web site or the Web site of the Model United Nations in the United States (MUN-USA) at http://www.unausa.org. Students can also learn more about the project by reading the e-news journal at http://groups.yahoo.com/group/mun-e-news/. A good videotape, *Model U.N. for Schools,* can be purchased through the UNA-USA Education Department.

First Amendment Schools Network

First Amendment Schools: Educating for Freedom and Responsibility is a national school reform initiative designed to help schools teach and practice the civic habits of heart, mind, work, and voice vital to democracy, freedom, and the common good. The initiative was launched through a partnership between the Association for Supervision and Curriculum Development (ASCD) and the First Amendment Center, and is now sustained by ASCD. First Amendment Schools (FAS) provides selected K–12 schools with resources on the First Amendment, democratic education, whole school

reform, and educational best practices; and it engages school communities, the public, the media, and policymakers in conversations that illustrate how the civic mission of education can frame school renewal initiatives. Schools in the FAS Network commit to providing all members of the school community with substantial opportunities to practice democracy; protecting inalienable rights and demonstrating civic responsibility; engaging all stakeholders; and translating civic education into community engagement. More information is available at www.firstamendmentschools.org.

The Peace Institute

In 1994 a project began at Northridge Middle School in Los Angeles, California, and ran for eight years in Los Angeles and Jackson, Mississippi. The project, called the Peace Institute, was designed to engage students in a topic they cared about—the study of peace. Attached to this broad goal was the participants' involvement in active response to incidents in their city, state, country, and world. The institute offered students the opportunity to become proactive in the peace process as they explored and researched essential questions pertaining to requisite conditions for peace in the world, the community, the school, and the self. The use of the word *institute* created a mind-set that differed from that found in a typical interdisciplinary team. Students and teachers became an organization within the school. The various Peace Institutes that developed shared the following characteristics:

• Interdisciplinary teaching teams responsible for 65 to 150 students, heterogeneously grouped and representing a wide range of ethnicities, ability levels, and age groups

• Team organization with consistent management and instructional methodology

• Ongoing development of an integrated curricular experience based on the yearlong theme of Diversity and World Peace and tied closely to state and district standards

• Extracurricular field trips

• Use of computer technology for computer literacy and production of student projects

• Use of art and music to express peace-related issues

• Training in conflict resolution and cultural diversity

• Proactive roles for students in becoming peer conflict mediators

• Various guest speakers

• A presence in the school and in the local community for community action

Team Organization

Each team had a team leader, team manager, curriculum coach, and a parent liaison whose focus was on issues of leadership, student discipline, learning outcomes, and strategies for re-engaging parents and the community (Shapiro & Klemp, 1996). The team roles allowed for more active participation in the management of the team to ensure that all teachers were involved.

Team meetings were held monthly unless there was a special reason to convene. On assembly days, students and teachers wore their Peace Institute T-shirts, which were the same for institutes at all schools. School names did not appear on the shirt, so when the students were involved in interschool projects, the shirts conveyed the image of one large institute. The goals of the Peace Institute (see Figure 5.1) helped to frame a sense of teamwork and provided a framework upon which the organization was based.

Classroom Methodology

Another component of the Peace Institute was reflected in the organization at the classroom level. Peace Institute classes were arranged into noncompetitive learning teams, or PODs, as described in Chapter 4 (Klemp, 1996; Klemp, Hon, & Shorr, 1993). In these Cooperative Literacy structures, students interact in a classroom organized around positive interdependence and peer accountability. The use of participatory work structures provides opportunities for the socialization process while satisfying students' needs to affiliate, to attach and bond to others (Arhar, 1997; Lipka, 1997). The overall pedagogy can be described in terms of some basic labels: cooperation, inclusion, critical thinking, participatory learning, empowerment and response, and the use of technology for action.

Integrated Curriculum

The Peace Institute did not use a packaged curriculum. Instead, teachers developed their themes based upon their areas of interest or the perceived needs and questions of the students. The teachers used the overarching concept of world peace and the following story line to guide them through their curricular emphasis:

> Mankind's efforts to achieve peace in the world involve a continual struggle to bring the world community together politically, economically, and socially, so that the human race may continue to thrive on our planet.

Other content areas promoted connections as students explored the theme through the various disciplines. For example, the Institute at Brinkley Middle School

Figure 5.1
Goals for Peace Institute Students

1. **Teamwork and collaboration:** Students will work collaboratively and interdependently in a variety of authentic settings with people of diverse backgrounds within the school.

2. **Problem solving/critical thinking:** Presented with a conflict or issue, students, working either independently or collaboratively, will use appropriate reasoning skills.

3. **Self-directed independent learning:** Students will acquire the means to work independently and gain knowledge for personal interest and academic growth.

4. **Communication/literacy skills:** Students will comfortably and effectively express opinions, deliver information, and communicate ideas using oral, written, and artistic mediums.

5. **Research/study skills:** Using available research and technology, students will effectively organize information, make inferences, and reach meaningful conclusions.

6. **Self-esteem/self-worth:** Through their achievements and participation as decision makers in the institute, students will gain knowledge, acquire confidence, and develop their sense of importance and self-worth.

7. **Responsibility and interdependence:** Students will recognize the value of each member of our culturally diverse and international community, while demonstrating individual and group responsibility.

8. **Enthusiasm, desire, motivation, pride:** Students will have a positive attitude and will interact within the school and community as they become energetic proponents of world peace.

in Jackson, Mississippi, was part of the Robert Moses Algebra Project, an experiential learning model that prepares middle school students for higher math. Mathematics was used to analyze information, and basic skills were reinforced through the use of graphs, charts, and tables. Science was applied to the theme in studies of adaptation and health-related information. The language arts permeated the whole endeavor as students composed letters, created brochures, prepared speeches, and wrote reports. Two institutes wrote and performed plays about violence. This integrative approach used Jim Beane's premise that "curriculum allows teachers to be facilitators of a search for self and social meaning" (1993, p. 89).

Engaging the Community

An additional component of the Peace Institute was the integration of what Banks (1993) calls a course of "social action," in which students approach key issues and plan responses or courses of action.

One of the institutes visited the Aids Project Los Angeles facility after studying a unit on sexually transmitted diseases. Another institute visited a children's hospital unit on Halloween to give candy to some of the pediatric patients. Other institutes participated in beach clean-ups, gutter clean-up patrols, tree plantings, and drives to support the Rainforest Coalition, food banks, aid to flood victims, and voter registration. Other activities included responses to local emergencies. An institute in the inner city of Los Angeles created a mural depicting the peace process in harmony with nature as part of their Dolphin Peace Institute motif. The U.S. Postal Service's pilot program called Let's Write assisted the institutes by sending two teachers and four Peace Institute students to Oklahoma City after the 1994 bombing of the Murrah Federal Building.

Each month all of the Peace Institutes published newsletters containing stories written by students telling of their experiences as participants in the program. All of these activities were, in the words of one of the institute students, "the kinds of things we could never learn in a book!"

The Future of Peace

In a compelling article, "Why We Must Teach Peace," Colman McCarthy (1992), director of the Center for Teaching Peace in Washington, D.C., states that "non-violence isn't just about ending wars. It's about creating peace in our own hearts, often the last place many people ever find it" (p. 9). The Peace Institutes provide a way of looking at the world through the filter of cause and effect. Students are offered the opportunity, and accept the responsibility, to become agents of peace. The rising tide of violence in schools challenges middle-level educators to present students with alternatives to violence through a curricular approach in an integrative experience. As a poster in a Peace Institute classroom reads, "Imagine a class where the homework involves saving the planet."

Recommendations for Promoting Civic Engagement in Schools

The models just described present some inspiring examples of what civic engagement can be. Before setting up a civic education program, teachers may want to evaluate the present status of student engagement in their school. The Center for Information & Research on Civic Learning & Engagement (CIRCLE) has created a Civic Engagement Quiz (2001). This instrument can be used to compare patterns of civic engagement in a particular school to others nationally. The instrument can also be given in pre- and post-test situations to measure changes produced by school programs. CIRCLE allows schools to use the quiz free of charge. A copy of this survey instrument appears in Appendix C. It also can be downloaded at www.civicyouth.org/PopUps/Civic_Inds_Quiz.pdf.

Helping students become engaged in their communities requires more than just covering the text in the social studies classroom. As the National Council for the Social Studies (1997) states:

> The cognitive outcomes of education are vital, but character is not formed solely on the basis of the study of traditional subject matter. Although subject matter is an essential component of the reflective process that leads to a mature understanding of the nature of civic life, the focus of social studies education needs to be widened to encompass the quality of the civic experiences that classrooms, schools, and communities provide to students.

The following are other recommendations culled from a multitude of sources used in the research for this book.

• Make educating for democracy a priority in your school. Ensure that government, civics, and social studies are part of your school standards and are assessed.

"School curriculum is devoted to the subjects tested, and in many cases class time is spent on test preparation. Without an inclusive place in the curriculum, civic learning is diminishing in grades K–12." (Campaign for the Civic Mission of Schools, 2004)

- Select themes in social studies that correlate highly with youth civic engagement. For example, when "great American heroes and the virtues of the American system" are emphasized, students are "more likely to trust other people, to trust the government, and to say that they have volunteered recently." When "problems facing the country today" are emphasized, students are "more likely to feel that they can make a difference in their communities and the most likely to think that voting is important." When "racism and other forms of injustice" are emphasized, students are "more likely to be engaged in community problem-solving and also most likely to be registered to vote." And when "the U.S. Constitution and system of government" is combined with lessons on "great American heroes and the virtues of the system of government," students are "civically engaged, across the board." (Levine & Lopez, 2004)

- Provide professional development for social studies teachers to help them understand both the cognitive and affective influences of schooling on a student's future civic engagement.

- Require students to take civics or government classes. When young people take such courses, they report that they are more likely to do the following:
  - Help solve a community problem
  - Believe they can make a difference in their community
  - Volunteer
  - Trust other people and government

  - Make ethical and political consumer decisions
  - Believe voting is important
  - Register to vote (CIRCLE, 2004; Kurtz, et al., 2003; Torney-Purta et al., 2001)

- Provide simulations of the democratic process in school, involving students in school governance, voting, trials, debate, and diplomacy.

- Establish time for discussion of current events—local, national, and international. "Reading political news in the newspaper is associated with the likelihood of voting in the United States." (Torney-Purta & Barber, 2004)

- Keep parents informed of what is being covered in the social studies and civics curriculum and encourage them to discuss schoolwork with their children. "At every grade level there is a positive association between frequency of discussion of schoolwork at home and average civics scale scores." (Lutkus et al., 1999)

- Provide youth organizations in which students can work with peers and see results from their efforts. "Such organizations can have positive effects on civic knowledge, attitudes and future engagement by giving students opportunities for participation in settings that matter to them." (Torney-Purta et al., 2001)

- Create cocurricular activities that involve school, community, and business institutions, providing students with opportunities to see positive civic role models in their community.

- Involve youth in the design, implementation, and evaluation of volunteering and political programs.

- Invite students to volunteer. "Being asked is the top reason motivating young people to volunteer (closely followed

by 'because it makes me feel good')."
(CIRCLE, 2002)

• Allow students to share their volunteer experiences. "Young people who discuss a volunteer experience are twice as likely as others to volunteer regularly. And, they are also 16 percentage points more likely to try to influence someone's vote!" (CIRCLE, 2002)

• Provide counseling and support to keep students in school as long as possible.

Resources

The Campaign for the Civic Mission of Schools (2004) provides an excellent guide for establishing civic education programs in schools. The site provides information on school and district models, overcoming key challenges, promising approaches, research, web links, and assessment tools. The site is located at www.civicmissionofschools. org/site/resources/challenges.html.

The Center for Information & Research on Civic Learning & Engagement has researched, collected, and annotated a list of more than 50 organizations created to promote civic engagement. The resources are divided into three main categories: political participation, youth civic engagement, and civic education. The list appears in Appendix C and is available at the CIRCLE Web site at www.civicyouth.org/ practitioners/org_links.htm.

And, finally, the greatest resource we have is our own vision and belief in the democratic process. To keep the democratic process alive we must ensure that we have an educated society that can understand and comprehend the issues that confront and challenge us on a daily basis. Democracy, literally the rule of the people, can exist only when our students are educated to be critical

readers and thinkers and shown how to be caring, compassionate beings.

*　*　*　*　*　*　*

As the Number 2 in each POD handed in the attendance and homework check, Mr. Reaf wrote the following words on the board: *Community Service Projects.*

"Hey, Mr. Reaf," called out Juan. "That looks like work to me."

Mr. Reaf smiled.

"Well, you're right, Juan. But I have a feeling this will be work you think about for a long time." He turned to face the whole class.

"Today I'm going to pass out material about our quarter project, which is part of our final assessment. Remember that one of the 'big ideas' that you wanted to deal with this year was Helping Others. Each POD is going to select a community service project. I have a list of suggested projects that groups in the past have really enjoyed, but don't feel you have to choose something from this list."

"How we gonna be graded, man?" called out Carlos. "I don't want to be doing a bunch of work and Marie here getting the credit." Carlos smiled at Marie, who slugged him in the arm.

"Great question, Carlos. Each group will be required to produce four pieces of work, one for each of you. Your POD will write a descriptive essay about how you began and carried out the community service. You must also produce an editorial relating your group's point of view about community service. The best of these will be sent to the school and local newspapers. Your POD will create charts, graphs, and maps if necessary so that you can show what your project produced. And, finally, your POD must produce a media presentation—for example, in PowerPoint or digital photography or video—to show other students what you accomplished. You'll need to use persuasive or propaganda techniques in both your media presentation and your editorial."

"Hey, Mr. Reaf!" called out Ramona. "We don't know anything about writing an editorial."

"That's OK, Ramona. That's what we'll be learning in class this quarter."

"But, Mr. Reaf," interrupted Sharisa. "Editorials are for English class."

"Well, I disagree, Sharisa. You see, part of social studies is learning to be connected and involved in the world around you. Every day people are expressing opinions in editorials found in newspapers, on TV, and in magazines. I bet sometimes you disagree with what they say."

"I heard that!" called out Jeffrey.

"Then it's time to learn how to express your opinion. That is the wonderful thing about a democracy. If you are literate and can think critically, you can make a difference in how others see the world.

"OK, Number 3s, come up and get the project description sheet and the suggested forms of community service. We've got work to do."

PART

2

Strategies for Textbook Literacy

The final three chapters of this book provide research-based, hands-on, practical strategies for teaching students to comprehend the materials they read, including textbooks, primary and secondary sources, and newspapers and magazines. This chapter focuses on reading social studies textbooks. The chapter is divided into the following lessons that teach specific strategies to help students become critical readers of textbooks:

- Previewing Texts
    Strategy: Making Preview Maps
- Activating Prior Knowledge
    Strategy: Creating a P.L.A.N.
- Determining Main Ideas
    Strategy: Using Pair Questions and Answers
- Organizing Information
    Strategy: Making Three-Column Notes
- Understanding Maps
    Strategy: Recognizing Key Map Terms and Features
- Interpreting Graphs
    Strategy: Understanding Pie, Line, and Bar Graphs
- Analyzing Charts
    Strategy: Synthesizing Data
- Summarizing Key Concepts
    Strategy: Using a Frayer Model

Each lesson has two parts:

1. A Teaching Model section that includes the following:
   - Description of the strategy
   - Introductory activity to motivate students
   - Step-by-step instructions explaining how to teach and model the strategy
2. A Student Strategy section that includes the following:

- Step-by-step instructions for guided practice
- Applying the strategy activities for further practice and assessment

Each lesson also includes practice pages—models of appropriate texts and reproducible graphic organizers for use with the models.

Previewing Texts
Teaching Model

Introducing the Strategy

Description: A Preview Map is a drawing of the main features of a textbook page. Begin by explaining to students that seeing a preview helps your brain search for information you already know about a subject. Bringing up background knowledge helps you better understand what you see and hear later.

Introductory Activity: Ask students to describe some movie previews they've seen. Pose the following question: What do previews have in common? Tell students to first work in pairs and then in fours, or PODs, to make a list of these traits on the board. Ask groups to make a list of at least five characteristics common to previews. Tell students to think about what a preview is trying to achieve and how it does it. Ask groups to share their ideas. Tell students they are now going to learn how to preview the chapter of a textbook.

Teaching the Strategy of Preview Maps

Step 1: Show a copy or transparency of the chapter opener (Figure 6.1). Ask students to note the main features on this page. Provide a model by pointing out the heading across the top under the section title. Help students see that headings, subheads, graphs, charts, photos, cartoons, maps, and special boxes of texts are all features they should notice.

Step 2: Explain to students that they are going to learn how to make a Preview Map of a textbook page. Show a copy of the Preview Map (Figure 6.2) of the chapter opener. Point out to students how this drawing represents the textbook page just seen.

Step 3: Point out that all the headings in bold print on the chapter opener are rewritten as questions on the Preview Map. For example, the heading "The Stirrings of Rebellion" becomes "What were the stirrings of rebellion?" Draw lines between sections of text.

Figure 6.1
Chapter Opener

The Stirrings of Rebellion

MAIN IDEA	WHY IT MATTERS NOW	Terms & Names
Conflict between Great Britain and the American colonies grew over issues of taxation, representation, and liberty.	The events that shaped the American Revolution are a turning point in humanity's fight for freedom.	• Stamp Act • Samuel Adams • Townshend Acts • Boston Massacre • committees of correspondence • Boston Tea Party • King George III • Intolerable Acts • martial law • minutemen

One American's Story

On the cold, clear night of March 5, 1770, a mob gathered outside the Customs House in Boston. They heckled the British sentry on guard, calling him a "lobster-back" to mock his red uniform. More soldiers arrived, and the mob began hurling stones and snowballs at them. At that moment, Crispus Attucks, a sailor of African and Native American ancestry, arrived with a group of angry laborers.

A PERSONAL VOICE JOHN ADAMS

" This Attucks . . . appears to have undertaken to be the hero of the night; and to lead this army with banners . . . up to King street with their clubs . . . [T]his man with his party cried, 'Do not be afraid of them. . . .' He had hardiness enough to fall in upon them, and with one hand took hold of a bayonet, and with the other knocked the man down."

—quoted in *The Black Presence in the Era of the American Revolution*

▲ **Crispus Attucks**

Attucks's action ignited the troops. Ignoring orders not to shoot, one soldier and then others fired on the crowd. Five people were killed; several were wounded. Crispus Attucks was, according to a newspaper account, the first to die.

The Colonies Organize to Resist Britain

The uprising at the Customs House illustrated the rising tensions between Britain and its American colonies. In order to finance debts from the French and Indian War, as well as from European wars, Parliament had turned hungry eyes on the colonies' resources.

THE STAMP ACT The seeds of increased tension were sown in March 1765 when Parliament, persuaded by Prime Minister George Grenville, passed the **Stamp Act.** The Stamp Act required colonists to purchase special stamped paper for every legal document, license, newspaper, pamphlet, and almanac, and imposed special "stamp duties" on packages of playing cards and dice. The tax reached into every colonial pocket. Colonists who disobeyed the law were to be tried in the vice-admiralty courts, where convictions were probable.

Source: From *The Americans*, by Gerald A. Danzer, J. Jorge Klor de Alva, Larry S. Krieger, Louise E. Wilson, and Nancy Woloch. Copyright © 2005 by McDougal Littell, a division of Houghton Mifflin Company. All rights reserved. Reprinted by permission of McDougal Littell, a division of Houghton Mifflin Company.

Figure 6.2
Preview Map

Chapter/Section: Chapter 4/Section 1   **Page**: 96

What were the stirrings of rebellion?

_____

What is the main idea?	Why does it matter now?	What are the terms and names?

Whose story is being told?

_____

Whose personal voice is this?

A picture of
Crispus Attucks

How did the American colonies organize to resist Britain?

_____

What was the Stamp Act?

Step 4: Model how to draw all pictures, maps, graphs, charts, or photos on the blank page to resemble the size and shape of the picture in the textbook. Then write the caption or title of the picture by the shape.

Step 5: Now have students use the instructions in the Student Strategy with the opening page of the next section they are about to read in their social studies text and make a Preview Map. Have students also choose one of the Applying the Strategy activities for more practice.

Student Strategy

Learning the Strategy

Step 1: A Preview Map is a drawing of the features of a page of your textbook. To make a Preview Map, first select one of your texts that you wish to read better. Then turn to the first page of the chapter or section that the class is going to read next.

Step 2: You will make a drawing of the features of this page. Use a blank sheet of paper with no lines on it. For all headings in bold print, rewrite them as questions. For example, rewrite the heading "The Stamp Act" to "What is the Stamp Act?" Write these questions on your blank paper in the same position as the corresponding headings appear on the textbook page.

Step 3: For all pictures or photos, draw a shape on your blank page that resembles the size and shape of the picture in the textbook. Then copy the title or caption of the picture underneath the shape.

Step 4: For all graphs, tables, or charts, make a simple drawing of the graphic on your blank page. Then copy the title or caption of the graphic underneath the drawing.

Step 5: Look for any information written in the margins of the text. For example, you may see something like "Vocabulary Tips" or "Real-life Connections." In the same place on your Preview Map, write a brief description of these features.

Step 6: Now share the information you've collected on your Preview Map with a classmate. Revise your map if you've left off something. Reread the questions and the information about any pictures or graphics. As you begin to read this page, use your questions to help you look for information to remember. Make sure you understand the text or pictures you've described on your Preview Map.

Applying the Strategy

Choice 1: Preview Maps are helpful in all subject areas, not just social studies. On blank transparency film, make a Preview Map for the opening page of a chapter from each of your textbooks from other classes. Share these maps with the class. Then borrow a textbook from a lower grade. Show a younger student how to make Preview Maps with his or her text.

Choice 2: How would you preview one of your textbooks to your classmates? Choose one of your textbooks and study its Table of Contents. What features would you highlight? What would get your classmates excited or interested in this subject? What real-life connections can you see between your text and your world? Create a storyboard, a PowerPoint slide show, or a video no more than a minute long that sells your text to your classmates.

Introducing the Strategy

Description: The strategy called P.L.A.N. provides a structure to help students organize their reading and reflect on the text in short chunks. Begin by explaining to students that having a plan to do any task makes the work easier and more efficient. This strategy will give them a plan to use when reading their textbooks.

Introductory Activity: Tell students to imagine they are going to debate the topic "The War in Iraq." They will need a plan to do research first. Write *The War in Iraq* within a rectangle on the blackboard. Ask students to call out major subtopics. As students call out subtopics, add them to your graphic, writing each one within an oval. Illustrate how information is organized by listing additional ideas under appropriate headings. For example, "Weapons of Mass Destruction" may be a subheading. Branching off from this topic may be the subheadings of "dirty bombs," "anthrax," and "poisonous gas." Now model how to note your familiarity with these topics. Place an *X* by topics that you know something about. As you write the *X,* say aloud something you know about this topic. Place a question mark by topics about which you know little. State that as you do more research, you'll add information to your chart.

Teaching the Strategy of P.L.A.N.

Step 1: Tell students that they can use the P.L.A.N. strategy for reading a section of text. Pass out copies of the P.L.A.N. Steps (Figure 6.3). Walk students through the steps, explaining that these are the same steps they just followed with the example of the debate on the war in Iraq. Tell students they are going to practice this strategy in their study of the U.S. Constitution.

Figure 6.3
P.L.A.N. Steps

1. **P**—Predict the main ideas. Plot how the ideas are organized in a graphic organizer.

2. **L**—Locate which of these topics you know something about and which topics you know little about.

   • Place an *X* by topics about which you already know something.

   • Place a question mark by topics that are unfamiliar to you.

3. **A**—Add information to your chart as you read.

4. **N**—Note what you learned by restating and reflecting on the information in your own words.

Source: From "PLAN: A Study-Reading Strategy for Informational Text," by D. Caverly, T. Mandeville, and S. Nicholson, November, 1995, *Journal of Adolescent & Adult Literacy, 39*(3), pp. 193. Copyright © 1995 by the International Reading Association. Adapted with permission.

Step 2: Show the textbook page titled "What Are Your Rights?" (Figure 6.4). Read the headings and bold words aloud. Tell students that you can now make predictions on your graphic organizer.

Step 3: Pass out copies of the partly filled-in graphic organizer on "What Are Your Rights?" (Figure 6.5). Read aloud the headings and bold words that have been filled in.

Step 4: Ask students to look at the textbook page. Model for them how to fill in the remaining sub-headings and bold words. Place an *X* by topics you already know something about. Tell students what you know and how you know it. Place a question mark by topics about which you know little.

Step 5: As you read this piece aloud, stop after each section and ask the class what new information can now be added to the chart. Add this information. When you have completed the chart, reflect back over your work, noting aloud what you have learned.

Step 6: Have students follow the steps in the Student Strategy, including choosing one of the Applying the Strategy activities for more practice and assessment.

Student Strategy

Learning the Strategy

Step 1: You will understand your textbook better if you make a plan for reading it. This strategy will show you how to "draw" a section of a textbook and react to what you read. The steps in P.L.A.N. are as follows:

1. **P**—Predict the main ideas and plot how they are organized.
2. **L**—Locate which of these topics you already know something about and which you know little about.
3. **A**—Add information to your chart as you read.
4. **N**—Note what you learned by restating and reflecting on the information in your own words.

Step 2: Choose a section of a chapter that you are about to read. On a blank sheet of paper, or using the P.L.A.N. handout (Figure 6.6), write the main title or heading within a rectangle in the center of the page. You will now predict and plot how the chapter is organized.

Step 3: Copy the bold subheadings from your text in ovals surrounding the square. Begin at the top oval (at 12 o'clock on a clock) and move to the right, or clockwise, filling in the ovals with the subheadings in the order that they appear in your book.

Step 4: You are now going to locate known and unknown information. Place one of the following symbols by each oval on your chart: an *X* means the information is familiar to you; a question mark means that you don't know much about this topic.

Step 5: Begin reading each subheading in your text. Add new information to your chart as you read. Add bold words from your text to your chart by the appropriate subheading. Be sure to add information to sections where you placed a question mark.

Step 6: Once you've finished reading, note what you have learned. Either try to redraw your P.L.A.N. from memory, rewrite your P.L.A.N. as a learning log in your notebook, or reteach the text to a classmate.

Applying the Strategy

Choice 1: P.L.A.N. is helpful in all subject areas, not just social studies. Choose another one of your textbooks. Following the same procedure as above, fill out a P.L.A.N. on the next chapter you are about to read. Share your charts with your teacher for that subject.

Choice 2: Imagine you want to do a survey of students about improving your school. Follow the P.L.A.N. steps to predict which major areas you'd like to improve. Locate which of these areas you know something about and which you know little about. Add information to your plan by interviewing classmates, adding what they know. Then note what you've learned by summarizing your survey in a written report or speech.

Figure 6.4
Textbook Page

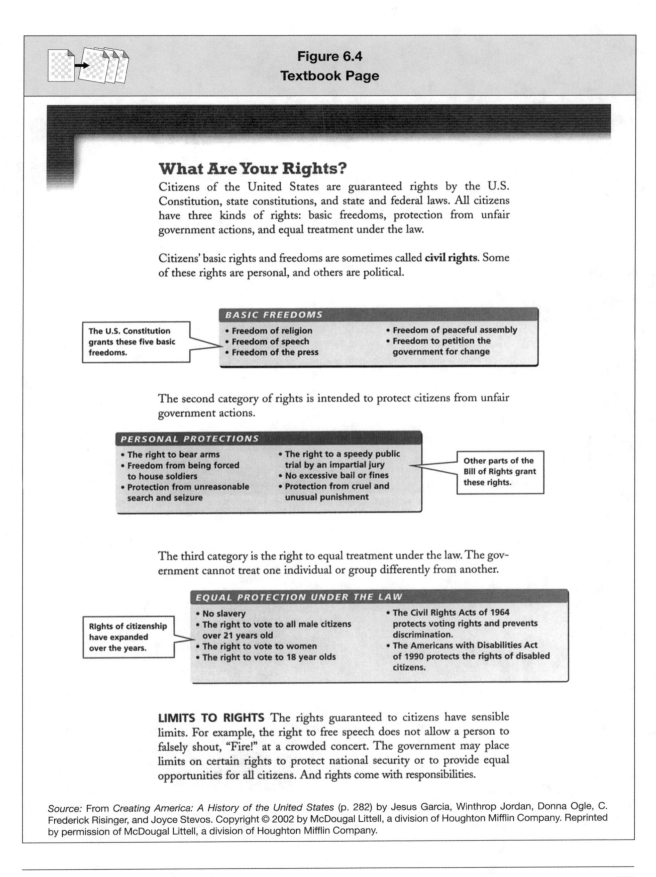

What Are Your Rights?

Citizens of the United States are guaranteed rights by the U.S. Constitution, state constitutions, and state and federal laws. All citizens have three kinds of rights: basic freedoms, protection from unfair government actions, and equal treatment under the law.

Citizens' basic rights and freedoms are sometimes called **civil rights**. Some of these rights are personal, and others are political.

The U.S. Constitution grants these five basic freedoms.

BASIC FREEDOMS
- Freedom of religion
- Freedom of speech
- Freedom of the press
- Freedom of peaceful assembly
- Freedom to petition the government for change

The second category of rights is intended to protect citizens from unfair government actions.

PERSONAL PROTECTIONS
- The right to bear arms
- Freedom from being forced to house soldiers
- Protection from unreasonable search and seizure
- The right to a speedy public trial by an impartial jury
- No excessive bail or fines
- Protection from cruel and unusual punishment

Other parts of the Bill of Rights grant these rights.

The third category is the right to equal treatment under the law. The government cannot treat one individual or group differently from another.

EQUAL PROTECTION UNDER THE LAW
- No slavery
- The right to vote to all male citizens over 21 years old
- The right to vote to women
- The right to vote to 18 year olds
- The Civil Rights Acts of 1964 protects voting rights and prevents discrimination.
- The Americans with Disabilities Act of 1990 protects the rights of disabled citizens.

Rights of citizenship have expanded over the years.

LIMITS TO RIGHTS The rights guaranteed to citizens have sensible limits. For example, the right to free speech does not allow a person to falsely shout, "Fire!" at a crowded concert. The government may place limits on certain rights to protect national security or to provide equal opportunities for all citizens. And rights come with responsibilities.

Source: From *Creating America: A History of the United States* (p. 282) by Jesus Garcia, Winthrop Jordan, Donna Ogle, C. Frederick Risinger, and Joyce Stevos. Copyright © 2002 by McDougal Littell, a division of Houghton Mifflin Company. Reprinted by permission of McDougal Littell, a division of Houghton Mifflin Company.

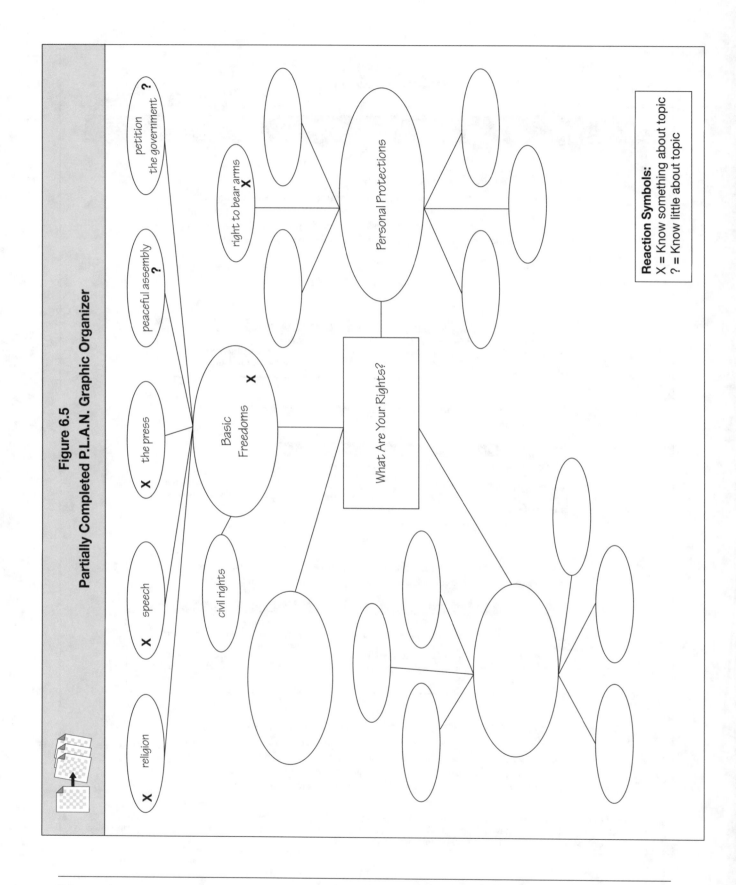

Figure 6.5
Partially Completed P.L.A.N. Graphic Organizer

Reaction Symbols:
X = Know something about topic
? = Know little about topic

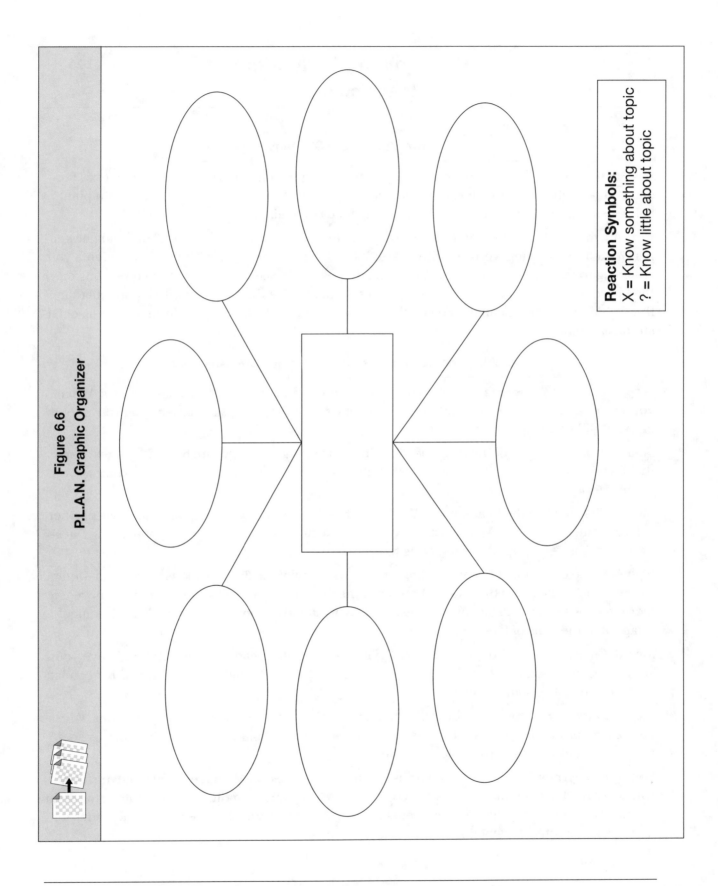

Figure 6.6
P.L.A.N. Graphic Organizer

Reaction Symbols:
X = Know something about topic
? = Know little about topic

Determining Main Ideas
Teaching Model

Introducing the Strategy

Description: Many students have difficulty determining the main ideas in a section of text. Students may confuse bits of information included to support or enliven the text with main points. Pair Questions and Answers will help students focus on main ideas.

Introductory Activity: Find an interesting sports article from either the school or local newspaper. Write the following words on the board: *Who? What? Where? When? Why?* Tell students you are going to read the article aloud. As you read, they are to see how many of the questions on the board they can answer. After reading, have students give their answers. Tell students that these simple questions can help guide them in determining the essential information in a social studies textbook.

Teaching the Strategy of Pair Questions and Answers

Step 1: Explain to students that history is about people and events that create changes. When you are looking for the main point of a section of text, you should ask yourself what this person or event did to change the lives of others.

Step 2: Pass out copies of the Pair Questions and Answers graphic (Figure 6.7) and the text page that includes the section "Tools of Protest" (Figure 6.8). Choose a student as your partner as you model the activity.

Step 3: First rewrite the heading as "What Were the Tools of Protest?" Explain that your partner will read the text to you. As you listen, you will make notes on a transparency of the Pair Questions and Answers graphic for the class to see.

Step 4: When the student begins reading, answer as many of the five questions as you can. Don't worry if you don't get all the information down the first time. Also, tell students you can have more than one answer to any of the questions. For example, under "Who?" include both Samuel Adams and the Sons of Liberty.

Step 5: Change places with your partner. This time you will reread the same text and have your student partner add more notes to the transparency. After two readings, you should have most of the five questions answered.

Step 6: Demonstrate for the students, by thinking aloud, how you determine the main idea. Focus on the actions of the colonists. Then ask for a volunteer to summarize the main idea of this section of text and write it in the space provided.

Step 7: Finally, rewrite the next heading as "What Was the Boston Massacre?" Tell students they will now practice the strategy. Pass out copies of the instructions in the Student Strategy for them to follow as they work. Then have students choose one of the Applying the Strategy activities for more practice and assessment.

Figure 6.7
Graphic Organizer for Pair Questions and Answers

Pair Questions and Answers

Partner 1: _____ Partner 2: _____

Title of Section: _____

Heading as a Question	
Who?	
When?	
Where?	
What?	
Why?	
Main Idea	

Figure 6.8
Text for Pair Questions and Answers

Determining the Main Idea

Directions: Use Pair Questions and Answers with a partner to determine the main ideas of the following two sections of text.

Tools of Protest

To protest the Townshend Acts, colonists in Boston announced another boycott of British goods in October 1767. The driving force behind this protest was **Samuel Adams,** a leader of the Boston Sons of Liberty. Adams urged colonists to continue to resist British control.

The boycott spread throughout the colonies. The Sons of Liberty pressured shopkeepers not to sell imported goods. The Daughters of Liberty called on colonists to weave their own cloth and use American products. As a result, trade with Britain fell sharply.

Colonial leaders asked for peaceful protests. Articles in the *Boston Gazette* asked the people to remain calm—"no mobs.... Constitutional methods are best." However, tempers were running high. When customs officers in Boston tried to seize the American merchant ship *Liberty,* which was carrying smuggled wine, a riot broke out. The rioters forced the customs officers to flee.

Fearing a loss of control, officials called for more British troops. A defiant Samuel Adams replied, "We will destroy every soldier that dares put his foot on shore.... I look upon them as foreign enemies."

The Boston Massacre

In the fall of 1768, 1,000 British soldiers (known as redcoats for their bright red jackets) arrived in Boston under the command of General Thomas Gage. With their arrival, tension filled the streets of Boston.

Since the soldiers were poorly paid, they hired themselves out as workers, usually at rates lower than those of American workers. Resentment against the redcoats grew. Soldiers and street youths often yelled insults at each other. "Lobsters for sale!" the youth would yell, referring to the soldiers' red coats. "Yankees!" the soldiers jeered. *Yankee* was supposed to be an insult, but the colonists soon took pride in the name.

On March 5, 1770, tensions finally exploded into violence. A group of youths and dockworkers— among them Crispus Attucks—started trading insults in front of the Custom House. A fight broke out, and the soldiers began firing. Attucks and four laborers were killed.

The Sons of Liberty called the shooting the **Boston Massacre.** They said that Attucks and the four others had given their lives for freedom. The incident became a tool for anti-British propaganda in newspaper articles, pamphlets, and posters. The people of Boston were outraged.

Meanwhile, the redcoats who had fired the shots were arrested for murder. **John Adams,** a lawyer and cousin of Samuel Adams, defended them in court. Adams was criticized for taking the case. He replied that the law should be "deaf ... to the clamors of the populace." He supported the colonial cause but wanted to show that the colonists followed the rule of law. Adams argued that the soldiers had acted in self-defense. The jury agreed. To many colonists, however, the Boston Massacre would stand as a symbol of British tyranny.

Source: From Creating America: A History of the United States, by Jesus Garcia, Winthrop Jordan, Donna Ogle, C. Frederick Risinger, and Joyce Stevos. Copyright © 2002 by McDougal Littell, a division of Houghton Mifflin Company. Reprinted by permission of McDougal Littell, a division of Houghton Mifflin Company.

Student Strategy

Learning the Strategy

Step 1: Pair Questions and Answers is an activity to help you figure out the main idea of what you are reading. First, choose a partner with whom you work well.

Step 2: Look at the title of this section of the chapter. Rewrite this heading as a question.

Step 3: Decide who will read the section first and who will listen and make notes. As one of you reads, the partner should make notes that answer the five questions on the sheet. Don't worry if you don't get them all answered during the first reading.

Step 4: When the first reader finishes, review the answers you have so far.

Step 5: Now switch roles. The note taker will reread the same section, and the first reader will add more information to the worksheet. Sometimes answers for all five questions may not be in the text. Sometimes you may have more than one answer to a question.

Step 6: History is about people and events that create change. When looking for the most important idea of a section of a chapter, ask yourself what this person or event did to change the lives of others. Look back at your notes. Which answer seems to have had the greatest effect on the lives of others? Discuss what you think the most important idea in this section might be.

Step 7: In the "Main Idea" section of your worksheet, write one sentence that summarizes the most important idea in this section. Tell why this idea is so important.

Step 8: Now rewrite the next heading as a question and read to find the answers.

Applying the Strategy

Choice 1: Pair Questions and Answers also works when you are reading fiction, or stories that are made up. Choose a story to read. Because there are no headings, you can skip the section on turning the heading into a question. As you read, make notes that answer the five questions. For a story, rename the "Main Idea" section as "Theme." The theme of a story is the lesson about life that the story teaches.

Choice 2: With a partner, use the Pair Questions and Answers strategy to analyze a news story in your local newspaper. Pick a story on the front page. As one of you reads, notice how quickly you are able to answer most of the questions. Newspaper writers include most of the important information at the beginning of the piece. In this way a reader can find out important points without reading the entire article. More detailed information is included later on in the article for those who wish to find out more. Using this format as a model, write a news story about an event at your school.

Organizing Information
Teaching Model

Introducing the Strategy

Description: Many students do not use text features and visual information to preview information and guide their note taking. They simply open a textbook and begin reading. Fluent readers use headings and pictures to organize the information they read.

Introductory Activity: Choose a page in your social studies textbook that has headings and at least two different types of visual information, such as pictures, maps, cartoons, graphs, or charts. Ask students to turn to that page and begin reading. After three minutes ask students to close their books and write down what was "on the page." Ask them to recall the headings or describe any visual information. (Most students will recall only part of the opening paragraph.) Tell them that you are going to model a strategy for using textbook headings and pictures to organize your thinking and your notes.

Teaching the Strategy of Three-Column Notes

Step 1: Show a copy or a transparency of "Costs of the War" (Figure 6.9), which describes the effects of the American Revolutionary War.

Step 2: Show students a copy of the model of a Three-Column Chart for this same page (Figure 6.10). Point out how the reader has copied the heading in the left-hand column, but rewritten it as a question—"What were the costs of the war?" Then point out how the reader described the "Background" and "Reading History" notes, copying the question from the second note—"Why do you think the Loyalists left the United States?"

Step 3: Explain to students that after they have copied main headings, side notes, and bold words in the left-hand column, they should describe any visual information on the textbook page in the center column of the graphic. Point out how the reader used the titles of the map and chart to help describe the two visual pieces. Also point out how the reader copied the questions from the bottom of the chart to answer later.

Step 4: Tell students that now the reader has properly previewed the text by noting the important written and visual information. The reader is ready to move to the right-hand column to begin taking notes and answering questions. Tell students that they may not be able to answer the main heading question until they've finished reading the entire section. Show students how the notes in the right-hand column refer to the questions and pictures in the left and center columns.

Step 5: Have students use the directions in the Student Strategy and a blank Three-Column Chart (Figure 6.11) to practice the strategy with another textbook page of their choice. Once students have filled out their charts, have them share their charts in pairs. Choose some of the best examples to share with the entire class. Students should also choose one Applying the Strategy activity as further practice and application of the strategy.

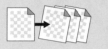

Figure 6.9
Textbook Page for Notes Using Three-Column Chart

Postwar Boundaries, 1783

Background Even after George Rogers Clark's Western victories, the British stayed at Fort Detroit.

Costs of the War

No one knows exactly how many people died in the war, but eight years of fighting took a terrible toll. An estimated 25,700 Americans died in the war, and 1,400 remained missing. About 8,200 Americans were wounded. Some were left with permanent disabilities, such as amputated limbs. The British suffered about 10,000 military deaths.

Many soldiers who survived the war left the army with no money. They had received little or no pay for their service. Instead of back pay, the government gave some soldiers certificates for land in the West. Many men sold that land to get money for food and other basic needs.

Both the Congress and the states had borrowed money to finance the conflict. The war left the nation with a debt of about $27 million—a debt that would prove difficult to pay off.

The losers of the war also suffered. Thousands of Loyalists lost their property. Between 60,000 and 100,000 Loyalists left the United States during and after the war. Among them were several thousand African Americans and Native Americans, including Joseph Brant. Most of the Loyalists went to Canada. There they settled new towns and provinces. They also brought English traditions to areas that the French had settled. Even today, Canada has both French and English as official languages.

Reading **History**
B. Analyzing Causes Why do you think the Loyalists left the United States?

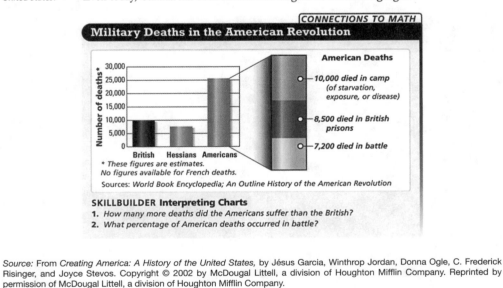

CONNECTIONS TO MATH

Military Deaths in the American Revolution

American Deaths

- 10,000 died in camp (of starvation, exposure, or disease)
- 8,500 died in British prisons
- 7,200 died in battle

* These figures are estimates. No figures available for French deaths.

Sources: *World Book Encyclopedia; An Outline History of the American Revolution*

SKILLBUILDER Interpreting Charts
1. *How many more deaths did the Americans suffer than the British?*
2. *What percentage of American deaths occurred in battle?*

Source: From Creating America: A History of the United States, by Jésus Garcia, Winthrop Jordan, Donna Ogle, C. Frederick Risinger, and Joyce Stevos. Copyright © 2002 by McDougal Littell, a division of Houghton Mifflin Company. Reprinted by permission of McDougal Littell, a division of Houghton Mifflin Company.

Figure 6.10
Example of Completed Three-Column Chart
Used for Textbook Page

Name: Sara Johnson   **Title or Heading:** Costs of the War   **Pages:** 213

Headings and Bold Words	Visual Information	Notes
What were the costs of the war? Background note about the British staying at Ft. Detroit. Reading History question—Why do you think the Loyalists left the United States?	A map showing the postwar boundaries of North America in 1783. A chart showing the number of military deaths in the American Revolution with two questions— (1) How many more deaths did the Americans suffer than the British? (2) What percentage of American deaths occurred in battle?	Map note—The Spanish still controlled most of North America. An estimated 25,700 Americans died and 1,400 were missing. The British lost about 10,000. Many people and the government were broke. Loyalists left because they lost their property and were traitors. Many Africans & Native Americans left looking for a better life. Chart Answers: (1) 15,000 (2) About 28%

Figure 6.11
Three-Column Chart for Textbook Notes

Name: _____   Title or Heading: _____   Pages: _____

Headings and Bold Words	Visual Information	Notes

Student Strategy

Learning the Strategy

Step 1: Three-Column Notes is a strategy that helps you preview the information in a textbook section. The graphic also provides a space for you to organize your notes.

Step 2: First get a blank copy of the Three-Column Chart. Review the three column headings. In the left-hand column you will rewrite headings as questions and copy down any bold words in the order that they appear. In the center column you will describe any visual information, such as pictures, cartoons, charts, colored boxes, or graphs. In the right-hand column you will take notes as you read.

Step 3: Using the page your teacher shows you, rewrite the first heading as a question in the left-hand column of your graphic. Move down the text page. Copy all bold or key words on your graphic in the order that you find them. Rewrite any additional headings as questions so that you will know what information you are looking for as you read.

Step 4: Start again at the top of your textbook section. Now, in the center column of your graphic, describe any visual information in the order that it appears. Read the titles and captions to find out what each visual piece is presenting.

Step 5: You are now ready to begin reading. As you read the section, define your key terms in the right-hand column. Also try to answer your headings rewritten as questions. Note how the visual information helps summarize, support, or clarify what you are reading. You now have excellent notes about what you have read.

Applying the Strategy

Choice 1: The Three-Column Notes strategy works with other content area textbooks. All students should know how to use this strategy. You are going to teach this strategy to either a younger student or a class at a lower grade. Get permission to borrow the student's or class text. Find out what chapter will be covered next. Create a model of a completed Three-Column Chart for the first section of this text. You can use either a transparency or a PowerPoint slide. Rehearse your presentation with a partner, your teacher, or in front of your class. Then teach your lesson to your student or group.

Choice 2: Whenever you do research using the Internet, texts, or magazines, it is important to keep good notes. The Three-Column Chart (Figure 6.12) is ideal for note taking while doing research. Choose a topic you want to know more about or one that has been assigned for a class. As you do your research, fill out a Three-Column Chart for each source. For an Internet article, be sure to note the author and the URL (uniform resource locator, or Web address). Also note the date. For books and magazines, include authors, copyright dates, publishers, and pages. Keeping this detailed information on your charts will save you much work later as you begin writing your research paper.

Figure 6.12
Three-Column Chart for Textbook Notes

Name:_____ Title/Author: _____

(From Print) Source: _____ Date: _____

(From Internet) URL address:_____

Headings and Bold Words	Visual Information	Notes

Understanding Maps
Teaching Model

Introducing the Strategy

Description: Social studies textbooks, magazines, and newspapers are filled with many types of maps. This activity will explain types of maps to students and show them how to interpret the information they provide.

Introductory Activity: Write the following quotation on the board: *If you don't know where you're going, you'll probably end up somewhere else.* Ask students to write two sentences about what this anonymous quotation means. Students should note that on a literal level, one can get lost; and on a symbolic level, not having a goal in life can leave one subject to the whims of others. Now ask students to draw a map from their house to school or to a major shopping center. Tell them to create symbols for houses, churches, stores, gas stations, restaurants, and their school and to place these symbols in the appropriate places on their maps. Finally, they must write specific directions telling every turn a person would have to make. If possible, have students draw their maps on a transparency. Then have students share their maps and directions with the class.

Teaching the Strategy of Recognizing Key Map Terms and Features

Step 1: Write the following terms on the board: *physical maps, political maps,* and *historical maps.* Ask students in pairs or PODs to come up with a one-sentence definition of what they think each of these kinds of maps might show. Help students understand that physical maps show natural features; political maps show boundaries, such as those between towns and countries. Historical maps show events such as battles or migrations.

Step 2: Tell students that maps have their own specialized vocabulary. Pass out a copy of Key Map Terms and Features (Figure 6.13). Read aloud the definitions on the page.

Step 3: Have students turn to a specific map you have chosen. In pairs or PODs, have students match the definitions on the Key Map Terms and Features sheet to objects on the map.

Step 4: Once groups are finished, ask specific students to point out specific key map terms and features. Be sure students point out the following:

- Map key—a box stating what key symbols mean
- Compass rose and pointer—an arrow that shows which way is north
- Scale—a small line that tells how distances are represented on the map
- Lines of latitude and longitude—lines that flow across the map (latitude) or up and down (longitude) to show the area's location on the earth

Step 5: Model how to interpret the information on this map by doing a "think-aloud," stating your thought processes aloud as you think through the map.

Step 6: Pass out the sheet Practice with Understanding Maps (Figure 6.14) for more practice.

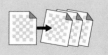

Figure 6.13
Key Map Terms and Features

Compass Rose—a pointer or arrow that shows which direction is north. A large *N* (for *north*) is usually placed by the arrow.

Inset—a smaller map placed in a corner of the larger map; the smaller map shows exactly where the larger map is located on a larger land mass or area.

Labels—words or phrases on the map that explain actions, places, or events.

Lines of Latitude—faint lines, often colored light blue, that flow across the map and show how far north or south the area is located.

Lines of Longitude—faint lines, often colored light blue, that flow up and down the map and show how far east or west the area is located.

Map Key or Legend—a box that shows what lines, colored areas, and symbols (such as stars, arrows, or dots) mean on a map.

Scale—a set of bars or lines that show how small distances on the map are equal to actual distances in the real world. For example, a scale may show that 1/2 inch on the map actually equals 100 miles in the real world. The scale is sometimes found inside the Map Key or Legend.

Types of Maps

- **Physical Map**—shows only natural features, such as mountains, rivers, and lakes.

- **Political Map**—shows man-made boundaries, such as states, countries, or towns.

- **Historical Map**—shows where and how some major event took place, such as a battle, or how a people spread from one land to another.

Student Strategy

Learning the Strategy

Step 1: This lesson will help you learn how to read a map. Choose a map that interests you from your textbook. Look at the title. Which one of the three types below is it?

- Physical map—shows only natural features, such as mountains, rivers, and lakes
- Political map—shows boundaries for things such as states, countries, or towns
- Historical map—shows where and how some major event took place, such as a battle, or how a people migrated from one land to another

Step 2: Look for any titles or captions on your map. If you find a title in **bold** print, rephrase it as a question. This will tell you what information to look for in the map.

Step 3: Now place your handout of Key Map Terms and Features beside your map. Match the symbols and words on your map to the definitions on your Key Map Terms and Features chart.

Step 4: Look for a *map key*—a box on the map that explains important symbols.

Step 5: Look for *lines of latitude* that flow across the map and *lines of longitude* that flow up and down the map. These lines are often colored a light blue and divide the map into boxes. The lines will have a number by them. The numbers tell you the location of this specific area on the earth.

Step 6: Find the *compass rose* so that you will know which directions are north, south, east, and west. Find the *scale* that tells you how to determine the distances on your map.

Step 7: Finally, reread all the labels, or words and phrases on your map. With the information you have gathered in the steps above, you are now ready to put it all together and interpret your map. Rehearse with your partner how you will explain the map. Ask the class to turn to the map you've chosen as you explain it.

Applying the Strategy

Choice 1: Redraw the map you originally made from your home to your school or to a shopping center. This time include a title, a map key, a compass rose, a scale, and lines of latitude and longitude. Then rewrite your directions but use only the terms *north, south, east,* and *west* instead of *right* and *left.*

Choice 2: Teach a younger student how to understand a map. Find a map in a textbook for a lower grade level. Study the map using the steps above. Think through how you would explain this map. Is there a title? Where would you begin? In what order would you describe the features on the map? Rehearse in your head how to explain the map to another student. Ask the student's teacher if you can teach the class a lesson on understanding maps. Use transparencies or a PowerPoint presentation.

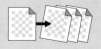

Figure 6.14
Practice with Understanding Maps

Directions: Use your chart of Key Map Terms and Features to help you answer the following questions about the map below. Answer on a separate sheet of paper.

1. What is the title of the map? Rewrite the title as a question.

2. Is this a physical, political, or historical map?

3. Where is the map key or legend on this map?

4. What six symbols are explained in the map key?

5. Where is the scale on this map?

6. About how many miles does a half inch equal?

7. Where is the compass rose on this map?

8. Where is the inset map on the larger map?

9. What part of the world does this map show?

10. What line of latitude runs through the country of Norway?

11. What line of longitude runs through the country of Italy?

12. What do all the arrows mean on this map?

13. Write an explanation of this map for a younger student.

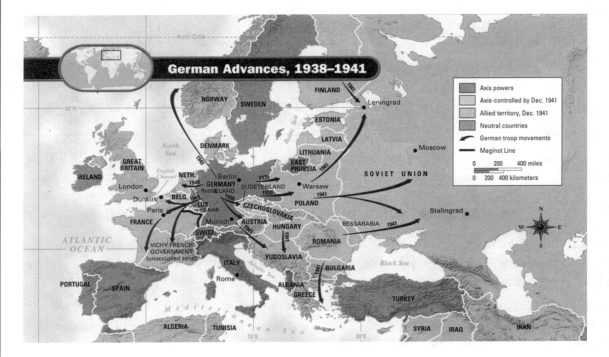

Source: From *The Americans,* by Gerald A. Danzer, J. Jorge Klor de Alva, Larry S. Krieger, Louis E. Wilson, and Nancy Woloch. Copyright © 2005 by McDougal Littell, a division of Houghton Mifflin Company. All rights reserved. Reprinted by permission of McDougal Littell, a division of Houghton Mifflin Company.

Interpreting Graphs
Teaching Model

Introducing the Strategy

Description: Graphs are used frequently in social studies texts and in the media to illustrate information in a visual format. This activity will explain types of graphs and show students how to interpret the information found in them.

Introductory Activity: Draw the graphs shown in Figure 6.15 on the board. Remind students that they have seen such graphs in their math and social studies texts. Tell students that different types of graphs are used to show different types of information. Make sure students understand the terms *vertical axis* and *horizontal axis*. Give students the following information and ask them (in pairs) to depict this information on one of the graphs on the board (students could use the pie graph or the bar graph):

> During the U.S. Civil War, soldiers on the Union, or Northern, side died in the following ways: Accidents—6.4 percent; Prisoners of War—7.7 percent; Combat—28.3 percent; and Disease—57.6 percent.

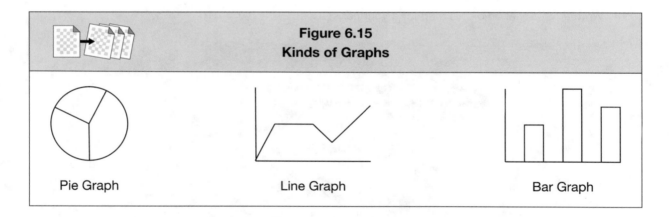

Figure 6.15
Kinds of Graphs

Pie Graph   Line Graph   Bar Graph

Teaching the Strategy of Understanding Pie, Line, and Bar Graphs

Step 1: Have volunteers draw their graph on the board, explaining how it depicts the information on Civil War casualty percentages. Note that a line graph would not work. Point out that pie graphs can show in percentages how much something is part of a whole.

Step 2: Explain that bar graphs compare quantities of things, such as groups, places, events, or categories. For example, you could use a bar graph to compare the number of hot dogs, hamburgers, and bags of popcorn sold at football games in a season.

Step 3: Tell students that line graphs are used for showing changes over time. Quantities or measurements are shown by points placed along both the vertical and horizontal axes. Write the following information on the board:

The U.S. Government spent the following sums of money for outer-space activities from 1959 to 1969: 1959—$1 billion; 1961—$1.9 billion; 1963—$5.2 billion; 1965—$7 billion; 1967—$6.8 billion; 1969—$6 billion (Source: NASA).

Draw the frame of a line graph on the board and ask pairs or PODs to transfer this information to the graph. When students have finished, have volunteers draw their versions on the board.

Step 4: Pass out copies of Practice with Interpreting Graphs (Figure 6.16) for more practice. Use these with the instructions in the Student Strategy section. Also have students choose one of the Applying the Strategy activities for further practice and assessment.

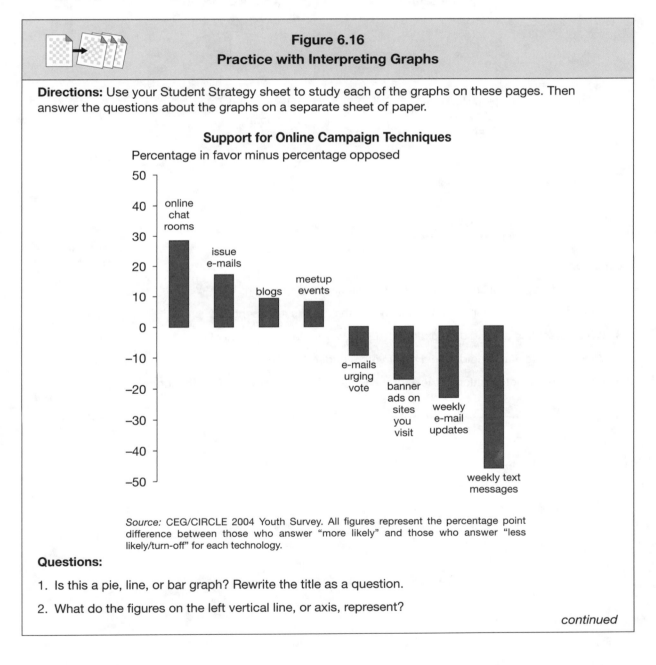

Figure 6.16
Practice with Interpreting Graphs

Directions: Use your Student Strategy sheet to study each of the graphs on these pages. Then answer the questions about the graphs on a separate sheet of paper.

Support for Online Campaign Techniques
Percentage in favor minus percentage opposed

Source: CEG/CIRCLE 2004 Youth Survey. All figures represent the percentage point difference between those who answer "more likely" and those who answer "less likely/turn-off" for each technology.

Questions:

1. Is this a pie, line, or bar graph? Rewrite the title as a question.

2. What do the figures on the left vertical line, or axis, represent?

continued

115

Figure 6.16 *Continued*

3. How many different forms of campaign techniques are being compared?

4. What was the most popular way among young voters to get information?

5. What was the least popular way among young voters to get information?

Presidential Choice of Young Voters—November 2004

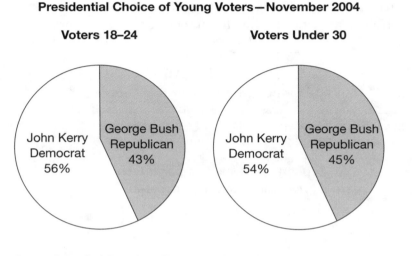

Source: Center for Information & Research on Civic Learning & Engagement (CIRCLE), November 9, 2004.

Questions:

1. Are these pie, bar, or line graphs? Rewrite the title as a question.

2. What is the difference in the information that the graphs represent?

3. Which presidential candidate did most 18-to-24-year-old voters select?

4. Which presidential candidate did most voters under 30 select?

5. How might the information in these graphs affect each party's actions in the future?

continued

Figure 6.16 *Continued*

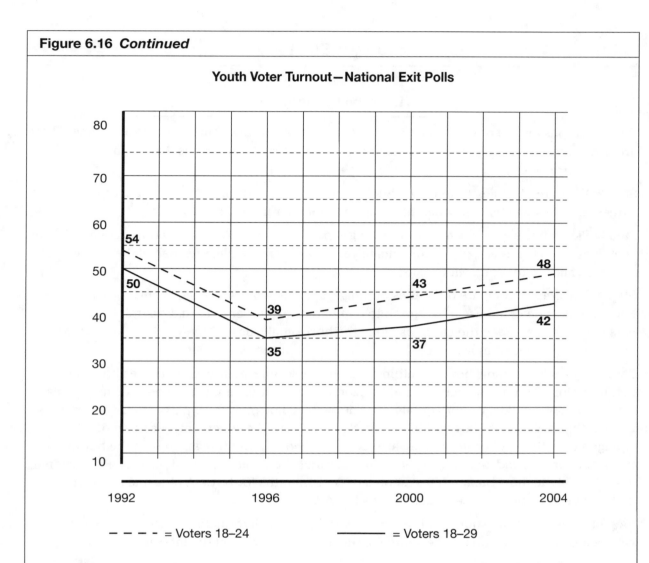

Youth Voter Turnout—National Exit Polls

− − − − = Voters 18–24   ———— = Voters 18–29

Source: Center for Information & Research on Civic Learning & Engagement (CIRCLE)
January 29, 2005.

Questions:

1. Is this a pie, line, or bar graph? Rewrite the title as a question.

2. What do the numbers along the vertical line, or axis, represent?

3. What do the numbers along the horizontal line, or axis, represent?

4. Why are there two different kinds of lines on the graph?

5. How did the turnout change from 1992 to 2004?

Student Strategy

Learning the Strategy

Step 1: Graphs are used to compare quantities and to show how things change over time. There are three main forms of graphs—pie graphs, bar graphs, and line graphs. Each is used for a specific purpose.

Step 2: When reading any graph, look first for titles or captions. If you find a title, rephrase it as a question. This will tell you what information to look for in the graph.

Step 3: Pie graphs show how much something is part of a whole. A "whole" always equals 100 percent. If half, or 50 percent, of the students in your school are female, then half of the pie, or circle, would be filled in to represent females.

Step 4: Bar graphs compare quantities of things, such as groups, places, events, or categories. For example, you could use a bar graph to compare the number of Ford, Chevrolet, and Toyota cars sold in a year. Read the captions along the horizontal axis and the vertical axis so that you know what is being compared.

Step 5: Line graphs show how something changes over time. Measurements are shown by regular points on both the vertical and horizontal axes. For example, time periods may be listed across the bottom line, or horizontal axis. The vertical line may show percentages or amounts of something. A crooked line within the graph shows how these percentages or amounts changed over time. A line graph may also compare two or more things. Look at the bottom of the graph for a *legend,* or explanation, that tells what each colored line stands for. For example, a red line might show the math test scores over six months for boys. A blue line might show math test scores over the same six months for girls.

Step 6: Finally, find the source of the graph. Where did this information come from? See if you can locate information about the source in the media center or on the Internet.

Applying the Strategy

Choice 1: Find out how many of your classmates speak one, two, or three languages. Present this information in the form of a pie graph.

Choice 2: Find out how many boys in your class played some kind of organized sport over the last three years. Find out how many girls played in an organized sport over the last three years. Present this information in the form of either a bar graph or a line graph.

Analyzing Charts
Teaching Model

Introducing the Strategy

Description: Charts are used frequently in social studies texts and in the media to illustrate information in a visual format. This activity will help students learn how information is categorized and presented within charts.

Introductory Activity: Write the following words on the board: *subway, skyscraper, restaurant, police officer, taxi, bank, shopkeeper, waiter, bus, judge, hotel, train.* Explain to students that when you "categorize" things, you group them together based on similarities. Draw a square on the board. Ask pairs or PODs to figure out the categories of the words on the board and to place them in the square so that others can see the order. Tell students that they must also create headings that explain each category and a title for their chart. Have students share their charts on the board. Students should have determined that the categories are Types of (Mass) Transportation, Types of Buildings, and Types of Workers (or People). The title for the chart can be "Things Found in Cities."

Teaching the Strategy of Synthesizing Data

Step 1: Ask students what the square they have filled out is called (a chart). Show students how charts are useful for organizing information in a simple format that is easier to read than a page of text.

Step 2: Explain to students that when reading a chart, they should always begin with the main title, which is usually in bold print at the top of the chart. As with graphs and maps, turning the title into a question will help students know what information to look for in the chart.

Step 3: Tell students that charts always have categories. These categories are displayed in columns and rows. Using the chart drawn on the board, make sure students understand the terms *column* and *row*.

Step 4: Explain that each category has its own heading. Tell students to read the headings next.

Step 5: Explain that the categories in charts can contain words, numbers, or pictures. Model for students how to look at the information under one category before moving on to the next column or row. Point out any patterns of organization, such as smallest to largest.

Step 6: Now do a "think-aloud," reflecting on the information presented in the chart and what it might mean. Finally, find the source of the information. Ask if this seems to be a trustworthy source.

Step 7: Pass out copies of Practice with Analyzing Charts (Figure 6.17) and the Student Strategy guide in the next section for more practice. Also have students choose one of the Applying the Strategy activities for more practice and assessment.

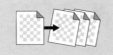

Figure 6.17
Practice with Analyzing Charts

Directions: Use your Student Strategy sheet to study each of the charts on these pages. Then answer the questions about the charts on a separate sheet of paper.

Federal Office Requirements

Position	Minimum Age	Residency	Citizenship	Length of Term
Representative	25	state in which elected	at least 7 years	2 years
Senator	30	state in which elected	at least 9 years	6 years
Supreme Court Justice	none	none	none	life
President	35	14 years in the United States	natural-born citizen	4 years; 8 if reelected

Questions:

1. What is the title of the chart? Rewrite the title as a question.

2. What does the word *federal* mean?

3. What are the bold headings in the chart?

4. Which federal employee on the chart serves the shortest term before seeking reelection?

5. Which federal employee can be born anywhere in the world and still serve in office?

6. The president selects the U.S. Supreme Court Justices. The candidates must be confirmed by the Senate. Why are the president's choices so important?

7. Can George W. Bush run for the presidency again?

8. If you were born in a foreign country and became a U.S. citizen, could you run for the presidency?

continued

Figure 6.17 *Continued*

Volunteers—Initial Involvement, 2003

Method of Involvement	16–18 years old	19–22 years old	23–25 years old	26+ years old
Individual approached an organization or school	42%	44%	40%	41%
Individual asked by someone	42%	44%	42%	44%
Individual asked by someone in an organization or school	23%	22%	23%	28%
Individual asked by a friend or family member	17%	15%	15%	12%

Source: From *How Individuals Begin Volunteering,* by S. Helms, January 27, 2005, CIRCLE. Retrieved January 2005 from www.civicyouth.org/PopUps/FactSheets/FS_How_vol_began.pdf.

Questions

1. What is the title of this chart? Rewrite it as a question.

2. How many age groups is the survey broken down into?

3. Under the column with the heading Method of Involvement, what is the difference between the first method and the next three listed?

4. For people 26 and older, what was the most common way they first got into volunteering?

5. What are the most common ways people age 16 to 18 get into volunteering?

6. Which is the least common way that people get into volunteering for all groups?

Student Strategy

Learning the Strategy

Step 1: Charts are used frequently in social studies texts, in magazines and newspapers, and on television to categorize information and make it easier to understand. This lesson will help you understand how to read a chart.

Step 2: When reading any charts, look first at the main title, which is usually written in **bold** print. When you find the title, rewrite it as a question. This will tell you what information to look for in the chart.

Step 3: Charts organize information in columns and rows. Columns are the rectangles that run vertically, or up and down, within the chart. Rows are the rectangles that run horizontally, or across, the chart.

Step 4: Each category in a chart has a heading. Read each of the headings next so that you will know what information has been categorized for you. If you don't understand what a heading means, ask someone and look for clues in the chart.

Step 5: Study the information under one heading at a time. Ask yourself what is important about this information. Does the information show amounts? Does it give descriptions or explanations? Does it give examples? Does it show order, such as largest to smallest? Look for a pattern to see how the information might be organized.

Step 6: Sometimes you'll find small symbols by the information in a chart, such as an asterisk (*). These symbols indicate footnotes, which appear at the bottom of the chart. These footnotes give important information about the part of the chart where the symbol is placed.

Step 7: Find the source of the chart. Where did this information come from? Can you trust the data you see in the chart? If you question the source, do further research.

Applying the Strategy

Choice 1: Pick something you know well, such as school, a sport, or a type of car, music, or clothing. Create a list of four categories for this topic. Then create a list of terms that fall under each category. Scramble the terms. Give the terms to others to see if they can figure out the main title and the headings and then draw a chart containing your information.

Choice 2: Find a chart about a topic that interests you in a newspaper, magazine, or textbook other than your social studies text. Follow the Student Strategy steps to analyze the chart. Imagine you are going to explain to a younger student how to understand this chart. Rehearse your lesson. Then present the lesson to your classmates.

Summarizing Key Concepts
Teaching Model

Introducing the Strategy

Description: Abstract terms that describe government, religion, economics, society, and philosophy are often used in social studies and the media. This activity will help students learn and summarize the key characteristics of such essential concepts.

Introductory Activity: Write the following two lists on the board:

Buddhism	town
democracy	person
truth	table
love	snow
capitalism	Jupiter

Ask students in pairs or PODs to figure out what the words in each list have in common. Help students to understand that List 1 names abstract concepts and List 2 names concrete, real objects. Ask students to come up with their personal definition for something that is "abstract." (Students should note that an abstract noun is something that is a quality, feeling, idea, belief, or state of being.) Tell students that social studies texts and the media use abstract terms all the time. Abstract terms often name the following:

- Government systems or theories, such as democracy
- Economic systems, such as capitalism
- Philosophy or ways of thinking, such as optimism
- Feelings, such as sadness
- Religions, such as Islam

Teaching the Strategy of Summarizing Key Concepts

Step 1: Either show a transparency of the graphic organizer in Figure 6.18 or pass out copies of it. Point out to students the five bold headings. These headings suggest different ways of describing an abstract term. (Students may need an example of a non-example, such as "football" is a non-example of a "water sport.")

Step 2: Tell students that this type of graphic, called a Frayer Model, is used to define abstract terms. Walk students through the model with the key word *democracy*.

Step 3: Based on what they've learned about democracy, ask students to suggest their own definitions of the key term. Write one of the students' suggestions under the part of the graphic labeled "Definition (in your own words)."

Step 4: Pass out a copy of the graphic organizer in Figure 6.19.

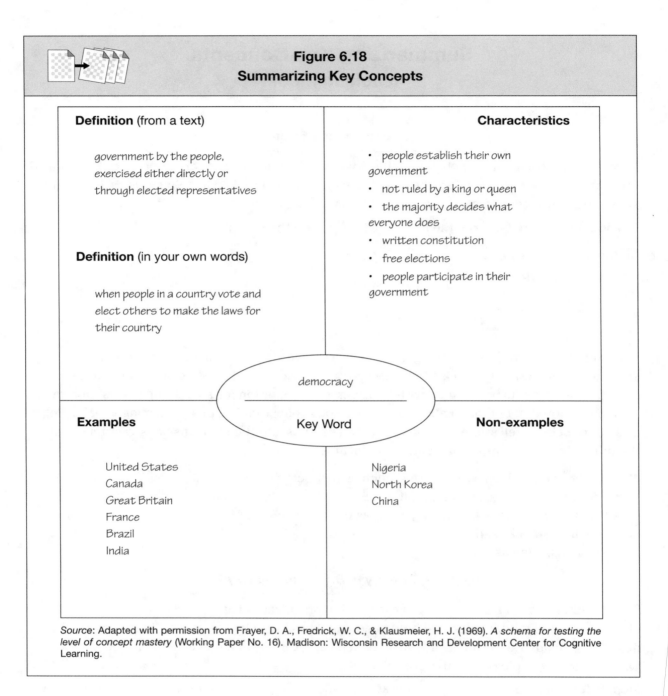

Figure 6.18
Summarizing Key Concepts

Definition (from a text)

government by the people,
exercised either directly or
through elected representatives

Definition (in your own words)

when people in a country vote and
elect others to make the laws for
their country

Characteristics

- people establish their own government
- not ruled by a king or queen
- the majority decides what everyone does
- written constitution
- free elections
- people participate in their government

democracy

Key Word

Examples

United States
Canada
Great Britain
France
Brazil
India

Non-examples

Nigeria
North Korea
China

Source: Adapted with permission from Frayer, D. A., Fredrick, W. C., & Klausmeier, H. J. (1969). *A schema for testing the level of concept mastery* (Working Paper No. 16). Madison: Wisconsin Research and Development Center for Cognitive Learning.

Step 5: For practice, have students write the term *capitalism* in the middle of the graphic organizer and follow the directions in the Student Strategy section.

Step 6: Instruct students to use these charts when they encounter difficult terms in their texts, including key terms in bold print. Also have students choose one of the Applying the Strategy activities for further practice and assessment. Students can use their texts or the Internet to gather information.

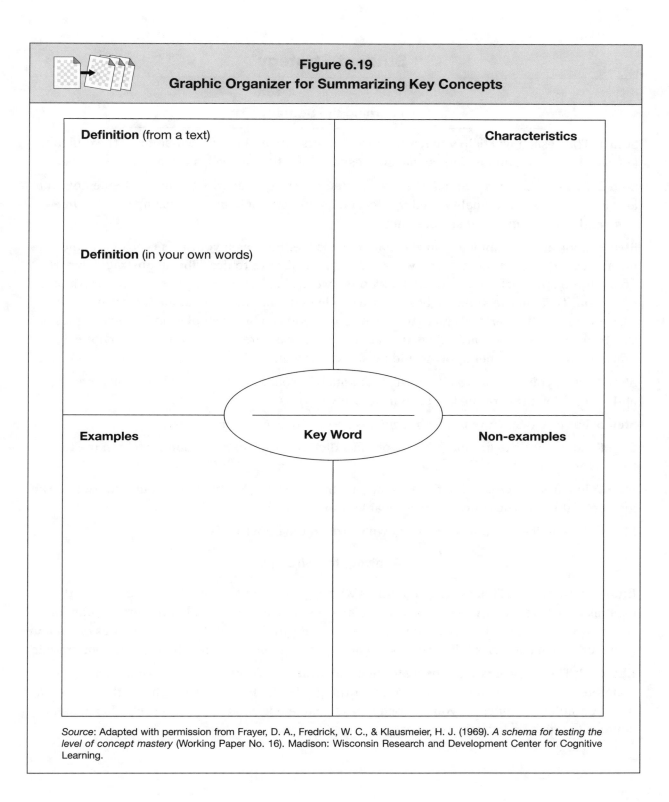

Figure 6.19
Graphic Organizer for Summarizing Key Concepts

Definition (from a text)

Characteristics

Definition (in your own words)

Examples

Key Word

Non-examples

Source: Adapted with permission from Frayer, D. A., Fredrick, W. C., & Klausmeier, H. J. (1969). *A schema for testing the level of concept mastery* (Working Paper No. 16). Madison: Wisconsin Research and Development Center for Cognitive Learning.

Student Strategy

Learning the Strategy

Step 1: This lesson will help you learn how to understand and remember some of the difficult key words that you find in your social studies texts and that you see and hear in the media.

Step 2: Key words in texts and in the media often describe an abstract concept. Remember that an "abstract" noun is a quality, feeling, idea, belief, or state of being. For example, *pride, freedom,* and *Christianity* are abstract nouns.

Step 3: Look at the graphic organizer that your teacher has given you. This type of graphic organizer is called a Frayer Model. You will see a number of ways to describe an abstract key term. To fill in the upper-left box, you can look up the word in a dictionary or textbook and write that definition. To fill in the upper-right box, you can list characteristics of someone or something that represents this term. To fill in the lower boxes you can list examples and non-examples of this term. Non-examples are things that are of a similar nature but differ in some major way. A non-example of a summer sport would be snowboarding.

Step 4: Once you are able to fill out the four squares, you can return to the upper-left square and write a definition of the key term in your own words.

Step 5: For practice, write the word *capitalism* in the oval on your handout.

Step 6: Look up the definition of this word in a dictionary or textbook and write it in the top of the upper-left square.

Step 7: In pairs or PODs, fill out the remaining three squares. You may use your textbook or the Internet if it helps you. Always use a reliable source.

Step 8: Now write a definition in your own words in the upper-left square.

Applying the Strategy

Choice 1: During the 20th century, countries whose governments promoted democracy and capitalism competed for world power with countries whose governments promoted communism. Do research to find out how pure "communism" is defined. Find out the characteristics of communism and which countries followed this political and economic system. Then fill out your graphic.

Choice 2: The graphic you are using to define abstract concepts also works well with many concrete nouns that name people, places, or things. Try filling out the graphic with the word *terrorist.* Complete as much as you can before you go to a textbook or the Internet. Then use these sources to finish and check your work.

Strategies for Reading Primary and Secondary Sources

7

This chapter is designed to help students learn specific strategies for reading primary and secondary sources. The chapter is divided into the following lessons that teach specific strategies to help students become critical readers:

- Interpreting Primary Source Documents
- Answering Document-Based Questions
- Evaluating Internet Sources

As in Chapter 6, each lesson has two parts:

1. A Teaching Model section that includes the following:

- Description of the strategy
- Introductory activity to motivate students
- Step-by-step instructions for how to teach and model the strategy

2. A Student Strategy section that includes the following:
- Step-by-step instructions for guided practice
- Applying the Strategy activities for further practice and assessment

Each lesson also includes practice pages—models of appropriate texts and reproducible graphic organizers for use with the models.

Interpreting Primary Source Documents
Teaching Model

Introducing the Strategy

Description: A major part of being a historian is using primary source documents, such as original records of events, newspaper accounts, photographs, speeches, and letters. Students can participate in the process of interpreting history by learning to use primary sources. This activity provides students with a set of questions to guide their reading of such documents.

Introductory Activity: Explain to students that historians develop an understanding of the past by examining and interpreting documents. Make either a transparency or copies of the Ohio editorial on women's suffrage (Figure 7.1). Write the following questions on the board:

- Who developed it?
- For what purpose?
- What does it tell about the United States in the early part of the 20th century?
- Why might a historian find this document interesting?

In pairs or groups of four (PODs), ask students to interpret this document. Discuss the students' responses once they have finished. Tell them that the strategy they are about to learn will help them read and understand primary sources.

Teaching the Interpretation of Primary Source Documents

Step 1: Tell students that historians are investigators looking for clues to piece together what happened in the past. These clues come from artifacts that earlier people left us. Pass out copies of the Student Strategy instructions and the Graphic Organizer for Interpreting Primary Sources (Figure 7.2). Using the Student Strategy as a guide, walk the students through the titles and secondary questions in each of the sections. For "Style," you may want to use the examples of *thee* and *thou* as unusual wording. For "Point of View," explain that first-person point of view uses the pronouns *I* and *we,* and third-person point of view uses the pronouns *he* and *she.*

Step 2: Pass out the letter written by Christina Kallstrom to her brother in Sweden in the late 1800s (Figure 7.3). Read the letter aloud to the students. Clear up any unclear or unknown terms.

Step 3: Have students work in pairs or PODs to answer as many of the questions as they can on their guide sheet. After a few minutes bring the class back as a whole group and have students share their responses. Write their findings on the board and discuss differences. Explain that as they use primary sources they need to think of the source of the document and the ideas and the point of view of the author or authors that are revealed.

Step 4: Now read the letter from S. M. Korling (Figure 7.4) to your students. Clear up any unknown terms, such as *emigrants.* This time have them work individually with their guide sheets to interpret the letter. Have them share their responses. For further practice and assessment, have students choose and complete one of the Applying the Strategy activities.

Figure 7.1
Primary Source Document: Editorial

EDITORIAL.

Women's Suffrage—We favor women's suffrage because it is right. The women are a part of our citizenship and have always been loyal regardless to the conditions they had to face. Thirty-five states including Ohio, have ratified the women's suffrage amendment. It only requires one more to ratify to write the amendment in our national constitution. It will mean much to the Colored women as they will interest themselves along with the White women in making a study of public problems.

With an equal opportunity to become properly informed the women will handle the ballot as well as any man and better than some men. Let her vote if she is twenty-one.

Figure 7.2
Graphic Organizer for Interpreting Primary Sources

Title of Document (if there is one): _____

Type of Document: (Is the document a letter, an article, an advertisement, or a government piece?)	**Author of Document:** (Who wrote the document)
Date of Document: (When was the document created?)	**Source of Document:** (In what city, town, or country was the document created?)
Style of Document: (What is unusual about the language used in the document?)	**Point of View of Document:** (Is the document written in the first person, using the pronoun "I"?)
Main Idea of Document: (What is the main point the writer is presenting?)	**Impact of Document:** (What feelings does the document bring up in you, the reader?)
Questions Raised by Document: (What do you want to know more about? What is still unknown?)	**Further Research:** (What are some other documents worth finding and reading?)

Figure 7.3
Primary Source Document: Letter

Excerpt from a letter written 4 March 1848 from Chicago, in the state of Illinois of North America

Dear Brother,

I must now tell you about my present circumstances and I must thank God for the priceless gift of health, which is the greatest treasure one can wish for in a foreign, faraway land. I and my children are living very well here and have, praise be to God, not suffered any want as far as the needs of this earthly life go, though it looked dark when we first came and was harder still when my husband died on 7 February a year ago. But praise be to Providence which has granted me and mine health up to the present. I long greatly to hear how you and your family and my children in Sweden are. I have sent greetings to them all but have not heard a word from any of my relatives. I beg of you, Brother, that you tell my children the contents of this letter and tell them all that we live better here than they can imagine, for whoever has health need fear no want. I have sent word several times to my girls, that if someone intends to come over here they should come along, for they would be much better off here than in Sweden. Until they learned the language they could not get more than four dollars a week plus food and gifts, but as soon as they got more used to things they could surely get more: women do not have to do any other work here but wash clothes and cups and keep the house tidied up and at some places also cook food. And here people live well, there is nothing but wheat bread. There is no need to tell about conditions, for word has surely spread through various letters that have been sent from here....

Christina Kallstrom

Source: From *Letters from the Promised Land: Swedes in America, 1840-1914,* by H. A. Barton, 1975, Minneapolis, MN: University of Minnesota Press. Copyright © 1975 by University of Minnesota. Reprinted with permission.

Figure 7.4
Primary Source Document: Letter from Sweden

Krisdala, Sweden, August 24, 1869

To the Editor of Hemlandet:

The undersigned, superintendent of the post office at Krisdala, hereby requests the editor to urge through the columns of his paper emigrant Swedes to send their correct addresses to their relatives here and also to address letters to Sweden so that they can be forwarded to the right parties.

The addresses on most of the letters from America are in all respects so obscure that they cannot be delivered to the right parties. To take one instance among many, "Nils Persson, Sislaa, Swerget." This letter is first sent to Kalmar and Cristwalla and returned. Then perhaps there are fifty persons in the parish bearing the name Nils Persson, and the letter must be opened to ascertain, if possible, the owner. If the letter is unsigned it will have to go the rounds of the parish until it reaches the right party.... Addresses sent home read "Wod hyl" or "Ward Hylt," etc.

The majority of emigrants cannot write Swedish, much less English. Notwithstanding this, certain emigrants, in order to advertise their proficiency in the new language to their relatives, put a good many English words in their letters; but as these words are incorrectly spelled and put together, the letters are unreadable to the recipient. He brings it to the preacher to have him read it. If he cannot, it remains unread.

Therefore, everybody who writes home, as they call it, is urged to consult somebody who is a good speller and who can write a legible address to send to the addressee and one to keep as a model when he addresses a letter. Do not use English words, because they do more harm than good....

Yours respectfully,

S. M. Korling

Source: From *Letters from the Promised Land: Swedes in America, 1840-1914,* by H. A. Barton, 1975, Minneapolis, MN: University of Minnesota Press. Copyright © 1975 by University of Minnesota. Reprinted with permission.

Student Strategy

Learning the Strategy

Step 1: When reading a document from the past, there are a set of steps you can follow to help you better understand the writing. First, look to see if the document has a title. If it does, rewrite the title as a question. This helps you know what information to look for.

Step 2: Examine the document. What type of document is it? Is it an old letter? Is it an advertisement or a newspaper article? Is it something published by a government? You may find clues in its form, such as a letter beginning with "Dear ...," and any official symbols such as a government stamp or seal.

Step 3: Determine who wrote the document. Look for any signatures or names.

Step 4: Look for a date on the document. If one doesn't exist, try to determine the date by studying the language or names. For example, a signature by a Lord Governor of Virginia would have to have taken place when Virginia was still part of England in the 17th and 18th centuries.

Step 5: Where was the document created? Can you determine the town and country in which it was written? Does the language used hold any clues?

Step 6: Is there unusual wording in the document? If so, do the words seem to indicate an earlier time or a foreign country?

Step 7: In what point of view is the document written? Does the writer use the pronouns *I* and *we?* If so, it's written in the first person. Or does the writer use the pronouns *he* and *she,* which indicate third person? Something written in the first person means you are reading someone's firsthand account.

Step 8: Now ask yourself what main point the writer was trying to express.

Step 9: Finally, you can begin to reflect on what you've learned. Think about any feelings you got from reading the document. What do you still wonder about? And what research would tell you more about this person or event?

Applying the Strategy

Choice 1: Find a primary source in a chapter you have read in your textbook. Apply the steps above and fill out your chart on this document. Share your findings with the class.

Choice 2: Pick a time period you have studied. Create an old primary source describing some event. Use your chart to be sure to include important information. Share your document with your classmates.

Answering Document-Based Questions
Teaching Model

Introducing the Strategy

Description: Historians learn about and interpret the past by reading documents and making inferences from them about historical periods and events. With a "big question" in mind, historians collect and study source documents. Individual documents provide some clues and information; however, many documents are needed to be able to construct an interpretation of events and movements.

Introductory Activity: Explain to students that historians often ask "big questions" and then use a variety of documents to help them find answers. For example, one question some historians have asked is, "How did adults think of teenagers during the turbulent 1970s?" What kinds of documents might be used to answer this question? (Elicit ideas such as these: teen magazines, movie advertisements, letters, adolescent novels, etc.) Then explain that there are some basic questions that historians ask of these documents. Ask, "What would you want to know if you had some of these source documents?"

Teaching the Strategy of Answering Document-Based Questions

Step 1: Explain that when we want to find answers to big questions, we need to look for sources that give us good information. Hand out the Document Analysis Grid (DAG) and show a transparency of it (Figure 7.5). As you highlight the sections, ask students why each is included.

Step 2: Explain that one big question still studied by many historians is "What was the role of women in the development of the United States in the 19th century?" Ask what they have already studied related to this question. Then give all students a copy of the document "Disappointment Is the Lot of Women," a speech given by Lucy Stone in 1855 (Figure 7.6). Ask them to read this document and work with a partner to fill in the first four sections of the DAG. Review their work and model on a transparency the information that should go on the DAG.

Step 3: Ask them to think about the big question as they read the document. They may read individually or you may need to read it orally to them. Next show them how to use the DAG to identify main ideas and information included in the document to help answer the big question. Model doing this with the class.

Step 4: Ask students to come together as a group and share their analysis of the document. Focus on how the document contributes to answering the big question. Also check on their understanding of the perspective and limitations of this data source.

Figure 7.5
Document Analysis Grid

Big question being addressed:	What I already know:
Name of document:	Source:
Primary source ___ Secondary source ___	Author: Date:
Main idea of the document:	Key information/data/quotations and location of that information:

Figure 7.6
Speech to Use with Document Analysis Grid

Disappointment Is the Lot of Women
Speech given by Lucy Stone at the Cincinnati Convention, 17–18 October 1855

From the first years to which my memory stretches, I have been a disappointed woman. When with my brothers, I reached forth after the sources of knowledge, I was reproved with "It isn't fit for you; it doesn't belong to women." Then there was but one college in the world where women were admitted, and that was in Brazil. I would have found my way there, but by the time I was prepared to go, one was opened in the young State of Ohio—the first in the United States where women and Negroes could enjoy opportunities with white men. I was disappointed when I came to seek a profession worthy an immortal being—every employment was closed to me, except those of the teacher, the seamstress, and the housekeeper. In education, in marriage, in religion, in everything, disappointment is the lot of woman. It shall be the business of my life to deepen this disappointment in every woman's heart until she bows down to it no longer. I wish that women, instead of being walking show-cases, instead of begging of their fathers and brothers the latest and gayest new bonnet, would ask of them their rights.

The question of Woman's Rights is a practical one. The notion has prevailed that it was only a ephemeral idea; that it was but women claiming the right to smoke cigars in the streets, and to frequent bar-rooms. Others have supposed it a question of comparative intellect; others still, of sphere. Too much has already been said and written about woman's sphere. Trace all the doctrines to their source and they will be found to have no basis except in the usages and prejudices of the age. This is seen in the fact that what is tolerated in woman in one country is not tolerated in another. In this country women may hold prayer-meetings, etc., but in Mohammedan countries it is written upon their mosques, "Women and dogs, and other impure animals, are not permitted to enter." Wendell Phillips says, "The best and greatest thing one is capable of doing, that is his sphere." ... Leave women, then, to find their sphere. And do not tell us before we are born even, that our province is to cook dinners, darn stockings, and sew on buttons. We are told woman has all the rights she wants; and even women, I am ashamed to say, tell us so. They mistake the politeness of men for rights—seats, while men stand in this hall to-night, and their adulations, but these are mere courtesies. We want rights. The flour-merchant, the housebuilder, and the postman charge us no less on account of our sex; but when we endeavor to earn money to pay all these, then, indeed, we find the difference. Man, if he have energy, may hew out for himself a path where no mortal has ever trod, held back by nothing but what is in himself; the world is all before him.... But the same society that drives forth the young man, keeps woman at home—a dependent—working little cats on worsted, and little dogs on punctured paper; but if she goes heartily and bravely to give herself to some worthy purpose, she is out of her sphere and she loses caste. Women working in tailor-shops are paid one-third as much as men. Some one in Philadelphia has stated that women make fine shirts for twelve and a half cents apiece; that no women can make more than nine a week, and the sum thus earned, after deducting rent, fuel, etc., leaves her just three and a half cents a day for bread. Is it a wonder that women are driven to prostitution? Female teachers in New York are paid fifty dollars a year, and for every such situation there are five hundred applicants.... The present condition of woman causes a horrible perversion of the marriage relation. It is asked of a lady, "Has she married well?" "Oh, yes, her husband is rich." Woman must marry for a home....

The widening of woman's sphere is to improve her lot. Let us do it, and if the world scoff, let it scoff—if it sneer, let it sneer....

Source: From *The History of Woman Suffrage* (ed. Elizabeth Cady Stanton), VOL. 1 (New York: Fowler & Wells, 1881).

Student Strategy

Learning the Strategy

Step 1: In history courses you may be given primary and secondary source documents related to a particular significant historical question and asked to use them to form an interpretation or answer to the question. A key to being successful with this kind of activity is to keep the big question in focus. Use of the DAG can help you develop this habit.

Step 2: Write the big question on the DAG. Think of what you already know related to this issue. Then examine the first document. Determine what kind of document it is. Is it a primary or secondary source?

Step 3: Look for the author and date of the document. Record these on the form.

Step 4: Try to determine the intended audience for the document. Also think of its original purpose.

Step 5: Read through the document and then summarize the main idea or theme. Think about how this relates to the main question.

Step 6: Make notes on key information and quotations that you think are particularly helpful in answering the question. Reflect on the relationship of the document to the question.

Applying the Strategy

Choice 1: Look through your textbook or course resource materials and find any documents that are related to either of the questions mentioned earlier—How were teenagers viewed in the 1970s? or What was the role of women in 19th-century America? Use the DAG to analyze the document you select.

Choice 2: Work with a partner and identify a big question in the unit you are studying in history or civics. Then go online and find a document related to that question and analyze it together using your DAG skills. (Hint: You may want to use the Library of Congress Web site, www.loc. gov, because it has thousands of good documents related to American history.)

Evaluating Internet Sources
Teaching Model

Introducing the Strategy

Description: Students are frequently on the Internet looking for information. Given the enormous number of sites available, it is important that students develop skill in evaluating the quality of sites by noting site sponsors and checking information provided against other sources.

Introductory Activity: Write on the board: *How do you know what to believe on the Internet?* Ask students how they verify information in what they read; list their ideas on the board.

Teaching the Strategy of Evaluating Internet Sources

Step 1: Explain to students that when they read information in a textbook or a published article, it has been "edited"—reviewed by persons considered authorities on the content. In contrast, anyone can create a Web site, and there is no review by experts of what is included.

Step 2: Make two columns on the board with the headings "edited" and "unedited." Put a list of sources beside these columns and ask students to sort the sources. (Some possibilities include the following: American Memory Web site; your history textbook; *Time for Kids* magazine articles; http://sun.menloschool.org; Wikipedia.org; *St. Louis Post Dispatch* newspaper). Discuss their work and clarify any points of confusion.

Step 3: Explain that because Internet sites aren't edited, it is important to check the information for accuracy. There are two easy ways to do this. The first is to identify the site sponsors. Explain that most sites include information about the people who maintain them. Show students a print copy of a Web page. Highlight the band with the link to the information or copy the band below.

Home	About Us	Get Involved	Contacts	Store	Members

Step 4: Explain that the other way to verify accuracy is to use a textbook or an encyclopedia. Give students a copy of the Grid for Evaluating Internet Source Accuracy (Figure 7.7) and explain its purpose. The first column is where students should write the information they are interested in using. Then they should locate the same topic in an "edited" source. If there are great differences, then further research is needed. Tell students that by keeping this information, they will always have a good reference if they need to confirm data later when doing research.

Student Strategy

Learning the Strategy

Step 1: When you use Internet sites as sources of information, it is essential to check the accuracy of the sites. This is a two-step process. First, check to see who sponsors the site. If the organization is reputable, like the Library of Congress or the Centers for Disease Control and Prevention, you can have confidence in the information.

Step 2: If you cannot be sure the sponsors of the site are reputable or have accuracy of information as part of their purpose, then try to verify the information from another reputable source or two. Use the Grid for Evaluating Internet Source Accuracy so you can always refer to your search strategy later.

Step 3: Summarize each key piece of information you think you will use in the left column of the grid. Indicate where you found the information, with the URL of the site and the location within the site, so you can return to it later.

Step 4: Select one or two other references that have been edited and are published by reputable publishing houses. If you are unsure, ask a teacher, librarian, or other knowledgeable person to help you. Locate information in those sources and make notes of what you found and where (author, title, publisher, and page).

Step 5: Compare the information you gathered from the sources. If there are differences, then continue to search in additional sources or ask a librarian for assistance. When you are sure the information is accurate, you can incorporate it in your paper or report.

Applying the Strategy

Choice 1: Select a contemporary political figure to research. Locate one or two Internet sites about this person. Use the Grid for Evaluating Internet Source Accuracy and write down some key information. Then use an edited biographical collection and news articles to confirm the information.

Choice 2: Work with a partner and visit a political Web site sponsored by a group with a clear agenda. Compare information on the site with what you can find in a reputable news magazine. Evaluate the Web site using the Grid for Evaluating Internet Sites (Figure 7.8).

	Figure 7.7 Grid for Evaluating Internet Source Accuracy		
Information	**Internet Source**	**Edited Source**	**Similar (+) or not (–)**

	Figure 7.8 Grid for Evaluating Internet Sites				
URL and Title of Site	Authorship and Publishing Group	Evidence of Bias and View	Evidence of Misinformation	Evidence of Disinformation	Latest Web Site Update

8

Strategies for Newspaper and Magazine Literacy

This chapter is designed to help students learn specific strategies for reading newspapers and magazines. The chapter is divided into the following lessons that teach specific strategies to help students become critical readers:

- Understanding Newspaper Articles
- Analyzing Magazine Articles
- Supporting Opinions in Editorials
- Reading and Analyzing Essays
- Identifying Bias
- Identifying Propaganda Techniques in Political Ads
- Analyzing Political Cartoons

As in Chapters 6 and 7, each lesson has two parts:

1. A Teaching Model section that includes the following:
   - Description of the strategy
   - Introductory activity to motivate students
   - Step-by-step instructions for how to teach and model the strategy

2. A Student Strategy section that includes the following:
   - Step-by-step instructions for guided practice
   - Applying the Strategy activities for further practice and assessment

Each lesson also includes practice pages—models of appropriate texts and reproducible graphic organizers for use with models.

Understanding Newspaper Articles
Teaching Model

Introducing the Strategy

Description: Newspapers are a major resource for keeping citizens informed on local, national, and world issues. Newspaper articles are meant to be read with efficiency, so they follow a style that is sometimes called an "inverted pyramid." This activity will show students how to follow the organization of a newspaper article.

Introductory Activity: Do a quick informal survey of how many of your students read the newspaper. Ask the following questions and put the results on the board:

- How many of you read the newspaper (pick one) once a week, twice a week, more than three times a week? (Have students raise their hands; record results for each choice.)
- How many of you read any of the following: school newspaper, local newspaper, or national newspaper, such as *USA Today?* (Have students raise their hands; record results for each choice.)
- What part of the newspaper do you read first—front page, editorials, sports, entertainment, classified ads? (Have students raise their hands; record results for each choice.)
- What parts of the newspaper do you *never* read? (Write responses on the board.)
- Why would some people feel that the newspaper is an important part of society? (Write responses on the board.)

Explain to students that the strategy they are about to learn will help them better understand what they read in newspapers.

Teaching the Strategy of Understanding Newspaper Articles

Step 1: Explain that each newspaper article begins with a "lead" that grabs the reader's attention and could be one of several types. Write the following types of leads on the board: leads that create an *impact,* leads that reveal a *quote,* leads that ask a *question,* and leads that are indirect because they create an *impression* before getting to the "details" of the article.

Step 2: Draw an upside-down pyramid on the board. Tell students that most news articles are written in a style known as an "inverted pyramid." Following the lead, newspaper writers give details in a descending order. Large, important ideas are presented first and supporting details are presented later. This style helps readers read more efficiently.

Step 3: Using the article "Small Nuclear Conflict Could Affect Globe" (Figure 8.1), read the first paragraph aloud to demonstrate how the lead works. Ask students to guess what type of lead they think is used in this article. (Correct answer is "lead that creates an impact.")

Step 4: Now read the rest of the article with the students. Walk students through the graphic organizer Understanding Newspaper Articles (Figure 8.2). Solicit responses from the students as they fill in the graphic organizer in a directed lesson. (See Figure 8.3 for an example of a completed version.)

Step 5: Have students share their responses. For further practice and assessment, have students choose one of the Applying the Strategy activities in the Student Strategy section.

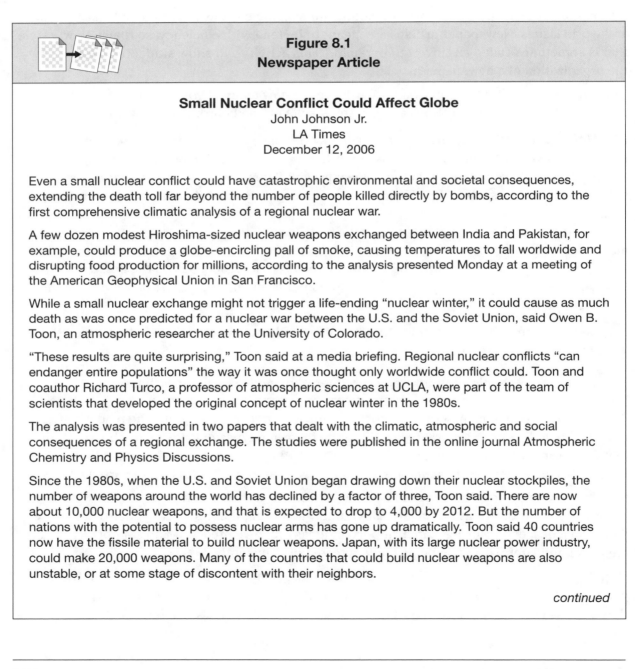

Figure 8.1
Newspaper Article

Small Nuclear Conflict Could Affect Globe
John Johnson Jr.
LA Times
December 12, 2006

Even a small nuclear conflict could have catastrophic environmental and societal consequences, extending the death toll far beyond the number of people killed directly by bombs, according to the first comprehensive climatic analysis of a regional nuclear war.

A few dozen modest Hiroshima-sized nuclear weapons exchanged between India and Pakistan, for example, could produce a globe-encircling pall of smoke, causing temperatures to fall worldwide and disrupting food production for millions, according to the analysis presented Monday at a meeting of the American Geophysical Union in San Francisco.

While a small nuclear exchange might not trigger a life-ending "nuclear winter," it could cause as much death as was once predicted for a nuclear war between the U.S. and the Soviet Union, said Owen B. Toon, an atmospheric researcher at the University of Colorado.

"These results are quite surprising," Toon said at a media briefing. Regional nuclear conflicts "can endanger entire populations" the way it was once thought only worldwide conflict could. Toon and coauthor Richard Turco, a professor of atmospheric sciences at UCLA, were part of the team of scientists that developed the original concept of nuclear winter in the 1980s.

The analysis was presented in two papers that dealt with the climatic, atmospheric and social consequences of a regional exchange. The studies were published in the online journal Atmospheric Chemistry and Physics Discussions.

Since the 1980s, when the U.S. and Soviet Union began drawing down their nuclear stockpiles, the number of weapons around the world has declined by a factor of three, Toon said. There are now about 10,000 nuclear weapons, and that is expected to drop to 4,000 by 2012. But the number of nations with the potential to possess nuclear arms has gone up dramatically. Toon said 40 countries now have the fissile material to build nuclear weapons. Japan, with its large nuclear power industry, could make 20,000 weapons. Many of the countries that could build nuclear weapons are also unstable, or at some stage of discontent with their neighbors.

continued

Figure 8.1 *Continued*

In conducting their research, the scientists looked at other global cataclysms, such as the 1815 eruption of the Tambora volcano in Indonesia. The eruption triggered what has come to be known as the Year Without a Summer, which caused killing frosts and crop losses in New England as well as crop failures and famine in Europe. The authors said even a limited nuclear conflict would be much worse, killing as many as 17 million in China alone.

The most significant atmospheric impact from a nuclear exchange would be the accumulation of smoke and soot in the atmosphere, said team member Georgiy Stenchikov, a professor of environmental science at Rutgers University. Stenchikov estimated that 5 million tons of soot could be thrown into the air by the explosion of about 100 15-kiloton nuclear weapons. The smoke and soot would ascend into the stratosphere and stay there for up to 10 years, causing temperatures to fall several degrees, the researchers said.

In areas far removed from the site of the explosions, growing seasons could be reduced by 10 days to a month, said Alan Robock, an environmental sciences professor at Rutgers who worked on the analysis.

One factor increasing the danger in densely populated areas is the proliferation of plastics, which in a firestorm would increase the soot released into the atmosphere. The production of plastics in the developed world has doubled in just the last two decades, Turco said.

Instead of feeling content that the U.S. and Russia are drawing down their nuclear arsenal, people should realize that they "are at a perilous crossroads," Toon said. "Nuclear proliferation and political instability form the greatest danger to human society since the dawn of mankind."

Copyright, 2006, Los Angeles Times. Reprinted with permission.

Figure 8.2
Graphic Organizer for Newspaper Articles

Understanding Newspaper Articles

Step 1: This lesson will help you learn how to read newspaper articles. Complete the graphic organizer below as you read a news article.

Title and date of article:

Where does the story take place?

What is the lead of this article?

What is the type of lead?

Step 2: As you read the article, fill in as much information as you can about the details of the article. (You might not fill in all the boxes.)

Important Details to Remember

Who	What	When	Where	Why/How

continued

Figure 8.2 *Continued*

Step 3: To support the information given in the article, reporters often quote their sources of information. Sources are people who witnessed the event or were in some way involved. In the table below, write in the quotes, or important parts of the quotes, that you determine to be important to what the article is discussing.

Person/Source	Quote

Step 4: In a sentence or two, describe the main topic or issue.

Main Focus of Article in My Own Words

Step 5: Write a sentence that describes your opinion, reaction, or evaluation of the article.

My Opinion/Evaluation

Figure 8.3
Sample of Completed Graphic Organizer
for Newspaper Articles

Title and Date of Article

"Small Nuclear Conflict Could Affect Globe"
December 12, 2006

Where does the story take place?

The story is written in San Francisco, California.

What is the lead part of this article?

Even a small nuclear war could have catastrophic societal and environmental consequences with higher death tolls than those people just killed with bombs.

What is the type of lead?

This is a lead that creates an impact because it describes a catastrophic result of even a small nuclear war.

Details to Remember

Who	What	When	Where	Why/How
Owen B. Toon	Much death would be caused by a nuclear war. Can endanger entire populations.	December 11, 2006	Meting of the American Geophysical Union in San Francisco	A pall of smoke would encircle the earth, causing temperatures to fall worldwide.
Richard Turco	Coauthor and professor of atmospheric sciences at UCLA	December 11, 2006	Meting of the American Geophysical Union in San Francisco	Part of a team that helped develop concept of nuclear winter in 1980s. Analysis was presented in two papers.
Owen B. Toon	Draw down of nuclear weapons	1980s	Soviet Union, United States	Reduced numbers of weapons to 10,000.
Scientists	Researchers/ Year Without Summer	From 1815 to present	Research report	Looked at causes of volcanoes and effects of frosts and crop failures.
Georgiy Stenchikov	Professor, Rutgers University	December 11, 2006	Research report	As much as 5 million tons of soot could be generated by 100 15-kiloton nuclear weapons. It would stay in atmosphere for up to 10 years, causing temperatures to drop.

continued

Figure 8.3 *Continued*

Person/Source	Quote
Owen B. Toon	"The results are quite surprising…it could cause as much death as was once predicted for a nuclear war between the U.S. and the Soviet Union!" "It could endanger entire populations…."
Authors of research report	"Even a limited nuclear conflict would be much worse, killing as many as 17 million in China alone."
Georgiy Stenchikov	"The most significant impact from a nuclear exchange would be the accumulation of smoke and soot in the atmosphere."
Alan Robock	"In areas far removed from the site of the explosions, growing seasons could be reduced by 10 days to a month."
Richard Turco	"One factor increasing the danger in densely populated areas is the proliferation of plastics, which in a firestorm would increase the soot released into the atmosphere. The production of plastics in the developed world has doubled in just the last two decades."

Main Focus of Article in My Own Words

The article's focus is the serious effects of a nuclear war, and in particular on the environment and the loss of life. Even a small nuclear war has dire consequences for many years to come based on its effect on the ability to sustain life on earth with all of the damage to the atmosphere.

My Opinion/Evaluation

The nuclear situation has other threats than just the death and destruction of the blasts. The aftereffects need to be considered and with ongoing nuclear proliferation, the threat continues, even after the cold war.

Student Strategy

Learning the Strategy

Step 1: This lesson will help you learn how to read newspaper articles. Using the article "Small Nuclear Conflict Could Affect Globe," your teacher will model the completion of the graphic organizer to help you understand how information is organized in newspaper articles. The steps shown in the graphic organizer include instructions for each part. Write the title and date of the article, and where the story takes place. Also copy the sentence that you think is the lead, and list the type of lead that best describes it.

Step 2: As you read the article with your teacher, fill in as much information as you can about the details of the article on the blank graphic organizer.

Step 3: To support the information given in an article, reporters often quote their sources of information. Sources are people who provide information about the topic of the article. In the graphic organizer, write the quotes, or important parts of the quotes, that you determine to be significant to what the article is discussing.

Step 4: In a sentence or two, describe the main focus or issue.

Step 5: Write a sentence or two that describes your opinion, reaction, or evaluation of the article.

Applying the Strategy

Choice 1: Choose an article that interests you from the front page of a newspaper. Analyze the article using the Understanding Newspaper Articles graphic organizer. Share your findings with the class.

Choice 2: Write a newspaper article on a topic that interests you. Before you write, use the graphic organizer to plan how you will write the article. Choose something that is newsworthy, whether it is about sports, politics, or the arts. Decide which type of lead you will use to begin your story. Then find sources who know something about your topic and whom you can quote. Submit your article to your school or local newspaper for publication.

Analyzing Magazine Articles
Teaching Model

Introducing the Strategy

Description: The strategy called KWL+ helps students engage actively while reading. Before reading, they activate what they know and ask questions about the text. During reading, they make notes related to answers to questions and new interesting information.

Introductory Activity: Ask students to list their favorite magazines. Ask them how they decide which articles to read and how they go about reading an article.

Teaching the Strategy of KWL+

Step 1: Explain that you are going to model with the class the use of a strategy called KWL+. Give each student a copy of the KWL+ graphic organizer (Figure 8.4). (See Figure 8.5 for a sample of a completed graphic organizer.)

Step 2: Put the title of the article "Cities Adopt a New Plan for the Homeless" (Figure 8.6) on the board or show the top part of the article on the overhead projector. Ask the students what they already know about the homeless and what they think this article will explain. Write their ideas on the board or on the transparency in the "**K**now" column.

Step 3: Have students bring in pictures of the homeless or show the clip art pictures presented in Figure 8.7. Ask students what these images portray about homeless people. Remind students that the pictures used in magazine articles are intended to reinforce the text or to promote a particular emotional response. What types of emotional responses do these pictures provoke? Do these pictures represent all homeless people?

Step 4: Pass out a copy of the article (Figure 8.6) to each student. Ask students to skim the article and note the graphics (picture, graphs, headings) and how the author has organized the sections. Ask what questions they think will be addressed in the article and what questions they have. Write these in the "**W**ant to Know" column.

Step 5: Read the first section orally to the class. Ask students what is new, is interesting, or answers their questions. Write that information on the KWL+ chart. Ask students to read the rest of the article with a partner or in groups of four (PODs), or read it to them.

Step 6: When they have finished with the article, model the creation of a graphic organizer of the text. Ask them to reflect on the purpose of this article and what they think the author was trying to communicate. Draw the categories on the board and ask partners to fill in information from their KWL+ charts.

Step 7: Bring the class back together and model how to write a summary of the article using the graphic organizer (see Figure 8.5).

Figure 8.4
Graphic Organizer for KWL+

What I Know	What I Want to Learn	What I Learned/ Still Need to Learn

Likely Categories	Summarizing Paragraph	Added Information
1.		1.
2.		2.
3.		3.
4.		4.

Figure 8.5
Example of KWL+ Chart Completed by Teacher

What I **K**now	What I **W**ant to Learn	What I **L**earned/ Still Need to Learn
People who are homeless usually beg for money. People who are homeless have drug problems. People who are homeless don't help themselves. People who are homeless always beg for money or food.	Why do people become homeless? What are we doing about it? How long has this been a problem? Which cities have the largest problem with this issue?	Primary cause is the rise in rent costs. People are either temporarily homeless or some are chronic and use half of the money allocated to treat the problem. Some cities have laws about the homeless. Some cities have programs to help the homeless.
Likely Categories	**Summarizing Paragraph**	**Added information**
1. Temporarily homeless 2. Chronically homeless 3. Cities with program 4. Cities with laws 5. State and federal programs to help with the problem	Homelessness is a problem across the country. Three million people will become homeless this year. Primary causes include high rent and loss of jobs. There are some programs that help and are funded by state and federal agencies. Some cities have plans in place to help the homeless.	1. Since 1980 the rising cost of rent has been the main reason for homelessness. 2. A person who has mental illness uses about $40,000 per year. 3. Cities like San Francisco and Alexandria, Virginia, have adopted long-range plans to help. 4. About three million Americans become homeless each year.

Figure 8.6
Newspaper Article to Use with KWL+ Chart

What's Happening

IN THE USA?

BY LAWRENCE GABLE

VOL 12, NO 9 MAY 2005

Cities Adopt a New Plan for the Homeless

In the past twenty years homelessness has become one of America's most difficult problems. In that time the number of homeless has doubled. Many cities have had programs to address the problem, but now they are taking a new approach. With it they are hoping to end homelessness in ten years.

The problem began in the 1970s. At that time there was plenty of affordable housing for low-income families. However, when many state and federal mental hospitals closed, they sent thousands of patients onto the streets. Churches and early homeless shelters helped, but suddenly there was not enough housing. By 2001 there were 4.7 million too few affordable housing units in the U.S.

Since the 1980s the rising cost of rent has become the primary cause of homelessness. Usually people spend no more than 30% of their monthly incomes on housing, but in many places people are spending more than half. Families give up their housing because they need the money for food, clothes and medicine. In some communities 40% of the homeless are working full time, but for low wages.

Experts divide homeless people into two groups. The majority is homeless only temporarily. These people are facing some kind of crisis, like losing a job or fleeing an abusive spouse. They get help from social services to resolve the crisis. Then they find housing within six months, and are never homeless again.

The minority is chronically homeless. These people go for more than a year without permanent housing, or end up homeless again and again. Although they are only 10% of the homeless population, they use 50% of the money, space and time that programs offer. Often they have mental, physical, or drug problems. Since most states have cut their treatment programs, they have received little help. Some of them can work, but they rarely earn enough to pay for housing.

Many cities have laws that affect the homeless. If they sleep on a sidewalk or beg for money, the police arrest them. They may even send the person for treatment at a hospital. Now cities are realizing that this makes the city look nicer and the public feel better, but it does not end chronic homelessness.

Programs to help the homeless have had some success. They provide many homeless people with temporary shelters. They also help them get support services from health departments, Veterans Affairs, the court system, and child protective services. Unfortunately, every night in America about 700,000 people still have no place to call home.

A study by the University of Pennsylvania has led cities to a new approach. It found that a homeless person with severe mental illness uses about $40,000 in services a year. The study also found that providing housing and support services costs about the same. That keeps the homeless out of jail and emergency rooms, and adds some stability and order to their lives.

Several cities already have new programs to provide housing and counseling. Alexandria, Virginia, adopted a 10-year plan in March. So far it has funded housing for 12 of the city's 100 chronically homeless. San Francisco started its 10-year program, "Care Not Cash," almost a year ago. It has reduced welfare checks to the homeless from $400 to $60. Instead it uses the money to pay for rent in renovated residence hotels. It also provides food, support services and counseling. More than 700 of the city's 3,000 chronically homeless now have a place to live.

On April 5 the U.S. Congress introduced legislation regarding homelessness. The "Services for Ending Long-Term Homelessness Act" could fund permanent housing and counseling for the chronically homeless around the country. Its goal is also to end chronic homelessness in ten years.

Three million Americans find themselves homeless every year. Many stay in a shelter, but others spend nights in cars, campgrounds and abandoned buildings, under bridges or on park benches. If the new programs address the causes of homelessness, not just its effects, then the number of homeless may start to fall.

Source: Reprinted with permission from Lawrence Gable, What's Happening Publications.

Figure 8.7
Picturing the Homeless

Student Strategy

Learning the Strategy

Step 1: When you are reading materials that you need to remember, the KWL+ strategy is a good one to use. Begin by listing what you think you know about the topic. Also, think of the major topics that the experts are likely to include. Jot those down. If you haven't mentioned anything about one or two areas, write questions in the "**W**ant to Learn" column. Other questions you have or think might be answered should be added to the chart. Then as you read, make notes.

Step 2: Choose an article you are reading for class or one from a news magazine on a related topic. Think of why you chose the article and what you already know about the topic. Write these ideas on your chart in the "**K**now" column. Think of how experts look at this topic and how they organize reports and books. What categories do you expect will be used to present the topic? Write these in the "**K**now" column, under "Likely Categories."

Step 3: Look through the article, noting the graphics, pictures, and bold headings. What focus does the author have? What might you learn as you read this text? Think of questions that might be answered and what you could learn. Then, write several questions in the center column reflecting what you "**W**ant to learn" as a result of your reading.

Step 4: As you read or when you finish each section, make notes in the "Learned" column of information you want to remember. Answers to your questions should be put here, and you may want to draw a line to the corresponding question in column 2.

Step 5: After you finish reading, think about the most important information and the important topics or categories. Create a graphic organizer with the title of the article in the center and use the main topics as the spokes. Add important details or examples under each area.

Step 6: Now write a summary of the article using the spokes as the topics of individual paragraphs. Add the supporting information from your organizer to explain each topic.

Applying the Strategy

Choice 1: Find a magazine article that contains issues and information that interest you. Use KWL+ with the informational articles you select to read, whether in social studies, science, or another course.

Choice 2: Try the KWL+ strategy on a chapter from your textbook. Based on your next assignment in your social studies class, apply the strategy and then compare with another student in your POD or in your class to determine how much of the information you remember.

Supporting Opinions in Editorials
Teaching Model

Introducing the Strategy

Description: Although students have opinions about everything, they may not be able to construct or analyze a well-supported argument. Part of being an engaged citizen is being able to read critically other people's opinions, especially in the form of editorials. To scaffold their reading of editorials, an Opinion Support Frame (Figure 8.8) serves as a graphic organizer to help them get through the editorial.

Introductory Activity: Have students choose a partner. Ask them to imagine that they are trying to convince students and parents that there is something going on at school that is unfair. It might be that there is too much homework, or that tests are all given on the same day, or that standardized tests are placing too much of a burden on students. Groups need to develop the following:

- Three reasons why the issue is thought to be unfair
- Two examples of how it affects students and teachers
- Two quotes from students and/or teachers that support the expressed view

Once students have crafted their argument, have volunteers present their opinions to the class.

Teaching the Strategy for Supporting Opinions in Editorials

Step 1: Ask the students if they know the word *editorial*. Make sure students understand that an editorial is a piece of writing, usually short, that gives an opinion about a particular topic or issue. Write the words *opinion* and *fact* on the board. Ask students to explain the difference. Students should know that an opinion is a belief, a feeling, or an attitude. A fact, however, is something that can be proved to be true. Tell students that writers who have strong opinions use facts, real-world examples, and quotes or information from experts to support their beliefs.

Step 2: Pass out a copy of the editorial "Kid Convicts" (Figure 8.9) by high school student Chris Morse.

Step 3: Based on the title of the editorial, ask students what they think the editorial is about and how they feel about the issue.

Step 4: Read the editorial aloud to the class. Write students' reactions on the board. Label students' responses with an *O* for opinion and an *F* for fact.

Step 5: Have pairs or PODs complete the Opinion Support Frame using the "Kid Convicts" article. Once students are finished, show a transparency of the completed graphic (Figure 8.10).

Step 6: For practice, pass out copies of a second editorial, "Steroids and Professional Sports" (Figure 8.11). After discussion, have students choose one of the Applying the Strategy activities as further practice and assessment.

Figure 8.8
Graphic Organizer for Analyzing Editorials

Opinion Support Frame: Editorials

What is the topic or title of the editorial?

What opinion is being stated in this editorial?

What facts are used to support this opinion?

What real-world examples are used to support this opinion?

What information or quotes from experts support this opinion?

Who is the author and what is his or her background?

What information might support an opposing viewpoint?

Do you agree with this editorial? Why or why not? (Answer on back)

Figure 8.9
Student Editorial

Kid Convicts
Chris Morse
Golden Valley High School

Imagine you are a well-known judge around the country and are given a new case. You say to yourself, "This case is fairly well cut and dried." You sit in your bench and wait for the defendant to walk into the courtroom. He walks in and you look upon his face. You take off your glasses and wipe them off to see if you are seeing things right. Who would have thought that a booster chair would ever be brought into a courtroom?

Under current Florida law even an 8-year-old child can be convicted and sent to jail for murder. "I'm sorry, I think that's wrong," said Florida Sen. Steven Geller in an interview on CBS news. Geller pointed out that this is the system we have for punishing juveniles who have committed crimes, and it is still not completely foolproof. In sentencing a child on crimes he or she has committed, age should be taken into account.

According to "Psychiatry for Medical Students" by Dr. Robert Waldinger, "It is easy to forget the fact that development does not stop in adulthood, because change in adult life is less rapid, and more easily overlooked than change in the childhood years." This means that in the periods of latency and adolescence, psychological reform is easier to attain. Therefore, child criminals should receive psychological help, and when deemed fit, given a second chance to experience life as if you have never done anything wrong. If you are 8 years old and murder someone, it was either an accident or you should be labeled insane. A 20-year-old can serve hard time for a crime committed when he was 10 years old!

If grown men like Charles Manson—who are set in their ways of self-indulgence, sexual offenses, murder, and other horrible criminal activity—are eligible for parole, why shouldn't an impressionable child be given the same chance as this evil character? In giving psychological help to children at the youngest age possible, we reduce the revenues that go into maintaining all the prisoners that don't deserve to be there. Of course, there are those cases that are considered beyond any kind of rehabilitation, but every child should at least be given a chance to live a life on their own.

Figure 8.10
Example of a Completed Graphic Organizer for Editorials

Opinion Support Frame: Editorials

What is the topic or title of the editorial?

The topic is whether young kids should be put away in prison for a long time when they have committed a serious crime.

What opinion is being stated in this editorial?

The writer thinks that juveniles should be given a chance at rehabilitation instead of being locked away at a great cost to the state.

What facts are used to support this opinion?

Under Florida law, young children can be put in prison for life for crimes they commit.

What real-world examples are used to support this opinion?

The author refers to a 20-year-old serving time for a crime committed when he was only 10 years old.

What information or quotes from experts support this opinion?

Florida Senator Geller—In sentencing a criminal, age should be taken into account. Dr. Robert Waldinger—Child criminals should receive psychological help, and when deemed fit, given a second chance to experience life.

Who is the author and what is his or her background?

The author is a high school student in California.

What information might support an opposing viewpoint?

Statistics might show how many of these young people continue to commit crimes when they get out.

Do you agree with this editorial? Why or why not? (Answer on back)

Figure 8.11
Student Editorial

Steroids and Professional Sports: Insert Needle Here
Chris Morse
Golden Valley High School

As we sat at home and watched baseball, we saw Mark McGuire, Sammy Sosa, and Barry Bonds slam homerun after homerun out of the stadium. These magnificent sluggers made the ball look like there was a magnet in the ball just waiting to stick onto a lonely car far out in the parking lot. A question comes to mind: how can one person hit these balls as if they were at batting practice? These super athletes want you to think it is all hard work in the gym and practicing on minuscule details for four hours. That might be how baseball should be practiced, but they "accidentally" might leave out their main ingredient that would help them become nationwide heroes. It's kind of like leaving the peanut butter out of the peanut butter and jelly sandwich: it is the most important part of the recipe. Steroids.

Androgenic-anabolic steroids may not be the secret ingredient for many players. Not every professional athlete uses them, but there is a large portion that do. And for those on the team who do, they become the leading factor on that team and make baseball become the Bash of the Brawns. Steroids are used to promote growth of skeletal muscles. Androgenic-anabolic steroids get their title from the two Greek words, andro and gennar, meaning "male-producing," and from another Greek word, anabold, which means "to build up." So as you watch these professional athletes break numerous records every day, you think, "What's so bad about taking steroids if it's going to make you a total superstar?" Steroids are like cheating on a test; you get paid to play baseball, not to take steroids and beat baseball at its own game. Oh yeah, steroids are also malevolent because it could stop your growth completely if you start using them at a premature age. Or maybe liver tumors, sterility, and coronary artery disease are looming on the horizon for later years.

Unfortunately, some high school teenagers are not getting the message and are taking these drugs anyway. According to the National Institute on Drug Abuse (NIDA), steroid use is increasing every year. A 1999 survey showed that 2.7% of 8th graders had used steroids at least once in their lives. Most users are male, but female steroid use is on the increase too. Most reasons young adults tend to use steroids is because they want to excel in athletics and this winning pattern will gain self-confidence for themselves. For the most part, teens use steroids just to get "popular."

Off-season training for many sports is spent inside the weight room for many hours. Football players spend all of their winter months preparing for the next year's summer camps just to gain an edge on the other competition they will face next year. Varsity football player James Lanphear knows everything about hard work and dedication. When asked his opinion if steroid use of professional players affects his decision to purchase and use steroids, he replies quickly, "That's their own decision to ruin their bodies. It in no way affects my decision."

Athletics is a huge factor here in Golden Valley High School. Any way you look at it, drugs are becoming more and more popular among professional sports players and students. Attributes of good athletes are not just speed or leadership or strength but also the will to make good decisions on an everyday basis.

Student Strategy

Learning the Strategy

Step 1: An editorial presents someone's opinion about an issue. Editorials appear in newspapers, magazines, and journals. When reading an editorial, first figure out the topic or issue being discussed. To figure out the topic, look at the title. Also read the first sentences very carefully. Writers often begin with a "topic sentence" that tells you the issue.

Step 2: Editorials always present a person's or group's opinion. Read the editorial carefully. Ask yourself what viewpoint is being expressed. What is the writer "for" or "against"?

Step 3: Now see how well the writer supported his or her opinion. Begin by thinking about what you already know about the issue. Then look for facts that the writer uses to support the opinion. Remember, a fact is something that can be proven to be true.

Step 4: Writers also use examples from world events to support an opinion. Check to see if the writers used examples. Ask yourself if these examples truly add support to the opinion.

Step 5: Writers also use statistics, or data, from research by experts who have studied the topic. A statistic is a number that measures some part of something, such as 50 percent of a group. Look to see how well this information adds support and if it seems accurate.

Step 6: People who write editorials do so to promote a particular view. Think about the background of the author. Why is he or she promoting this view? What personal interest does the author have in the topic? Does he or she stand to gain anything by convincing others to believe what he or she believes?

Step 7: Finally, ask yourself if you agree with the author's opinion. Was the opinion well supported? Did the author provide an opposing viewpoint and support for that view? Is it in the best interest of society to accept this person's opinions?

Applying the Strategy

Choice 1: Editorials appear in a newspaper on what is called the "Op-Ed" page, which stands for "opinions" and "editorials." Look through your local paper for a number of days. Find an editorial that interests you. Use your Opinion Support Frame to analyze it. Then present your findings to your classmates.

Choice 2: Write an editorial about a school-related issue. Choose something that you have strong feelings about. Remember that editorials are usually only about 300 words, so you have to be brief.

Reading and Analyzing Essays
Teaching Model

Introducing the Strategy

Description: Essays are a type of explanatory writing. Whether short or long, essays serve many functions. The structure of an essay often mirrors its purpose. Essays may explain comparisons and contrasts, causes and effects, sequence, or problems and solutions. Essays may also define, persuade, classify, or describe. Essays also have a consistent structure that comprises an introduction to state the topic, a body of supporting details, and a concluding statement.

Introductory Activity: Write the following statement on the board: *Sixteen-year-olds should be allowed to vote in elections.* Assign pairs or PODs to take a position, either for or against this issue. Ask pairs or PODs to come up with a list of reasons for their position. When students have finished, have volunteers list their reasons on the board under the categories "For" and "Against." Explain that in a written essay, these reasons would be the bulk of the article.

Teaching the Strategy of Reading and Analyzing Essays

Step 1: Either pass out a copy or show a transparency of the blank graphic organizer Reading and Analyzing an Essay (Figure 8.14, p. 167). Walk students through the organizer. Explain to students that titles of essays normally give a good idea of the topic.

Step 2: Tell students that when analyzing an essay, they will need to read it more than once. In the first reading, they should look for any unknown words that hamper comprehension. Students should use context clues, word structure, and a dictionary to make sure they understand the essay.

Step 3: After one reading, students should know the thesis statement, or the main idea or purpose of the writer. Students should also be able to tell who the intended audience is.

Step 4: A well-written essay has facts, statistics, examples, anecdotes, and quotes from experts to support its thesis statement. Tell students that an essay is judged on how well the writer supports his or her points.

Step 5: Explain that there are many kinds of essays, depending on the purpose of the writer. Write the following terms and their definitions on the board and discuss them with students.

  compare/contrast—explaining similarities and differences between two things

  cause/effect—explaining how the action of something makes other things happen

  problem/solution—explaining one or more solutions for a problem

  sequence—explaining the order that something is done

  classify—explaining how things relate to each other

---

analysis—explaining what makes up something

definition—explaining how something is seen or defined

persuasion—explaining something to convince readers to believe as the writer does

Step 6: Distribute copies of the essay "Teens and Voting: A Good Idea?" (Figure 8.12) and the completed graphic organizer (Figure 8.13). Walk students through the completed graphic organizer. Have students choose one of the Applying the Strategy activities for more practice and assessment.

Figure 8.12
Student Essay

Teens and Voting: A Good Idea?
Chris Morse
Golden Valley High School

Teenagers are often treated like adults when it comes to taxes, jobs, and most often in court. So why not when it comes to voting? The question in many legislatures around the U.S. concerns whether or not to give younger people, as young as 16- and 17-year-olds, the right to vote in elections that are both state and national.

Currently only adults over the age of 18 have the right to vote, and this starts American voters off on the wrong foot. At 19, the average American teenager is not interested in voting or in elections. The normal teenager is off to college or starting new life indulging in the freedoms that accompany becoming an adult. These newly eligible voters are too distracted by the new challenges of life on their own to become aware of the local issues. This is precisely why voter turnout of 18–24-year-olds has been slowly declining in the past few elections, even though people predicted a high turnout in the recent election for president.

If these new adults had the experience of voting while at a very impressionable age and still were enrolled in school, participating in elections would simply be second nature to them. While in school, teenagers are often required to take civics classes and learn the importance of their vote. Making voting an early habit would increase the chances that they would vote in future elections.

Some politicians question whether the government can trust teenagers to vote. But it wasn't too long ago that women were not given the right to vote. Among those who didn't trust women were important men like George Washington. Washington, however, supposedly used alcohol and rum to win over his voters. As proved by some outcomes of elections, many people who are uninformed may choose the wrong candidate over the right one. Many teenagers are too impressionable. Besides, some consider their impact to be negligible. Since they probably wouldn't vote they would not influence the outcome of the election.

Age should not be a source of fear since the number of voters introduced to the polls would hardly sway an election in a great number, but as citizens of the U.S., teenagers would be given the voice they are entitled to. This may produce a few immature voters, but their numbers would be greatly outweighed by the improved poll turnout and democratic representation for the future.

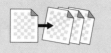

Figure 8.13
Example of a Completed Graphic Organizer
for Reading and Analyzing an Essay

Reading and Analyzing an Essay

Title of essay: *Teens and Voting: A Good Idea?*

Unfamiliar Words:

legislatures   indulging

eligible   impressionable

_____   _____   _____

_____   _____   _____

Thesis statement (in your own words): *Sixteen- and 17-year-olds should be allowed to vote in elections.*

Audience:

Lawmakers and the voting public that might change the present law

Other teenagers who might work to win the vote

Supporting Details:

Detail 1: Teenagers are old enough to pay taxes, work, and go to court.

Detail 2: Eighteen- and 19-year-olds are too distracted to learn about voting issues.

Detail 3: Voting would become a habit when teenagers are more impressionable.

Detail 4: Other groups once not allowed to vote, such as women, have done fine.

Detail 5: New numbers of voters wouldn't be enough to sway an election.

Structure or Purpose of Essay (compare/contrast, cause/effect, problem/solution, description, definition, sequence of events, analysis, classify, persuade):

Persuade—The writer is trying to persuade others to let 16- and 17-year-olds vote.

Reaction (Does this essay make sense to you? Are the supporting details logical or accurate? Do you hold a different belief or opinion? Why or why not?):

I don't think the writer gives enough evidence that 16- and 17-year-olds can make mature decisions.

Student Strategy

Learning the Strategy

The steps below will show you how to fill out the graphic organizer.

Step 1: Read the title of the essay. Then read the essay once, jotting down unknown words. Use context clues, word parts, and a dictionary to figure out what these words mean.

Step 2: Readers must determine what the thesis statement of the essay is. In pairs or PODs, determine which sentence best tells the thesis, or main idea, of the essay. Once you figure it out, write the thesis statement in the box.

Step 3: Based on the thesis, do you think you know for whom this essay is written? Who is the intended audience?

Step 4: Now find the reasons the writer provides to support his or her thesis. The number of supporting details will vary. In a compare/contrast essay, two different views will be presented.

Step 5: Now determine the structure or purpose of the essay. Ask yourself what the writer was trying to achieve.

Step 6: What is your reaction to the essay? Answer the questions in the box provided.

Applying the Strategy

Choice 1: Read the essay entitled "Comfort Gone Wrong" (Figure 8.15), which your teacher will provide. Use your graphic organizer (Figure 8.14) to analyze the essay. Compare your results with those of a classmate.

Choice 2: Now that you know the structure of an essay, you can try writing one. First pick a topic you're interested in. Use your graphic organizer to guide you.

Figure 8.14
Graphic Organizer for Reading and Analyzing an Essay

Reading and Analyzing an Essay

Title of essay:

Unfamiliar words:

_____   _____   _____

_____   _____   _____

_____   _____   _____

_____   _____

Thesis statement (in your own words):

Audience:

Supporting details:

Detail 1:

Detail 2:

Detail 3:

Detail 4:

Detail 5:

Structure or Purpose of Essay (compare/contrast, cause/effect, problem/solution, description, definition, sequence of events, analysis, classify, persuade):

Reaction (Does this essay make sense to you? Are the supporting details logical or accurate? Do you hold a different belief or opinion? Why or why not?):

Figure 8.15
Student Essay

Comfort Gone Wrong
Chris Morse
Golden Valley High School

Completely surrounded by comfort and leisure, we use modern conveniences to our advantage. Though these appliances provide an ever-increasing amount of relaxation, there are limits. Convenience is a luxury at times, but when people start complaining about making dinner or washing dishes it just adds up to "sheer laziness." For instance, washing dishes is not really all that bad. Turn on the hot water, put on those nice yellow rubber gloves, and put some soap on a sponge. Start rubbing the plates and before you know it, you are done. But let's complicate the process, because the TV looks much more enticing than a pile of dishes. After years of work, here is the dishwasher. A completely revolutionary item that costs $1,000 for that extra seven minutes you can be in front of the TV.

Another completely revolutionary idea that reinvents the word lazy is the Internet. Let's say I want to listen to a brand new Britney Spears CD but didn't want to go over to Best Buy. All right, I will just log on to a local PC and buy her latest album. Let's say I am also hungry too. Just log on to a local PC and buy groceries on Albertsons.com and have it delivered to my house. Let's say I also have an important message I have to give to my boss. Go on a computer and e-mail a message right on over instead of walking that extra 10 feet to the telephone, which could be twice as safe and twice as elaborate, which can save you your job maybe later on. The possibilities are endless, and your laziness has exceeded itself.

With the idea implanted in your brain that you can get away with half the effort, you also buy a microwave and a satellite dish. TV dinners are a must have when microwaves are available and require only the rip of the cover and the push of a button. Ovens work perfectly too and make any piece of food twice as good. But no, microwaves are much easier and can cook a 30-minute meal in four minutes. So what if that extra 26 minutes actually cooks the meal while you sit and gobble down the rubber substance you call food. Satellite dishes work the same way. You can watch concerts, movies, shows, and anything else you would possibly want.

Food has now been reduced to mini-meals that you can eat when you're too tired to cook. For this one you need a microwave though, because Campbell's has now made a new energy-saving product. Why waste valuable energy cooking when your hand can man the remote control? Their new product "Soup at Hand" implies that when you are on the go or just too tired to lift a spoon you can heat this up and eat it to go. I say you get off the couch and turn off the TV and for once do something full heartedly. Convenience can be good, but when convenience becomes like this it's going overboard.

Identifying Bias
Teaching Model

Introducing the Strategy

Description: Citizens need to be critical readers and writers. Politicians and special interest groups often compose advertisements, essays, articles, and stories to promote a certain viewpoint. Written material that presses the reader to agree with a view are "biased," or slanted in a specific direction.

Introductory Activity: To begin the lesson on bias, ask the students to give examples of some of the best movies they have ever seen. Write some examples on the board or an overhead transparency. In pairs or PODs, have students write a paragraph designed to convince everyone to go see this movie. Then ask a few students to share their examples. As they read, listen for any loaded language, such as adjectives and descriptive phrases that signal a bias toward this movie. Then have students exchange paragraphs, turning each other's positive remarks into negative ones.

Teaching the Strategy of Identifying Bias

Step 1: Write the words *loaded language* on the board. Tell students that the descriptive words they used in both their paragraphs, whether positive or negative, were examples of loaded language. Ask students if they can give a definition of loaded language. Help students understand that loaded language consists of words that are used to influence a person's attitude or feelings either positively or negatively.

Step 2: Write the phrases *purr words, snarl words,* and *weasel words* on the board. Tell students that these terms describe three types of loaded language. Have them guess what the phrases might mean. Help students understand that *purr words* produce nice or positive images or feelings, and *snarl words* produce bad, mean, or negative images or feelings. To help students understand *weasel words,* give examples such as *almost, sometimes,* and *nearly.*

Step 3: Write the word *bias* on the board. Ask students what it means to be biased toward or against something. If students are unsure, give them the following context clue: Explain that loaded language shows a writer's or speaker's bias.

Step 4: Now write the word *balanced* on the board. Ask students how a balanced report or story would be different. Help students understand that a balanced report or story does the following: treats all sides of an issue equally; presents people in a neutral way, neither all bad nor all good; does not show stereotypes or prejudice; and does not leave out important background material.

Step 5: Read aloud the essay "Terminate This Epidemic" (Figure 8.16). Guide students through the analysis of this essay using the graphic organizer Identifying Bias and Loaded Language (Figure 8.17). A partially completed sample is provided in Figure 8.18.

Student Strategy

Learning the Strategy

An author's position can sometimes be detected by specific sentences. Remember that the author is trying to persuade you to take on his or her point of view. It's important to realize the author's intent as you read the article. As you read the essay your teacher has provided, record sentences or phrases that reveal the author's view.

Step 1: What words or phrases did the author use to show bias toward the issue? Put a *P* for *purr,* an *S* for *snarl,* and a *W* for *weasel* to show the type of words or phrases that the author used to emphasize his or her view.

Step 2: Now that the work has been explored and biases revealed, readers must then determine how they view the issue. Are you for or against—do you support what the author says, or is the author totally off base?

Applying the Strategy

Choice 1: Discuss with another student some beliefs on a topic that generates strong opinions, such as teenage voting, teenage driving, or drug use among athletes. Use the graphic organizer Identifying Bias and Loaded Language (Figure 8.17) to plan an editorial about your topic.

Choice 2: Read the essay "Teenagers and Smoking: 'There Oughta Be a Law!'" (Figure 8.19). Using the graphic organizer, analyze the author's bias to determine if your view agrees with his.

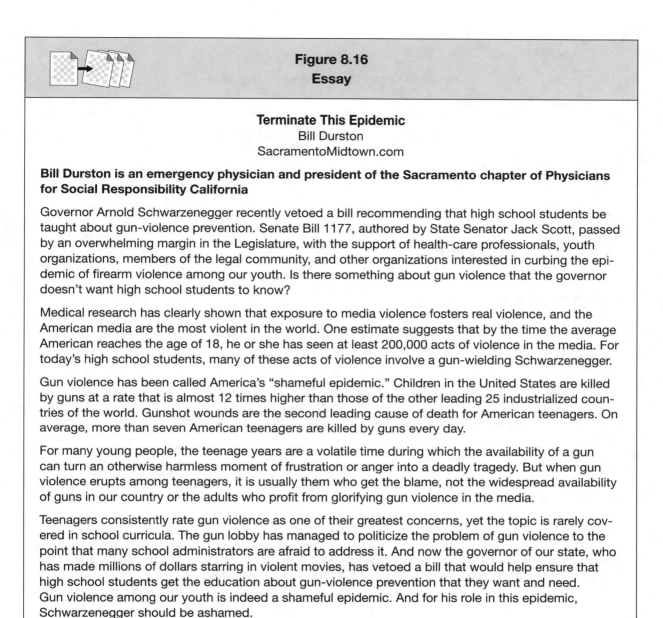

Figure 8.16
Essay

Terminate This Epidemic
Bill Durston
SacramentoMidtown.com

Bill Durston is an emergency physician and president of the Sacramento chapter of Physicians for Social Responsibility California

Governor Arnold Schwarzenegger recently vetoed a bill recommending that high school students be taught about gun-violence prevention. Senate Bill 1177, authored by State Senator Jack Scott, passed by an overwhelming margin in the Legislature, with the support of health-care professionals, youth organizations, members of the legal community, and other organizations interested in curbing the epidemic of firearm violence among our youth. Is there something about gun violence that the governor doesn't want high school students to know?

Medical research has clearly shown that exposure to media violence fosters real violence, and the American media are the most violent in the world. One estimate suggests that by the time the average American reaches the age of 18, he or she has seen at least 200,000 acts of violence in the media. For today's high school students, many of these acts of violence involve a gun-wielding Schwarzenegger.

Gun violence has been called America's "shameful epidemic." Children in the United States are killed by guns at a rate that is almost 12 times higher than those of the other leading 25 industrialized countries of the world. Gunshot wounds are the second leading cause of death for American teenagers. On average, more than seven American teenagers are killed by guns every day.

For many young people, the teenage years are a volatile time during which the availability of a gun can turn an otherwise harmless moment of frustration or anger into a deadly tragedy. But when gun violence erupts among teenagers, it is usually them who get the blame, not the widespread availability of guns in our country or the adults who profit from glorifying gun violence in the media.

Teenagers consistently rate gun violence as one of their greatest concerns, yet the topic is rarely covered in school curricula. The gun lobby has managed to politicize the problem of gun violence to the point that many school administrators are afraid to address it. And now the governor of our state, who has made millions of dollars starring in violent movies, has vetoed a bill that would help ensure that high school students get the education about gun-violence prevention that they want and need. Gun violence among our youth is indeed a shameful epidemic. And for his role in this epidemic, Schwarzenegger should be ashamed.

Source: Copyright 2004 by William Durston. Reprinted with permission.

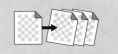

Figure 8.17
**Graphic Organizer for Identifying Bias
and Loaded Language**

Identifying Bias and Loaded Language

Title of work:

Author:

Author's purpose:

Intended audience:

Unfamiliar words: (Make sure that you understand these words when you read the article the second time.)

Topic or issue:

Significant sentences: (The author's position can sometimes be detected by specific sentences. In the space below, record sentences or phrases that reveal the author's view.)

Word choice: P = Purr, S = Snarl, W = Weasel

What is the author's view?

How balanced is this piece, and what is your reaction? (Answer on back)

Figure 8.18
Example of Partially Completed Graphic Organizer
for Identifying Bias and Loaded Language

Identifying Bias and Loaded Language

Title of work: "Terminate This Epidemic"

Author: Bill Durston

Author's purpose: The author is writing about the need to teach teenagers about gun violence.

Intended audience:
Audience could include teenagers, parents, teachers, and concerned voters.

Unfamiliar words:
(Make sure that you understand these words when you read the article the second time.)

epidemic, overwhelming, fosters, margin, volatile, erupts, veto, glorify

Topic or issue: The governor of California has vetoed a bill to teach high school students about gun violence.

Significant sentences: (The author's position can sometimes be detected by specific sentences. In the space below, record sentences or phrases that reveal the author's view.)

Gov. Schwarzenegger recently vetoed a bill recommending that high school students be taught abut gun-violence prevention.

Medical research has clearly shown that exposure to media violence fosters real violence.

Gun violence has been called America's "shameful epidemic."

And now the governor of our state, who has made millions of dollars starring in violent movies, has vetoed a bill that would help ensure that high school students get the education about gun violence that they want and need.

Word choice: P = Purr, S = Snarl, W = Weasel

What is the author's view?

How balanced is this piece, and what is your reaction? (Answer on back)

Figure 8.19
Essay

Teenagers and Smoking: "There Oughta Be a Law!"
Chris Morse
Golden Valley High School

It is a fact that there are more than 400,000 deaths in the U.S. each year from smoking-related illnesses, so here is the question: why? For example, if one product causes approximately 2,100 adults in Maine to die each year, why do the companies of cigarettes allow this? Millions of packs of cigarettes are sold in Maine, one of the smallest states in the country, each year. If the distribution of cigarettes were illegal in Maine, we would save thousands of lives on a yearly basis in just that state alone.

A law like this is a very unrealistic goal. This law in theory would make the distribution of cigarettes illegal but wouldn't take away the right to smoke. Smoking should one day be totally abolished and this law would be a starting punch to make this happy dream come true. Not many would like to travel miles and miles in order to buy a pack of cancer-causing cigarettes for $10.

Many would say that a law like this would never be given a chance, but how many smokers really want to keep smoking for the rest of their lives? Those who do smoke would completely vote against this law but would know that it would be for the better. If stores did not carry cigarettes, wouldn't that provide an incentive for people to quit?

But what about all those shopkeepers who make a living off other people's despair? Their sales would decrease substantially. But isn't saving a few million lives more enjoyable than a couple of bucks? Aren't we losing a major portion of the U.S.'s money by investing in health treatment for all the smokers out there? These questions can only be answered when we take actions.

Not only are smokers killing themselves in a long-term view, they are also killing the ones they love around them. Over 50,000 people (which include 6,000 children) die every year from secondhand smoke alone. What if you found out that your 7-year-old son died because you were smoking in the same room with him? Did you know that secondhand smoke triggers 26,000 new cases of asthma? Maybe it is a coincidence, but I have a very strong feeling of why kids get asthma at such a high rate.

Smoking is a very casual thing now even for America's youth. It's estimated that 3.4 million packs of cigarettes are sold or bought by kids every year. Imagine if you found out your 12-year-old Johnny was caught smoking on the corner of a street. It is a fact that many kids 18 years of age or younger will die prematurely from smoking. I strongly believe that if an anti-smoking law were passed it would be a step towards not only a smoke-free state but also a smoke-free country. Big companies like Camel and Marlboro are lighting their cigars with billions and billions of dollars without even justifying why kids can get a package of cigarettes. The only way we can change this is if we take a stand.

Identifying Propaganda Techniques in Political Ads
Teaching Model

Introducing the Strategy

Description: In our media-driven society, students are inundated with advertisements. To be critical viewers and readers, students need to recognize the persuasive techniques that politicians and lobbyists use in their political advertisements and campaign literature. This lesson will teach students how to recognize common types of propaganda.

Introductory Activity: Put students into pairs. Tell them that one of them will be running for office as King of the School, with absolute powers. The other partner is his or her campaign manager. Write the following terms on the board: *humor, testimonial, product comparison, security, bandwagon, name calling, purr words, individuality, slogan, transfer, plain folks.* Without defining these terms, tell students that these techniques can sway people's minds. Have students choose one technique and in 10 to 20 minutes design a quick campaign to present. After the presentations, the class will vote on who is King of the School.

Teaching the Strategy of Identifying Propaganda Techniques

Step 1: As students present their campaign advertisements, have the class guess which propaganda technique each group used. To arrive at a clear understanding, also ask students to describe the effect each ad has on the audience.

Step 2: Pass out copies of Propaganda and Persuasion Techniques (Figure 8.20). Then distribute a handout with the following sentences on it:

1. Every one of your classmates is voting for Terry.
2. Terry is an experienced leader, but John has never held an office.
3. Terry will make sure every student gets candy and free soda at break.
4. Should John win, you will lose all your privileges and rights as a student.
5. Terry has such a warm, delightful, and funny personality.
6. John is stupid and couldn't lead his way out of a paper bag.
7. "Terry Is Terrific—Terry Is Tops"
8. People who think for themselves will vote for Terry.
9. Terry is as groovy as a Chris Rock movie.
10. You can trust Terry because she doesn't act special; she's just like us.
11. President Bush says voting for Terry is "the right thing to do."
12. If you vote for Terry, we'll all be as happy and successful as she is.

Read through the handout. Have students match each of the techniques to the sentences. (Correct answers are as follows: 1—bandwagon; 2—product comparison; 3—rewards; 4—security; 5—purr words; 6—name calling; 7—slogan; 8—individuality; 9—humor; 10—plain folks; 11—testimonial; 12—transfer.)

Figure 8.20
Propaganda and Persuasion Techniques

Technique	Definition	Intended Effect on Audience
Bandwagon	Says that everyone else is buying this product or is for this person	To make a person feel left out if he or she doesn't do what others do
Humor	Presents a comic message that makes the consumer laugh	To make the consumer associate good feelings with the product
Individuality	Says that people who believe in themselves will like this product or person	To make the person feel self-secure in following his or her own beliefs
Name calling	Uses negative images and words to demean another product or person	To make the consumer dislike the other product or person
Plain folks	Says that good, simple, ordinary people like this product or person	To show that a product is not too complex for, or a person is not too different than, the consumer
Product comparison	Compares the benefits of one product or person to another	To show point-by-point how one product or person is better
Purr words	Uses words and phrases that produce positive thoughts and feelings in the consumer	To make the product or person desirable by appealing to the emotions
Rewards	Promises emotional, physical, financial, or psychological benefits for choosing the product	To create a need in the audience and make them want the reward as much as the product or person
Security (fear)	Uses words and images that make the consumer feel safer with a product or person	To make the audience fearful to choose the other product or person
Slogan	Uses a "catchy" phrase that sticks in the consumer's mind	To keep the product or person in the mind of the consumer
Testimonial (celebrity endorsement)	Uses a famous person, such as an actor or sports star, to promote the product or person	To impress the audience that someone who has achieved stardom chooses the product
Transfer (emotional appeal)	Makes the consumer feel emotions or a desire to be happy, sad, excited, athletic, comfortable, or sexy	To make the audience transfer or associate strong emotions to the product or person

Step 3: Review the answers to the activity with the class. Make sure students explain which words in the sentence provide the clue to the propaganda technique.

Step 4: Show students the examples of political and commercial ads illustrated in Figures 8.21 and 8.22, respectively. Have students determine the types of propaganda used in each. Then have students choose one of the Applying the Strategy activities for further practice and assessment.

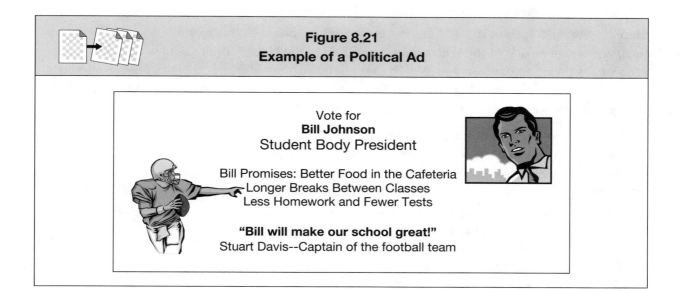

Figure 8.21
Example of a Political Ad

Vote for
Bill Johnson
Student Body President

Bill Promises: Better Food in the Cafeteria
Longer Breaks Between Classes
Less Homework and Fewer Tests

"Bill will make our school great!"
Stuart Davis--Captain of the football team

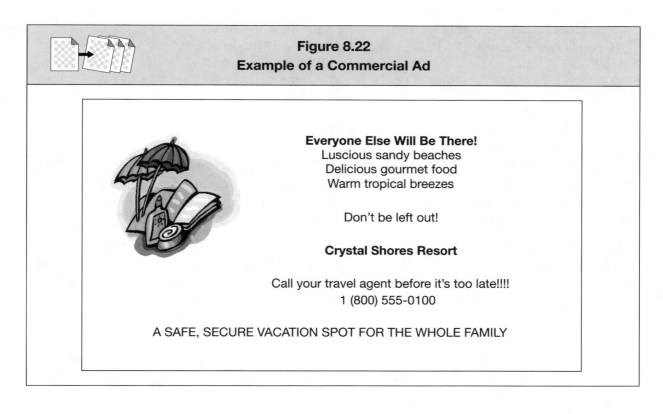

Figure 8.22
Example of a Commercial Ad

Everyone Else Will Be There!
Luscious sandy beaches
Delicious gourmet food
Warm tropical breezes

Don't be left out!

Crystal Shores Resort

Call your travel agent before it's too late!!!!
1 (800) 555-0100

A SAFE, SECURE VACATION SPOT FOR THE WHOLE FAMILY

Student Strategy

Learning the Strategy

Step 1: Advertisements use propaganda to persuade you to buy a product or vote for a person. Study the techniques on the Propaganda and Persuasion chart.

Step 2: Now read each of the sentences below. Each sentence is from a school political advertisement and uses one of the techniques described in the chart. Think about what effect each sentence is trying to have on you. Match that effect with one described in the chart to determine which technique is being modeled. Write your answers on a separate sheet of paper. Check your answers with your classmates when everyone is finished.

1. Every one of your classmates is voting for Terry.
2. Terry is an experienced leader, but John has never held an office.
3. Terry will make sure every student gets candy and free soda at break.
4. Should John win, you will lose all your privileges and rights as a student.
5. Terry has such a warm, delightful, and funny personality.
6. John is stupid and couldn't lead his way out of a paper bag.
7. "Terry Is Terrific—Terry Is Tops"
8. People who think for themselves will vote for Terry.
9. Terry is as groovy as a Chris Rock movie.
10. You can trust Terry because she doesn't act special; she's just like us.
11. President Bush says voting for Terry is "the right thing to do."
12. If you vote for Terry, we'll all be as happy and successful as she is.

Step 3: Now look at the examples of political and commercial ads your teacher has shown you. Using your chart, determine what propaganda technique each ad is using.

Applying the Strategy

Choice 1: Look through magazines and campaign literature. Try to find examples of all 12 of the propaganda techniques. Either post your pictures on a display or scan your images into PowerPoint and make a slide show for the class. Have your classmates determine the types of propaganda techniques that are used.

Choice 2: Pair up with a partner. One of you will be the politician running for office and the other will be the campaign manager. Write an effective political campaign ad that makes voters want to vote for you. Use one or more of the propaganda techniques you've learned. If possible, videotape your ad to share with your classmates.

Analyzing Political Cartoons
Teaching Model

Introducing the Strategy

Description: Students may have a lot of experience reading cartoons in comic books or in the comics section of the newspaper. Political cartoons are of a different nature in that they are drawn to depict a situation that has significance locally, nationally, or internationally, requiring much prior knowledge on the part of the reader. Consequently, the messages or opinions expressed in political cartoons may be lost if the reader doesn't know how to analyze the images and words.

Introductory Activity: Ask students in pairs to describe the types of printed cartoons they know. Then ask students to list reasons people create and read political cartoons. Lead a discussion on the purposes of political cartoons, such as criticizing government policies or people, making fun of science or technology, or pointing out the failures of social institutions. Write these on the board.

Teaching the Strategy of Analyzing Political Cartoons

Step 1: Write the word *caricature* on the board. Ask students if any of them can define this word. Point out that a caricature is a drawing of a person that exaggerates some physical features, often to make a point. Show a transparency of the cartoon in Figure 8.23. Ask students if they recognize any characters or objects in the cartoon. How are they depicted? Are they being made fun of? What are they doing?

Step 2: Tell students that after they identify the characters in a cartoon, they should read any captions, making sure they understand unknown terms, phrases, or abbreviations.

Step 3: Explain that a symbol represents something, like the flag of a country represents that country. Ask students if there are any well-known symbols in the cartoon. Based on this information, ask students what the subject and point of the cartoon may be.

Step 4: Explain that political cartoons always express one point of view. Ask students if they think this cartoon is effective. Why or why not? Then ask students what an opposing point of view might be.

Student Strategy

Learning the Strategy

You will understand political cartoons better if you follow a series of steps that involve self-questioning. Follow these steps with the Analysis Tool for a Political Cartoon (Figure 8.24) to help you to think through and understand political cartoons.

Step 1: Political cartoons present a particular view of something that has recently happened in the world. When reading a political cartoon, it is helpful to ask yourself questions about the topic. By answering these questions you can better understand the meaning of the cartoon. Look at the cartoon your teacher has provided (Figure 8.23). First, ask yourself who the characters are in the cartoon. What do you already know about them?

Step 2: What does the print say? Read any captions, titles, dialogue, or other print. Are there terms or abbreviations that you need to understand?

Step 3: Are there any well-known symbols in the cartoon that represent such things as countries, governments, religions, or social institutions?

Step 4: Based on this information, ask what the subject and point of the cartoon may be. What viewpoint is the cartoonist taking? What is the cartoonist making fun of? What is he or she for or against?

Step 5: Do you think the cartoonist was effective in presenting his or her viewpoint? Why or why not?

Step 6: Do you agree with the viewpoint of the cartoonist? Why or why not?

Applying the Strategy

Choice 1: Select a political cartoon from a newspaper or magazine, or use one your teacher provides (Figure 8.25). Use the Analysis Tool for a Political Cartoon (Figure 8.24) to analyze the cartoon. Make a transparency of the cartoon to show your classmates. Exchange your cartoon with a partner. Analyze each other's cartoons. Discuss what each of you discovered about your cartoons. Then model for your classmates how you analyzed the cartoon.

Choice 2: Create your own political cartoon. Think of an issue you feel strongly about. The issue may be related to your friends, your school, your local community, government policies, or happenings in the world. When you create a political cartoon, the object is to make fun of those who have done or are doing something you feel is wrong. Because you have only one panel or square to express your ideas, ask yourself if there is an action you can portray that expresses how bad this person's or group's decisions are. Can you draw your opponents as a caricature—in other words, in a way that exaggerates their worst qualities? What could you have them say that makes them look silly or incorrect? Are there any symbols that carry a lot of meaning for the reader that would make sense to add to your cartoon? Once you've drawn your cartoon, share it with a classmate and ask him or her to analyze it using the Analysis Tool for a Political Cartoon. If something is unclear to your reader, ask him or her how you can change your cartoon to make your point more clear. Then make a transparency of your cartoon to share with the class. You may want to publish your cartoon in the school or local newspaper.

Figure 8.23
Example of a Political Cartoon

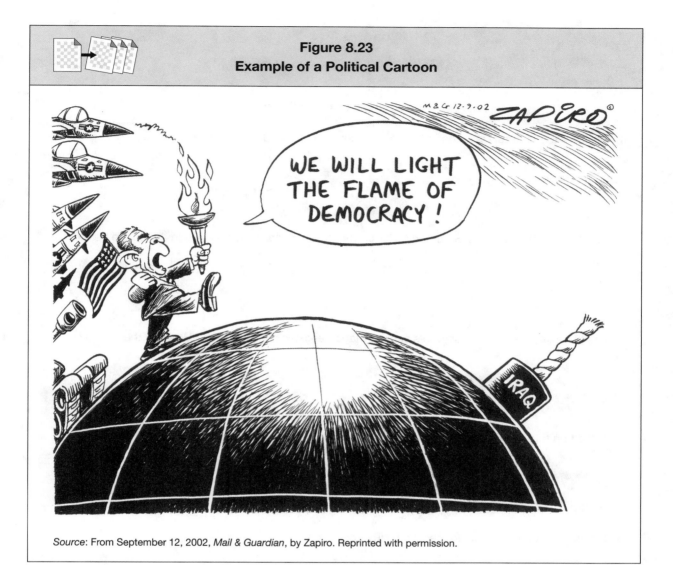

Source: From September 12, 2002, *Mail & Guardian*, by Zapiro. Reprinted with permission.

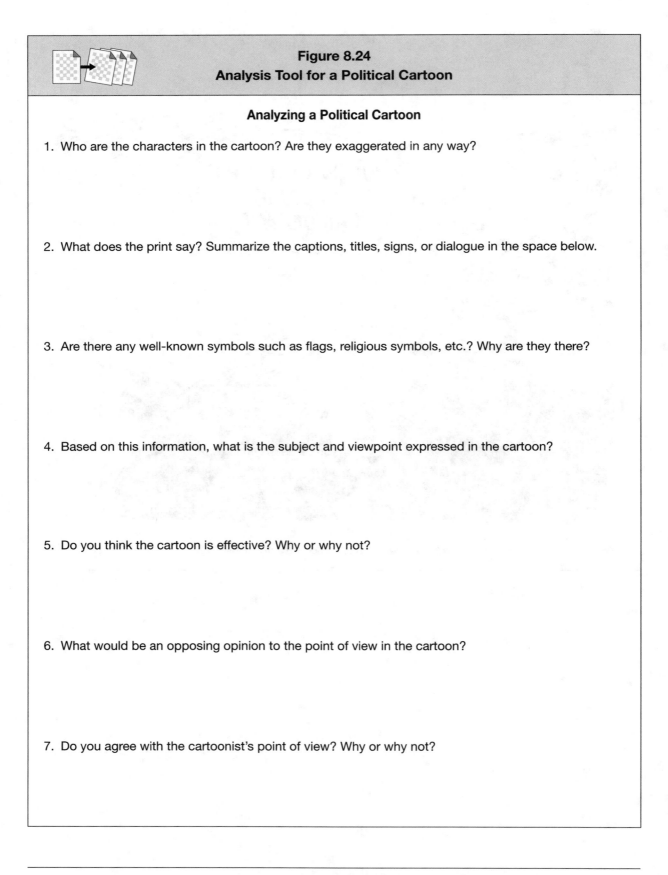

Figure 8.24
Analysis Tool for a Political Cartoon

Analyzing a Political Cartoon

1. Who are the characters in the cartoon? Are they exaggerated in any way?

2. What does the print say? Summarize the captions, titles, signs, or dialogue in the space below.

3. Are there any well-known symbols such as flags, religious symbols, etc.? Why are they there?

4. Based on this information, what is the subject and viewpoint expressed in the cartoon?

5. Do you think the cartoon is effective? Why or why not?

6. What would be an opposing opinion to the point of view in the cartoon?

7. Do you agree with the cartoonist's point of view? Why or why not?

Figure 8.25
Example of a Political Cartoon

Source: Landfill and Surfer, © Seppo Leinonen, www.seppo.net. Reprinted with permission.

Unit Example: Immigration to the United States

Theme: Immigration is changing the United States/How is immigration changing the United States?

Questions for Final Papers: What does immigration mean to the United States in the 21st century? Why do immigrants continue to come? How has immigration changed over the last two centuries? What impact is immigration having on U.S. communities? Can immigrants' dreams be realized? What does it feel like to be an immigrant? (Can you imagine yourself in this role?)

Teacher Read-aloud Materials: Biographies of recent immigrants like *New Kids in Town*

Central Vocabulary: *immigration, emigration, culture, Ellis Island, passages, infectious disease, job market, prejudice*

Text Materials:

- Textbook chapter
- American Memory video clip of boat arriving at Ellis Island
- Interviews with teenage immigrants, *New Kids in Town* (Scholastic)
- Graphs of shift in immigration from 1900 to 2000 (*Newsweek, Time* magazine)
- Articles from major magazines on changing patterns of immigration
- *American Memory* interviews with and journals of immigrants
- *Cobblestone Magazine* issue on new immigrants

Instructional Activities:
1. Anticipation (Activation of Knowledge and Experiences)

Teacher explains the unit design and time frame.

Students are given a timetable of activities and their final project expectations.

Initial activity: The teacher writes the word *IMMIGRATION* on the board and asks students to make associations with the term; the teacher then writes associated terms around the central term. The teacher asks students if they associate the term *immigrant* with themselves. Students are asked to think for a few minutes and then draw themselves as "immigrants." Students share their visual images, and as they discuss the drawings, the teacher listens for words they use and writes key terms on the board.

Vocabulary preparation: The teacher distributes a Vocabulary Knowledge Rating Chart [see Chapter 3, page 49] with some of the key terminology and asks students to reflect on their familiarity with these terms. After doing the activity individually, the students share their responses, and the teacher helps build shared definitions of the terms that students write in their notes.

Focusing on the content: The class reads from a current news magazine about the trend in immigration to the United States. It contrasts the immigration of the 1800s with that of the 1990s. As part of the reading, students are asked to contribute what they know about the current status of immigrants. (On a subsequent day the teacher will read from *New Kids in Town,* narratives from contemporary teens who have come to the United States.) The teacher may do most of this reading because it is the first encounter with the topic. After this reading the teacher explains that students will read more about immigrants and asks students to select one group of immigrants they will study and then report on to the class. (The teacher has selected the following groups from which students may choose: European immigrants at the turn of the 20th century, Asian immigrants in the 1880s, South Asian immigrants following the Vietnam War, and Mexican immigrants today.)

2. Building Knowledge

• Students will read their textbook section on 20th Century Immigration. They will also check earlier references to immigration.

• They will use class time to explore some of the resources on the Library of Congress Web site that have been bookmarked by the teacher and librarian working together.

• The teacher will create a large Venn diagram for a class discussion on the differences that they find between the various waves of immigration. They will define some key areas for comparison and contrast among the immigrant groups—for example, How were the immigrants received when they arrived? What jobs were available to them? Were there specific sections of the United States that became their homes?

• Students will learn how to conduct interviews. They will practice developing good questions and do a mock interview with a volunteer adult from the school (another teacher, the principal, or a resource person) and then invite a recent immigrant to come to the class.

• Students will contribute to the class bulletin board news articles about immigration and share what they read and hear in class when time is allocated for "Making Current News Connections."

• Teacher and students will build a resource list of Web sites and collect a file of good materials on immigration and share these with each other.

3. Consolidating Learning

Students engage in a class discussion sharing their perspectives on the questions for inquiry that the teacher laid out at the beginning of the unit. Students prepare their individual papers responding to the questions using data from their readings to support their point of view. The teacher may ask students to position themselves on a value line to show the range of perspectives on any one of the questions.

Individual student research: Each student will prepare a three-to-five-page report on his or her chosen group of immigrants. Students will include an interview with immigrants or their descendents and provide evidence of research done on Web sites (Library of Congress and others). In addition to explaining the basic information about the immigrant group (one to two pages), the students can take on a particular role (an immigrant or a local community member) and personalize the immigration process using the RAFT writing strategy.

Group presentations: The group will prepare and share with the whole class a report on their immigrant group. Credit will be given for presentation (including quality of visuals, variety of modes of presentation, clarity of presentation) and quality of content.

Reflection on learning: After all reports are presented, the teacher will return to the initial activity of brainstorming words associated with immigration and ask students individually to make a list of terms they think are essential to the topic. The original Knowledge Rating Chart of vocabulary terms will be reviewed, and students will evaluate their growth in understanding these essential terms. Finally, students will summarize individually what they have learned about immigration from their efforts.

B Graphic Organizers and Resources for Vocabulary Development

Internet Resources for Vocabulary

Resources for All Learners

Educator's Reference Desk

http://www.eduref.org/cgi-bin/lessons.cgi/Language_Arts
The Educator's Reference Desk includes vocabulary lesson plans, most of which cover grades 4 through 12. Plans include Beach Ball Vocabulary, Defining Ecology, Dictionary Game, Einstein Club, Euphemisms, Homophone Bingo, Lexicon Challenge, SAT or Foreign Language Vocabulary, and Vocabulary—Unfolding Meaning.

Surf the Net with Kids

http://www.surfnetkids.com/games/Word_Games/
Surf the Net with Kids is a great site for students age 8 to 17. It has free online games and puzzles, including a variety of crossword puzzles and games on topics related to science, adolescent literature such as Harry Potter, math, civil rights, and grammar.

Santa Clara County Office of Education

http://www.isb.sccoe.org/
The Web site of the Santa Clara County Office of Education includes a Math Mentor TV program and language arts information, including 6 + 1 Traits of Good Writing. In the Writer's Workshop section are Fun and Games, including vocabulary games such as Latin and Greek Root Word and Science PowerPoint in the style of a well-known game show.

Vocabulary University

http://www.vocabulary.com/

Vocabulary University has interactive vocabulary puzzles and Latin and Greek root activities separated into three levels. Activities include Fill-in-the-Blanks, Definition Match, Synonym & Antonym Encounters, Crosswords, Word Finds, True/False, and Word Stories. Twenty-five thematic topics are also included on diverse subjects from wizards to elections to character education.

Sarasota County Public School District

http://www.sarasota.k12.fl.us/sarasota/interdiscrdg.htm
The Web site of the Sarasota County Public School District in Florida includes information on reading strategies, vocabulary building, graphic organizers, journals, note taking, and semantic mapping. The vocabulary section includes Concept Cards, Photographed Vocabulary, Previewing Words in Context, Semantic Feature Analysis, and Word Sort Using Concept Cards.

Omaha Public Schools Teachers' Corner

http://www.ops.org/reading/secondarystrat1.htm
Omaha Public Schools Teachers' Corner provides reading strategies, vocabulary activities on context clues, roots and affixes, comprehension activities, and test taking strategies. The vocabulary section includes Decoding Multisyllabic Words, Prefixes/Suffixes, Content Area Vocabulary, Feature Analysis Map, Using Context Clues, and Unknown Words in Context.

Word Focus

http://www.wordfocus.com/vocabulary-resources.html
The Word Focus site focuses on Latin and Greek roots. The site contains an abundance of activities, including Word Units with Definitions, Self-Scoring Quizzes, Word Quests, Logo Focus on etymology, and Word Sources on such topics as filibuster, malaria, robots, dinosaurs, the sandwich, phobias, the planets, the arena, and bad days.

Literacy Web

http://www.literacy.uconn.edu/compre.htm
The Literacy Web at the University of Connecticut has excellent articles and activities in the Reading Comprehension section. Subjects include Vocabulary Cartoons, Word Play, Writing Den, Instructional Tips, and an Index of Vocabulary Web sites.

Reading Quest

http://readingquest.org/
Reading Quest is an excellent site for materials related to content area reading, vocabulary development, and word study. It includes vocabulary puzzles at Vocabulary University, a crossword puzzle creator, research on vocabulary acquisition and instructional implications, Merriam-Webster online, and Latin and Greek roots.

Web English Teacher

http://www.webenglishteacher.com/vocab.html
The Web English Teacher has a Vocabulary section that includes the following: Building a Better Vocabulary, which discusses Latin and Greek roots and prefixes and suffixes; Calliope, Muse of Eloquence, which has interactive Web-based lessons on Latin and Greek mythology; Changing Language, Beowulf to Buzzwords, which has activities showing how the English language has changed; The Dictionary Game, which brings Pictionary to the classroom; Finding New Ways to Say Something, which teaches about synonyms; Kid Crosswords and Other Puzzles; and a variety of games at Learning Vocabulary Can Be Fun.

Resources for English Language Learners

Internet TESL Journal

http://iteslj.org/links/
The Internet TESL Journal's page of links provides more than 12,000 links to instructional resources for English learners. The site is divided between Links of Interest to Students and Links of Interest to Teachers. The vocabulary section for students alone has more than 140 links, including sites such as English for You—Visual Veggies, SAT Vocabulary Builder, Language Zoo, Common Errors in English, Arabic Number to English Convertor, Word Safari, Vocabulary Self-Study Quizzes, and Language Adventure—Picture Quiz.

Englishpage.com

http://www.englishpage.com/
Englishpage.com focuses on English learners. Printable activities include Ordering in a Restaurant, Getting an Apartment, Returns and Refunds, Grocery Store Choices, Telecommunications, Humor, Internet 101, Turn Off the TV, and Presidential Elections.

Self-Study English Vocabulary Quizzes

http://a4esl.org/q/h/vocabulary.html
This site has a large collection of quizzes and games on three levels. Easy activities cover topics such as soccer vocabulary, words beginning with *A* and the other letters of the alphabet, colors, and school subjects. More difficult activities cover topics such as food and nutrition, abbreviations for companies, sports, employment ads, auto sales, government agencies, road vocabulary, and prepositions.

Interesting Things for ESL Students

http://www.manythings.org/
Interesting Things for ESL Students provides word games, puzzles, slang terms, and many other activities, including Vocabulary Study Using a Cell Phone. Puzzles include Word Web Games, Anagrams, Scrambled Words, Jumbles, and Crosswords.

Book Pass Choices

Your name: _____ **Date:** _____

Instructions:

1. Choose one book to review.
2. Copy the title in the left column.
3. Read the summary from the back or inside cover flap.
4. Read the first page.
5. Check the reading difficulty by opening the book in the middle and reading two or three paragraphs.
6. Place a check in the column that describes how you feel about the book.
7. Pass your book on to the next student and take another.

Title of Book	I want to read	I might read	I don't want to read
1.			
2.			
3.			
4.			
5.			
6.			
7.			
8.			
9.			
10.			
11.			
12.			
13.			
14.			
15.			
16.			
17.			
18.			
19.			
20.			
21.			
22.			
23.			
24.			

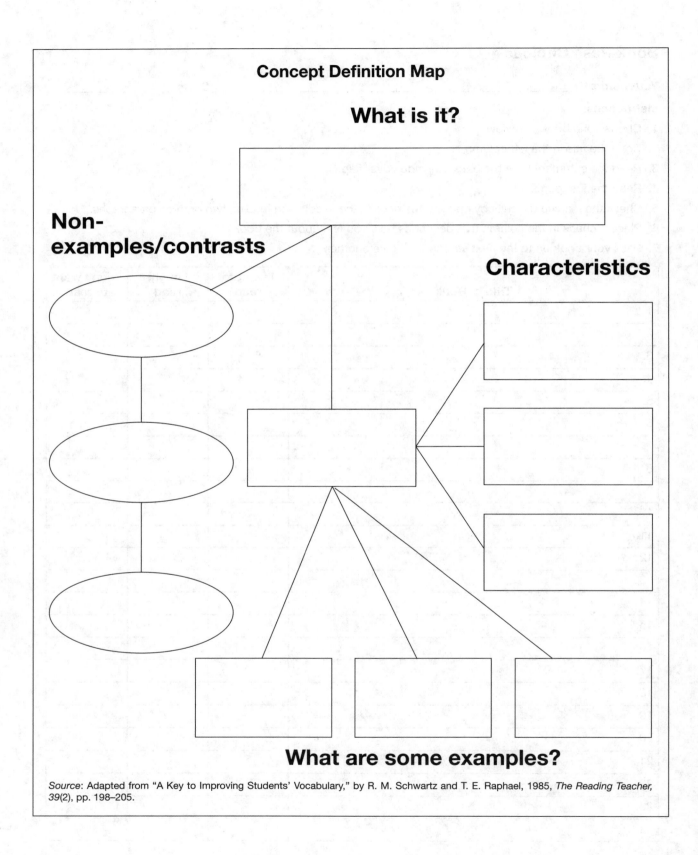

Concept Definition Map

What is it?

Non-examples/contrasts

Characteristics

What are some examples?

Source: Adapted from "A Key to Improving Students' Vocabulary," by R. M. Schwartz and T. E. Raphael, 1985, *The Reading Teacher*, 39(2), pp. 198–205.

Compare/Contrast Y-Chart
Summarizing Differences and Similarities

Topic:

_____

_____

_____

_____

_____

_____

_____

Topic:

_____

_____

_____

_____

_____

_____

_____

Similarities:

_____

_____

_____

_____

_____

_____

_____

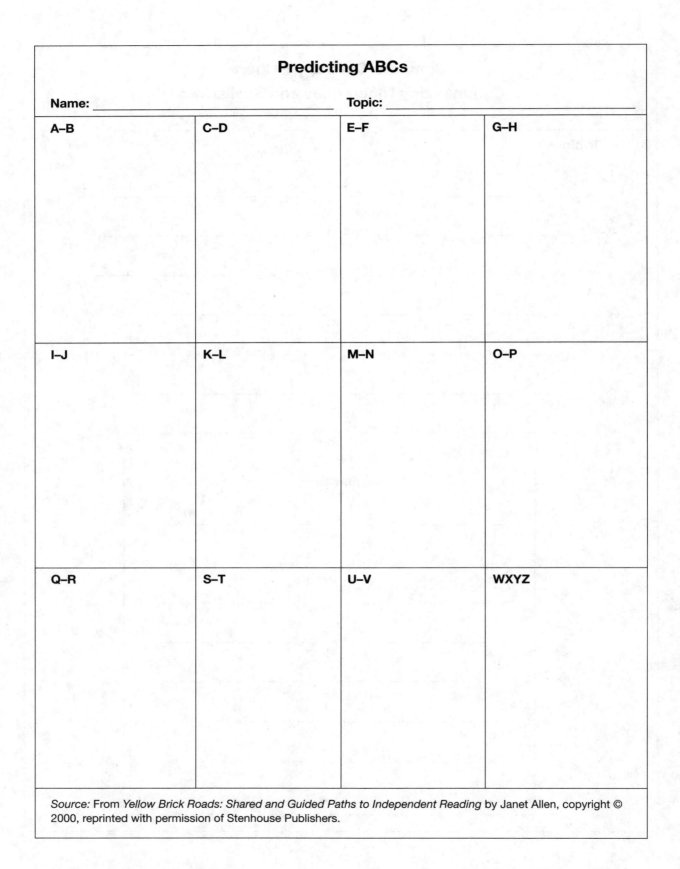

Predicting ABCs

Name: _____ **Topic:** _____

A–B	C–D	E–F	G–H
I–J	**K–L**	**M–N**	**O–P**
Q–R	**S–T**	**U–V**	**WXYZ**

Source: From *Yellow Brick Roads: Shared and Guided Paths to Independent Reading* by Janet Allen, copyright © 2000, reprinted with permission of Stenhouse Publishers.

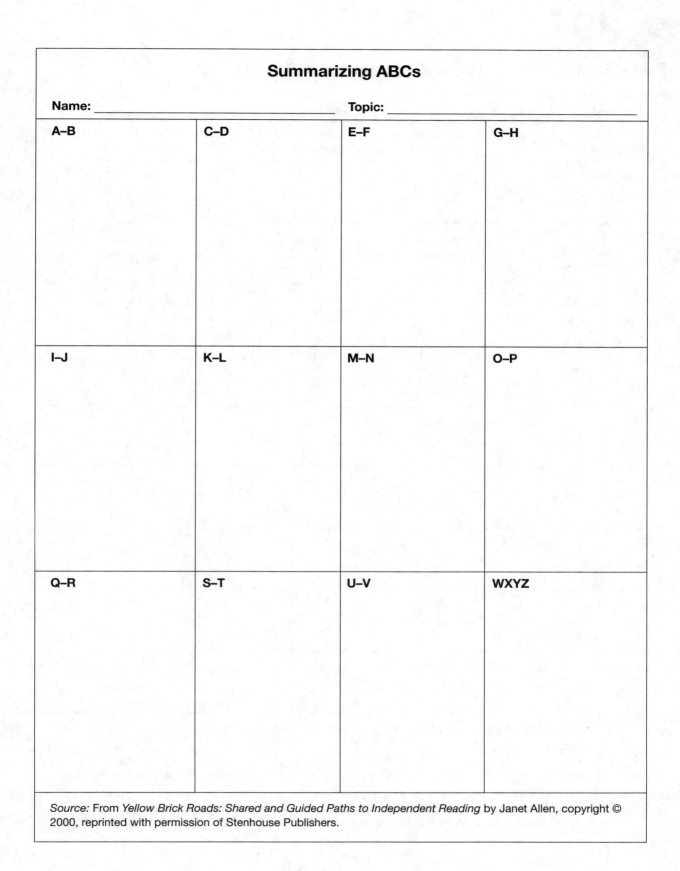

Summarizing ABCs

Name: _____ Topic: _____

A–B	C–D	E–F	G–H
I–J	K–L	M–N	O–P
Q–R	S–T	U–V	WXYZ

Source: From *Yellow Brick Roads: Shared and Guided Paths to Independent Reading* by Janet Allen, copyright © 2000, reprinted with permission of Stenhouse Publishers.

Vocabulary Knowledge Rating Chart

Name: _____ **Topic:** _____

Term	Know It	Not Sure	Don't Know It	Definition

Source: Figure from Blachowicz, Camille L. Z. (1986, April). Making connections: Alternatives to the vocabulary notebook. *Journal of Reading, 29*(7), 643–649. Reprinted with permission of Camille L. Z. Blachowicz and the International Reading Association. All rights reserved.

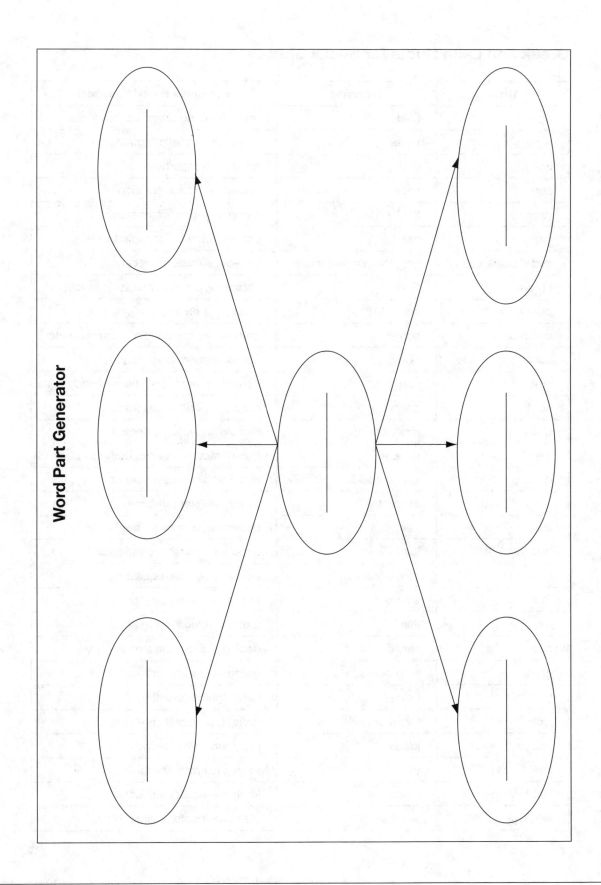

Greek and Latin Roots for Social Studies

Root	Meaning	Examples (Word Families)
agri	field	agriculture, agrarian, agribusiness
aqua	water	aquarium, aquatic, aqueduct
art	skill	artist, artisan, artistry
aud	hear	audience, audio, audition
cam	field	camp, campus, campaign
cap	head	captain, capitol, decapitate
cede, ceed, cess	go, yield, *or* give away	secede, secession, recede
chron	time	chronology, synchronize, chronicle
cise, cide	cut *or* kill	scissors, homicide, regicide
commun	common	communal, community, communicate
corp	body	corps, corpse, corporation
crat	rule	democrat, aristocrat, bureaucracy
cred	believe	credit, incredible, discredit
cycl	circle *or* ring	bicycle, recycle, cyclone
dem	people	democracy, epidemic, demographics
dic	say *or* speak	dictator, dictionary, verdict
div	separate	divide, division, divorce
domin	rule	dominate, dominion, domineer
duc, duct	lead	conduct, educate, conductor
equ, equi	same *or* equal	equality, equate, equilateral
form	shape	formation, transform, uniform
fug	flee	fugitive, refuge, refugee
geo	earth	geology, geography, geological
grad	step *or* stage	graduate, grade, gradual
hab, hib	hold	habit, inhibit, prohibit
ject	throw *or* hurl	project, projectile, reject
jud, jur, jus	judge	judgment, jury, justice
liber	free	liberty, liberate, liberal
loc, locat	place	location, locality, relocate
log, logy	word	dialogue, geology, chronology

continued

Building Literacy in Social Studies

Greek and Latin Roots for Social Studies *(Continued)*

mar	sea	marine, maritime, submarine
mech	machine	mechanic, mechanical, mechanism
migr	depart	migrate, migrant, immigrant
miss, mit	send	missile, transmit, transmission
mob, mot, mov	move	mobile, promote, motion
mort	death	mortal, mortality, mortuary
nat	born	native, nation, nature
nav	ship	navy, navigate, naval
orig	beginning	origin, originate, aborigine
path	feeling	apathy, sympathy, empathy
pel, puls	drive *or* thrust	propel, pulse, propeller
pop	people	popular, populace, population
pos, posit	put *or* place	position, positive, deposit
scend	climb	ascend, descend, transcend
spec, spect, spic	look *or* see	spectacles, spectator, inspect
sum	highest	summary, summation, summit
terr	land	territory, territorial, terrain
trib	give	tribute, contribute, distribute
urb	city	urban, suburban, urbane
ver, vert	turn	reverse, revert, divert

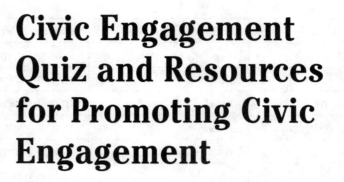

Civic Engagement Quiz and Resources for Promoting Civic Engagement

CIRCLE Civic Engagement Quiz

The indicators can be used in two ways to measure civic engagement for a group. First, they can be used to compare the pattern of civic engagement in a group of people to the pattern of civic engagement found nationally. Second, these indicators can be used to measure changes in civic engagement after a group has been exposed to a program or other treatment.

Several cautions should be noted about using the indicators to measure the effectiveness of a youth program, an organization, or a specific curriculum, or just to compare a group to the levels of civic engagement observed nationally:

• Many programs that are valuable to youth may not spark an immediate change in these indicators, particularly if the program is run over a short period of time or is not very intensive. In such a case, giving young people the indicators in the form of a pre- and post-test may not always yield results, and most likely will not capture new changes. The most appropriate measures may be more specific to the content of a project. For example, students in an environmental service-learning program should learn about the particular ecosystem in which they are working. The indicators will not reflect changes in environmental knowledge. Only if the project is intense or lasts for a considerable period of time would we anticipate changes in the civic indicators.

• All of the indicators measure behavior that can be quantified. Some types of civic values, motives, and behaviors may be better assessed through qualitative measures such as open-ended interviews where young people can describe their activities and intentions. If you are using the indicators to assess civic engagement in an organization or program, adding qualitative methods to your evaluation will give a richer picture of your program and the youth involved.

• The indicators were developed from a national sample, and as a result, reflect civic actions that can be measured on a national scale, but may not always be community specific. For instance, the national sample had a low representation of Native American youth. Consequently, the indicators do not include civic activities that may be common on a reservation or in a tribal community. Similarly, if you are working with extremely engaged youth, their civic behaviors may not be reflected in the indicators. Please adapt the indicators to fit your needs, and add new indicators to the list. Supplement any evaluations with additional measures and other types of data—particularly qualitative data that will give you a better idea of the uniqueness of your program and the young people you work with.

Please mark an "X" in the appropriate box(es). Once completed, use the tables to compare your responses to those of a nationally representative sample.

Civic Indicators

Community problem solving **1.** Have you ever worked together with someone or some group to solve a problem in the community where you live?	( ) Yes, within the last 12 months	( ) Yes, but not within the last 12 months	( ) No, never
Volunteering **2.** Have you volunteered or done any voluntary community service for no pay?	( ) Yes, within the last 12 months	( ) Yes, but not within the last 12 months	( ) No, never

Indicate whether you have volunteered with any of the following types of organizations or groups:			
2A. Religious group	( ) Yes, I have volunteered within the last 12 months	( ) Yes, I volunteer once a month or more	( ) Not within the last 12 months
2B. Environmental organization	( ) Yes, I have volunteered within the last 12 months	( ) Yes, I volunteer once a month or more	( ) Not within the last 12 months
2C. Civic or community organization involved in health or social services	( ) Yes, I have volunteered within the last 12 months	( ) Yes, I volunteer once a month or more	( ) Not within the last 12 months
2D. An organization for youth, children, or education	( ) Yes, I have volunteered within the last 12 months	( ) Yes, I volunteer once a month or more	( ) Not within the last 12 months
2E. Any other group: _____ (describe the group)	( ) Yes, I have volunteered within the last 12 months	( ) Yes, I volunteer once a month or more	( ) Not within the last 12 months

continued

Group membership		
3A. Do you belong to or donate money to any groups, either locally or nationally, such as a youth group like 4-H, Girl Scouts, or a Poetry Slam chapter, a charity, a PTSA or other association, a labor union, a political or social group, a sport team, or any other kind of group?	( ) Yes	( ) No

3B. Are you an active member of this group or any of these groups, a member but not active, or have you given money only? Mark all that apply.	( ) Active member of at least one of them	( ) Member, but not active in at least one of them	( ) Given money only	( ) No

Participate in run/walk/ride			
4. Have you personally walked, ran, or bicycled for a charitable cause? (This is separate from sponsoring or giving money to this type of event.)	( ) Yes, have done it within last 12 months	( ) Yes, but not within last 12 months	( ) No, never
Donate to a charity 5. Besides donating money, have you ever done anything else to help raise money for a charitable cause?	( ) Yes, have done it within last 12 months	( ) Yes, but not within last 12 months	( ) No, never

Electoral Indicators

Voter registration			
6A. Many people are not registered to vote because they are too busy or move around often. Are you currently registered in your election district, or not?	( ) Yes, definitely	( ) I think so	( ) No
Voting 6B. We know that most people don't vote in all elections. Do you vote in both national and local elections?	( ) Yes, always	( ) Yes, usually	( ) No
Volunteer for a candidate or political campaign 7. Have you volunteered for a political organization or candidate running for office?	( ) Yes, within the last 12 months	( ) Yes, but not within the last 12 months	( ) No, never
Persuade others to vote for a candidate or party 8. When there is an election taking place, do you try to convince people to vote for or against one of the parties or candidates, or not?	( ) Yes, always	( ) Yes, usually	( ) No
Display campaign button or sticker 9. Do you wear a campaign button, put a sticker on your car, or place a sign in front of your house?	( ) Yes, always	( ) Yes, usually	( ) No
Contributing to a campaign, party, or group 10. Have you given money to a candidate, political party, or organization that supported candidates?	( ) Yes, within the last 12 months	( ) Yes, but not within the last 12 months	( ) No, never

continued

Indicators of Political Voice

Have you done any of the following to express your views?			
Contacted a public official **11.** Contacted or visited a public official—at any level of government—to express your opinion?	( ) Yes, within the last 12 months	( ) Yes, but not within the last 12 months	( ) No, never
Contacted a newspaper **12.** Contacted a newspaper or magazine to express your opinion on an issue?	( ) Yes, within the last 12 months	( ) Yes, but not within the last 12 months	( ) No, never
Contacted a radio or television talk show **13.** Called in to a radio or television talk show to express your opinion on a political issue, even if you did not get on the air?	( ) Yes, within the last 12 months	( ) Yes, but not within the last 12 months	( ) No, never
Protested **14.** Taken part in a protest, march, or demonstration?	( ) Yes, within the last 12 months	( ) Yes, but not within the last 12 months	( ) No, never
Signed an e-mail petition **15.** Signed an e-mail petition about a social or political issue?	( ) Yes, within the last 12 months	( ) Yes, but not within the last 12 months	( ) No, never
Signed a written petition **16.** Have you ever signed a written petition about a political or social issue?	( ) Yes, within the last 12 months	( ) Yes, but not within the last 12 months	( ) No, never
Boycotted **17.** Have you ever NOT bought something from a certain company because you disagree with the social or political values of the company that produces it?	( ) Yes, within the last 12 months	( ) Yes, but not within the last 12 months	( ) No, never
Buycotted **18.** Have you *bought* something because you like the social or political values of the company that produces or provides it?	( ) Yes, within the last 12 months	( ) Yes, but not within the last 12 months	( ) No, never
Canvassed **19.** Have you worked as a canvasser—going door to door for a political or social group or candidate?	( ) Yes, within the last 12 months	( ) Yes, but not within the last 12 months	( ) No, never

Classifying Individuals by Type of Engagement

One of the many innovations of *The Civic and Political Health of the Nation* report is a "typology of engagement." This typology classifies individuals into four groups based on their participation in a range of civic and electoral activities. The checklist below lists the questions one should use to measure civic activities and electoral activities from the civic engagement quiz, and provides an easy way to add up the number of activities an individual is involved in. Each box in this checklist corresponds to a quiz question with the same number. After administering the quiz, place a check in each box to which a respondent gave a positive answer. Then count the number of boxes you checked in each column.

Typology of Engagement Checklist

Civic Activities			Electoral Activities			Political Voice Activities		
Q#	Activity/Question	Yes?	Q#	Activity/Question	Yes?	Q#	Activity/Question	Yes?
1	Worked to solve a community problem		6B	Always vote in elections (regular voting)		11	Contacted/visited a public official	
2A	Volunteered regularly for religious group		7	Volunteer for a political campaign or candidate		12	Contacted a newspaper or magazine	
2B	Volunteered regularly for an environmental group		8	Persuade others to vote		13	Contacted a radio or television talk show	
2C	Volunteered regularly for a civic or community organization		9	Wear a campaign button or put a sticker on your car		14	Protested	
2D	Volunteered regularly for an organization for youth, children, or education		10	Work or contribute money to a candidate, political party, or organization that supported candidates		15	Signed an e-mail petition	
2E	Volunteered regularly for any other group					16	Signed a written petition	
3B	Active member of a group					17	Boycotted a company	
4	Personally walked, ran, or bicycled for a charitable cause					18	Buycotted or bought something to support the values of a company	
5	Besides donating money, done anything else to help raise money for a charitable cause					19	Canvassed—going door to door for a social or political group	
	Total Number of Activities (add number of affirmative responses)			*Total Number of Activities (add number of affirmative responses)*			*Total Number of Activities (add number of affirmative responses)*	

Once survey results have been tabulated for an individual, respondents can be classified in the following way:

- *Disengaged:* 0 or 1 checks in BOTH columns
- *Civic Specialist:* 2 or more checks in the civic column and 0 or 1 in the electoral column
- *Electoral Specialist:* 2 or more checks in the electoral column and 0 or 1 in the civic column

- *Dual Activist:* 2 or more checks in BOTH columns

Nationally, based on the 2002 survey from the *Civic and Political Health of the Nation,* 16 percent of all adults 15 and older are *Dual Activists;* 16 percent are *Civic Specialists;* 20 percent are *Electoral Specialists;* and 48 percent are *Disengaged.*

Table 1—National Survey Results for 19 Measures of Civic Engagement from *The Civic and Political Health of the Nation,* 2002

	Age		Age						
	15+	Civic Indicators	15–18	19–22	23–25	15–25	26–37	38–56	57+
1	21%	Community problem solving	25%	16%	21%	21%	22%	25%	15%
2A1 to 2A5	24%	"Regular" volunteering for a non-electoral organization	27%	16%	22%	22%	25%	26%	19%
3B	31%	"Active" member in group or organization	25%	18%	23%	22%	29%	39%	27%
4	14%	Participating in fund-raising run/walk/ride	16%	15%	17%	16%	16%	15%	8%
5	31%	General fund raising for charity	31%	22%	30%	28%	29%	37%	26%
		Electoral Indicators							
6B	51%	Always vote (for age 20 and older)	—	21%	27%	24%	34%	53%	72%
7	6%	Volunteering for a candidate or political organization	3%	3%	2%	3%	5%	8%	6%
8	33%	Persuading others to vote for a particular candidate or party	38%	33%	35%	36%	33%	32%	32%
9	26%	Displaying campaign buttons, signs, stickers	24%	15%	19%	20%	18%	28%	34%
10	13%	Contributing to a campaign, party, or group	3%	3%	7%	4%	11%	17%	17%
		Indicators of Political Voice							
11	18%	Contacting officials	9%	8%	14%	10%	16%	20%	21%
12	10%	Contacting the print media	11%	9%	10%	10%	8%	12%	12%
13	8%	Contacting the broadcast media	6%	9%	8%	7%	7%	10%	8%
14	4%	Protesting	6%	8%	7%	7%	5%	3%	3%
15	12%	"Signing" e-mail petitions	12%	16%	16%	14%	15%	11%	9%
16	23%	Signing written petitions	15%	24%	23%	20%	23%	24%	21%
17	38%	Boycotting	33%	39%	45%	38%	43%	41%	28%
18	35%	Buycotting	33%	34%	40%	35%	42%	37%	25%
19	2%	Canvassing	2%	*	2%	2%	2%	3%	4%

Civic Engagement Resources

The following resources are provided by the Center for Information & Research on Civic Learning & Engagement (CIRCLE). The resources are divided into three main categories: Political Participation, Youth Civic Engagement, and Civic Education. You can find this same listing with links to each organization at the CIRCLE Web site at http://www.civicyouth.org/practitioners/org_links.htm.

Political Participation Resources

American Political Science Association

http://www.apsanet.org/
This site offers resources for teaching civic engagement and responsive government. It includes links to online political science textbooks, core history documents, and teaching resources including college-level service learning syllabi at http://www.apsanet.org.

Arsalyn Program of Ludwick Family Foundation

http://arsalyn.org/home.asp
This nonpartisan, non-issue-based organization encourages young Americans to become informed and active participants in the electoral process.

Center for Democracy and Citizenship

http://www.excelgov.org/index.php?keyword=a43 2929c8e1952
Based at the Council for Excellence in Government, the center identifies and implements ways to improve the performance of representative democracy in the United States.

Declare Yourself

http://www.declareyourself.com/
This site supports a nonpartisan campaign committed to registering and empowering young voters.

Eagleton Institute's Civic Engagement and Political Participation Program

http://www.eagleton.rutgers.edu/CEPP/CEPP/describe.html
Oversees several projects aimed at increasing voter turnout, political participation, and Americans' involvement in civic life.

Freedom's Answer

http://www.freedomsanswer.net
A movement led by high school students to encourage voting.

Hip-Hop Summit Action Network

http://www.hsan.org/Content/Main.aspx?pageId=1
Dedicated to engaging the hip-hop community in community development, this organization sponsors Hip-Hop Summits around the United States.

Moving Ideas Network

http://www.movingideas.org/youthpolitics.html
This project of *The American Prospect* is dedicated to explaining and popularizing complex policy ideas to a broader audience. This link is to the magazine's Special Report on Youth and Politics.

MTV's Choose or Lose Campaign

http://www.mtv.com/chooseorlose/
This site provides online voter registration, information on candidates, and polls on issues of interest to youth.

National Coalition on Black Civic Participation

http://www.bigvote.org/
This organization fights to eliminate remaining barriers to civic participation. Black Youth Vote!, its youth program, represents the combined efforts of coalition members to reach out to all segments of the youth population, including high school, college, street, and incarcerated youth.

New Millennium Young Voters Project

http://www.stateofthevote.org/duh.html
This national youth voter campaign by the National Association of Secretaries of State is designed to encourage political and civic participation in young people ages 18 through 24.

New Voters Project

http://www.newvotersproject.org/
The largest grassroots youth voter mobilization campaign in history combines nonpartisan voter registration, list building, and grassroots Get-Out-the-Vote (GOTV) strategies in six states: Colorado, Iowa, Oregon, Wisconsin, New Mexico, and Nevada.

Partnership for Trust in Government

http://www.excelgov.org/index.php?keyword=a4329511cee703
A project of the Council for Excellence in Government and the Ford Foundation, the partnership is a diverse alliance of nongovernment organizations working to improve and sustain government's place in the understanding and esteem of the American people.

Project Vote Smart

http://www.vote-smart.org/
PVS is a citizen's organization dedicated to serving all Americans with accurate and unbiased information for electoral decision making. Its Web site includes free classroom and teacher resources at http://www.vote-smart.org/resource_classroom.php.

Rock the Vote

http://www.rockthevote.com/
Rock the Vote engages youth in the political process by incorporating the entertainment community and youth culture into its activities.

Smackdown Your Vote!

http://vote.wwe.com/
This is the World Wrestling Entertainment's campaign, in conjunction with the League of Women Voters, Hip-Hop Summit Action Network, Youth Vote, and others, to increase youth voter participation.

State Public Interest Research Groups (PIRGs)

http://www.pirg.org/
State PIRGs are an alliance of state-based, citizen-funded organizations that advocate for the public interest.

Take Your Kids to Vote

http://www.excelgov.org/index.php?keyword=a432e9fc383051
A campaign of the Council for Excellence in Government, this program encourages families to make voting a tradition.

What Kids Can Do

http://www.whatkidscando.org
This site offers a feature called "Kids on the Trail," with writings and essays by youth active in politics, along with resources on voting and activism for youth.

Youth Vote Coalition

http://www.youthvote.org/
This the largest nonpartisan coalition in the United States working to increase the political involvement of 50 million Americans who are 18 to 30 years old.

Youth Civic Engagement Resources

Campus Compact

http://www.compact.org/
This site provides information and resources on civic engagement and service learning in higher education. It also offers activism resources for students.

Center for Civic Education

http://www.civiced.org/index.php
This organization offers civic education curriculum at both the high school and middle school levels. Visit its We the People program site at http://www.civiced.org/programs.php#wtp for more information.

Center for Democracy and Citizenship at the University of Minnesota

http://www.publicwork.org/
The Center sponsors a number of public work initiatives including the Jane Addams School for Democracy (http://www.publicwork.org/jas/), Public Achievement (http://www.publicachievement.org/), and the Community Information Corps.

Changemakers

http://www.changemakers.net/
Changemakers is an initiative of Ashoka: Innovators for the Public that provides inspiration, resources, and opportunities for those interested in social change throughout the world.

Civic Practices Network

http://www.cpn.org/
CPN is a collaborative and nonpartisan project bringing together a diverse array of organizations to bring practical methods for public problem solving into every community.

Do Something

http://www.dosomething.org/
This organization helps youth get involved in their communities, and has a special Educator Web site.

Forum for Youth Investment

http://www.forumforyouthinvestment.org/
The forum works to increase the quality and quantity of youth investment and youth involvement by building connections, increasing capacity, and tackling persistent challenges across the allied youth fields.

Innovation Center for Community and Youth Development

http://www.theinnovationcenter.org/
This organization offers articles, workshops, trainings, and consultations to help organizations and communities involve youth in meaningful decision-making roles.

LISTEN

http://www.lisn.org/
The Local Initiative Support Training and Education Network (LISTEN) identifies, convenes, trains, and supports urban youth age 14 to 29 to serve as assets in transforming their communities and solving urban programs.

Movement Strategy Center

http://www.movementstrategy.org/
The center supports joint vision and collective action among youth and adults in order to bring about strategic community change.

National Council of La Raza–Center for Emerging Latino Leadership

http://www.nclr.org/
The center is designed to increase the number, skills, and influence of young Latino leaders in the United States by building a national network that supports and strengthens programs and organizations that develop Latino youth.

National 4-H Council

http://www.fourhcouncil.edu/
The council provides grants, establishes programs and initiatives, designs and publishes curriculum and reference materials, and creates linkages fostering innovation and shared learning to advance the 4-H youth development movement, building a world in which youth and adults learn, grow, and work together as catalysts for positive change.

Search Institute

http://www.search-institute.org/
The institute provides leadership, knowledge, and resources to promote healthy children, youth, and communities.

Study Circles Resource Center

http://www.studycircles.org
This organization helps communities organize small-group, democratic, peer-led discussions that bring together diverse people to address critical issues; it has resources to help communities involve young people in study circle programs.

What Kids Can Do

http://www.whatkidscando.org/
This site includes examples of how young people have worked with adults on projects that combine powerful learning with public purpose.

YMCA Civic Engagement Initiative

http://www.ymcacivicengagement.org/
This YMCA initiative promotes the development of civic engagement attitudes, skills, and behaviors in young people.

Youth in Focus

http://www.youthinfocus.net/
This organization supports youth-led research, evaluation, and planning to create organizational and community change.

Youth Noise

http://www.youthnoise.com/
This Web site links young people around the United States with news and nonprofit partners to spark youth action and youth voice.

Youth on Board

http://www.youthonboard.org/
This organization strives to revolutionize the role of young people in society by preparing youth to be leaders and decision makers in all aspects of their lives, and ensuring that policies, practices, and laws reflect young people's role as full and valued members of their communities.

Youth Service America

http://www.ysa.org/
This resource center partners with thousands of organizations committed to increasing the quality and quantity of volunteer opportunities for young people in the United States. It also sponsors a database of volunteer opportunities at http://www.servenet.org.

Civic Education Resources

Carnegie Foundation for the Advancement of Teaching

http://www.carnegiefoundation.org/
The foundation is a major center for research and policy studies about teaching.

CHOICES Program at Brown University

http://www.choices.edu/
The program engages students at the secondary level in international issues and contributes to a renewal of civic engagement among young people in the United States. The Web site offers "Teaching with the News" curriculum materials.

Constitutional Rights Foundation

http://www.crf-usa.org/
The foundation seeks to instill in youth a deeper understanding of citizenship through values expressed in the Constitution of the United States and its Bill of Rights, and educate them to become active and responsible participants in U.S. society. The Web site includes online lesson plans, teaching resources, and a service learning mini-grant competition.

International Consortium for Higher Education, Civic Responsibility and Democracy

http://iche.sas.upenn.edu/
This Web site has a page of online resources for civic education at http://iche.sas.upenn.edu/online/civic.htm.

KidsVotingUSA

http://www.kidsvotingusa.org
This organization works with schools and communities to enhance civics education and provide youth an authentic voting experience. Participat-

ing students visit official polling sites on election day, and cast a ballot similar in content to the official ballot.

National Alliance for Civic Education (NACE)

http://www.cived.net/
The alliance is a network of about 150 people and organizations dedicated to promoting civic education.

National Center for Learning and Citizenship

http://www.ecs.org/html/projectsPartners/clc/clc_main.htm
The center, operated by the Education Commission of the States, works on several interrelated fronts: leadership and service learning, citizenship and civic education, and policy. It provides resources to help teachers, administrators, policymakers, and leaders use and promote service learning and citizenship education.

National Student/Parent Mock Election

http://www.nationalmockelection.org/
The National Student/Parent Mock Election makes students and parents aware of the power of their ballot by actively involving them in a full-fledged campaign and national election; it also sponsors corresponding educational curriculum for schools.

PBS Democracy Project

http://www.pbskids.org/democracy/
This PBS Web site includes online lessons on voting and government for kids.

Project 540

http://www.gse.upenn.edu/cssc/project540/
Based at Providence College, Project 540 gives 100,000 students nationwide the opportunity to talk about issues that matter to them and to turn these conversations into real school and community change. In face-to-face and online dialogues, students explore what concerns them most and make specific recommendations to transform high schools and communities into places of genuine engagement.

Public Achievement

http://www.publicachievement.org/
This international youth initiative focuses on the most basic concepts of citizenship, democracy, and public work. Public Achievement draws on the talents and desires of ordinary people to build a better world and to create a different kind of politics.

Youth Leadership Initiative

http://www9.youthleadership.net/index.jsp
This Web site provides free civic education classroom resources to teachers. Each fall, YLI conducts the largest online mock election in the nation, using individualized e-ballots.

Bibliography

Adams, M., & Collins, A. (1979). A schema-theoretic view of reading. In R. Freedle (Ed.), *New directions in discourse processing.* Norwood, NJ: Ablex.

Alexander, P., & Murphy, P. (1998). The research base for APA's learner-centered principles. In N. M. Lambert & B. L. McCombs (Eds.), *Issues in school reform: A sampler of psychological perspectives on learner-centered schools* (pp. 25–60). Washington, DC: American Psychological Association.

Alexander, P. A., Kulikowich, J. M., & Schulze, S. K. (1994). The influence of topic knowledge, domain knowledge, and interest on the comprehension of scientific exposition. *Learning and Individual Differences, 6,* 379–397.

Allen, J. (1999). *Words, words, words.* Portland, ME: Stenhouse Publishers.

Allen, J. (2000). *Yellow brick roads: Shared and guided paths to independent reading 4–12.* Portland, ME: Stenhouse Publishers.

Allen-Meares, P., Washington, R., & Welsh, B. (1996). *Social work services in schools.* Boston, MA: Allyn & Bacon.

Alvermann, D. (2001). *Effective literacy instruction for adolescents.* Chicago: National Reading Conference.

Anderson, R., Wilson, P., & Fielding, L. (1988). Growth in reading and how children spend their time outside of school. *Reading Research Quarterly, 23,* 285–303.

Anderson, R. C., & Pearson, P. D. (1984). A schema-theoretic view of basic processes in reading comprehension. In P. D. Pearson (Ed.), *Handbook of reading research* (pp. 255–291). New York: Longman.

Arhar, J. (1997). The effects of interdisciplinary teaming on teachers and students. In J. Irvin (Ed.), *What current research says to the middle level practitioner* (pp. 49–58). Columbus, OH: National Middle School Association.

Armbruster, B. (1996). Considerate texts. In D. Lapp, J. Flood, & N. Farnan (Eds.), *Content area reading and learning: Instructional strategies* (pp. 47–57). Needham Heights, MA: Allyn & Bacon.

Armbruster, B., & Anderson, T. (1984). Structures of explanations in history textbooks or so what if Governor Stanford missed the spike and hit the rail? *Journal of Curriculum Studies, 16,* 181–194.

Au, K. (1993). *Literacy instruction in multicultural settings.* Orlando, FL: Harcourt Brace.

Baldwin, R. S., Ford, J. C., & Readance, J. E. (1981). Teaching word connotations: An alternative strategy. *Reading World, 21,* 103–108.

Banks, J. (1993). Approaches to multicultural curriculum reform. In J. Banks & C. Banks (Eds.), *Multicultural education: Issues and perspectives* (2nd ed., pp. 195–214). Boston, MA: Allyn & Bacon.

Baumann, J. F., Kame'enui, E. J., & Ash, G. (2003). Research on vocabulary instruction: Ode to Voltaire. In J. Flood, J. M. Jensen, D. Lapp, & J. R. Squire (Eds.), *Handbook on teaching the English language arts* (2nd ed., pp. 752–785). Mahwah, NJ: Lawrence Erlbaum.

Beane, J. (1993). *A middle school curriculum: From rhetoric to reality* (2nd ed.). Columbus, OH: National Middle School Association.

Beck, I., McKeown, M. G., Hamilton, R., & Kucan, L. (1997). *Questioning the author.* Newark, DE: International Reading Association.

Beck, I. L., McKeown, M. G., & Kucan, L. (2002). *Bringing words to life: Robust vocabulary instruction.* New York: Guilford Press.

Blachowicz, C. (1986). Making connections: Alternatives to the vocabulary notebook. *Journal of Reading, 29*(2), 643–649.

Blachowicz, C., & Lee, J. (1991). Vocabulary development in the whole literacy classroom. *The Reading Teacher, 45*(3), 188–194.

Blachowicz, C., & Ogle, D. (2001). *Reading comprehension: Strategies for independent learners.* New York: Guilford Press.

Boone, B. (2000). Lessons from a vocabulary journal. *Voices from the Middle, 7*(4), 18–23.

Brady, C., & Roden, P. (2002) . *The DBQ Project.* Evanston, IL: Authors.

Bransford, J. D., Brown, A., & Cocking, R. R. (1999). *How people learn: Brain, mind, experience, and school.* Washington, DC: National Academies Press.

Britt, M., Rouet, J., Georgi, M., & Perfetti, C. (1994). Learning from history texts: From causal analysis to argument models. In G. Leinhardt, I. Beck, & C. Stainton (Eds.), *Teaching and learning in history* (pp. 47–84). Hillsdale, NJ: Lawrence Erlbaum.

Brophy, J. (1998). *Motivating students to learn.* Boston: McGraw-Hill.

Buehl, D. (2001). *Classroom strategies for interactive learning* (2nd ed.). Newark, DE: International Reading Association.

Buikema, J. L., & Graves, M. F. (1993). Teaching students to use context cues to infer word meanings. *Journal of Reading, 36*(6), 450–457.

Burden, Paul. (2003). *Classroom management; creating a successful K-12 learning community.* Hoboken, NJ: Wiley Jossey-Bass.

California State Department of Education: Middle School Task Force. (1987). *Caught in the middle: Educational reform for young adolescents in California public schools.* Sacramento, CA: California State Department of Education.

Campaign for the Civic Mission of Schools. (2004). *Resources and strategies.* Retrieved October 2006 from http://www.civicmissionof schools.org/site/resources/edresources

Carnegie Council on Adolescent Development. (1989). *Turning points: Preparing American youth for the 21st century.* New York: Carnegie Corporation.

Carr, E., & Ogle, D. (1987). KWL-Plus: A strategy for comprehension and summarization. *Journal of Reading, 30,* 626–631.

Caverly, D., Mandeville, T., & Nicholson, S. (1995). PLAN: A study-reading strategy for informational text. *Journal of Adolescent & Adult Literacy, 39,* 190–199.

Checkley, K. (2004, August). Meeting the needs of the adolescent learner. *ASCD Education Update, 46*(5).

Ciborowski, J. (1998). *Textbooks and the students who can't read them: A guide to teaching content.* Cambridge, MA: Brookline Books.

CIRCLE: The Center for Information & Research on Civic Learning & Engagement. (2001). *Civic engagement quiz—full version.* Retrieved February 2007 from http://www.civicyouth.org/PopUps/Final_Civic_Inds_Quiz_2006.pdf.

CIRCLE: The Center for Information & Research on Civic Learning & Engagement. (2002).

Quick facts. Retrieved January 2005 from http://www.civicyouth.org/quick/volunteer.htm

CIRCLE: The Center for Information & Research on Civic Learning & Engagement. (2004, February). *Themes emphasized in social studies and civics classes: New evidence.* Retrieved January 2005 from http://www.civicyouth.org/PopUps/fact_sheet_civic_ed.pdf

CIRCLE: The Center for Information & Research on Civic Learning & Engagement. (2005, January). *Youth voting in the 2004 election.* Retrieved January 2005 from http://www.civicyouth.org/PopUps/FactSheets/FS-PresElection04.pdf

Cobblestone Magazine. (2004). Voting rights. *25*(3).

Cole, R. (Ed.). (1998). *Educating everybody's children.* Alexandria, VA: Association for Supervision and Curriculum Development.

Cooper, L., Allen, D., & Newman, S. (2003, March/April). Keeping it real. *Harvard Education Letter.*

Cunningham, A., & Stanovich, K. E. (1998). What reading does for the mind. *American Educator, 22*(1), 8–15.

Curtis, M., & Longo, A. (2001, November). *Teaching vocabulary to adolescents to improve comprehension.* Retrieved May 15, 2005, from http://www.readingonline.org/articles/curtis/index.html

Darling-Hammond, L. (2000). [Speech], Association for the Advancement of International Education, San Francisco.

Doty, J., Cameron, G., & Barton, M. (2003). *Teaching reading in social studies.* Aurora, CO: Mid-continent Regional Educational Laboratory.

Duke, N., & Pearson, D. (2002). Effective practices for developing reading comprehension. In A. Farstrup & S. J. Samuels (Eds.), *What research has to say about reading instruction* (pp. 205–242). Newark, DE: International Reading Association.

Eccles, J., & Wigfield, A. (1997). Young adolescent development. In J. Irvin (Ed.), *What current research says to the middle level practitioner* (pp. 15–30). Columbus, OH: National Middle School Association.

Fabes, R. A., Carlo, G., Kupanoff, K., & Laible, D. (1999). Early adolescence and prosocial/moral behavior: The role of individual processes. *Journal of Early Adolescence, 19*(1), 5–19.

Far West Laboratory. (1989). *Cooperative learning in the classroom.* San Francisco: Far West Laboratory.

Frayer, D. A., Frederick, W. C., & Klausmeier, H. J. (1969). *A schema for testing the level of concept mastery* (Technical Report No. 16). Madison, WI: University of Wisconsin Research and Development Center for Cognitive Learning.

Gee, J. (1996). *Social linguistics and literacies: Ideologies in discourses* (2nd ed.). London, England: Taylor & Francis.

Glenn, J., & Hergert, L. (2004). The civic mission of schools. In Carl Glickman (Ed.), *Letters to the next president: What we can do about the real crisis in public education* (pp. 201–206). New York: Teachers College Press.

Glickman, C. (Ed.). (2004). *Letters to the next president: What we can do about the real crisis in public education.* New York: Teachers College Press.

Graves, M., & Hammond, H. (1980). A validated procedure for teaching prefixes and its effects on students' ability to assign meaning to novel words. *Perspectives on Reading Research and Instruction: Twenty-ninth Yearbook of the National Reading Conference, 29,* 184–188.

Greaney, V. (1980). Factors related to amount and type of leisure reading. *Reading Research Quarterly, 15,* 337–357.

Grinder, J., & Bandler, R. (1976). *The structure of magic.* Palo Alto, CA: Science and Behavior Books.

Guthrie, J. T., & Davis, M. H., (2003). Motivating struggling readers in middle school through an engagement model of classroom practices. *Reading & Writing Quarterly, 19,* 59–85.

Haley, A. N., & Watson, D. C. (2000). In-school literacy extension: Beyond in-school suspension. *Journal of Adolescent & Adult Literacy, 43,* 654–661.

Hayes, D., & Ahrens, M. (1988). Vocabulary simplification for children: A special case of "motherese." *Journal of Child Language, 15,* 395–410.

Hegarty, M., Carpenter, P., & Just, M. (1991). Diagrams in the comprehension of scientific texts. In R. Barr, M. Kamil, P. Mosenthal, & P. Pearson (Eds.), *Handbook of reading research II* (p. 652). White Plains, NY: Longman.

Heimlich, J.E., & Pittelman, S.D. (1986). *Semantic mapping: Classroom applications*. Newark, NJ: International Reading Association.

Helms, S. (2005, January). *How individuals begin volunteering*. Center for Information & Research on Civic Learning & Engagement (CIRCLE). Retrieved January 2005 from http://www.civicyouth.org/PopUps/FactSheets/FS_How_vol_began.pdf

Hoffman, J.V. (1992). Critical reading/thinking across the curriculum: Using I-charts to support learning. *Language Arts, 69,* 121–127.

Holt, T. (1995). *Thinking historically*. New York: College Board.

Ivey, G., & Baker, M. (2004, March). Phonics instruction for older students? Just say no. *Educational Leadership, 61*(6), 35–39.

Jenkins, J.R., Matlock, B., & Slocum, T.A. (1989). Approaches to vocabulary instruction: The teaching of individual word meanings and practice in deriving word meaning from context. *Reading Research Quarterly, 24,* 214–235.

Jensen, E. (1998). *Teaching with the brain in mind*. Alexandria, VA: Association for Supervision and Curriculum Development.

Johnson, D., Johnson, R., & Holubec, E. (1994). *The new circles of learning*. Alexandria, VA: Association for Supervision and Curriculum Development.

Johnson, D.D., & Pearson, P.D. (1984). *Teaching reading vocabulary* (2nd ed.). New York: Holt, Rinehart, & Winston.

Johnson, D.D., Toms-Bronowski, S., & Pittelman, S.D. (1982). *An investigation of the effectiveness of semantic mapping and semantic feature analysis with intermediate grade level students*. (Program Rep. No. 83-3). Madison, WI: University of Wisconsin, Wisconsin Center for Educational Research.

Johnston, J. (1992). Youth as cultural capital: Learning how to be. In J. Irvin (Ed.), *Transforming middle level education: Perspectives and possibilities* (pp. 46–62). Needham, MA: Allyn & Bacon.

Jones, B.F., Palincsar, A.S., Ogle, D., & Carr, E. (1987). *Strategic teaching and learning: Cognitive instruction in the content areas*. Alexandria, VA: Association for Supervision and Curriculum Development.

Kagan, S. (1992). *Cooperative learning*. San Juan Capistrano, CA: Cooperative Learning Resources for Teachers.

Klemp, R. (1996). Cooperative literacy through cooperative discipline: A management system to support cooperative learning ventures in middle level classrooms. *Journal of the New England League of Middle Schools, 9*(1), 18–23.

Klemp, R. (1999, Spring). The middle school peace institutes. *In Focus, 38,* 4–12.

Klemp, R. (2002, Fall). Peer to peer accountability through cooperative literacy. *In Focus, 31,* 20–29.

Klemp, R., Hon, J., & Shorr, A. (1993). Cooperative literacy for the middle school: A learning strategy based approach. *Middle School Journal, 24*(3), 19–27.

Kobrin, D. (1996). *Beyond the textbook: Teaching history using documents and primary sources*. Portsmouth, NH: Heinemann.

Kurtz, K., Rosenthal, A., & Zukin, C. (2003). *Citizenship: A challenge for all generations*. Retrieved January 2005 from http://www.ncsl.org/public/trust/citizenship.pdf

Laflamme, J.G. (1997). The effect of the multiple exposure vocabulary method and the target reading/writing strategy on test scores. *Journal of Adolescent and Adult Literacy, 40*(5), 372–381.

Lenski, S., Wham, M.A., & Johns, J. (1999). Reading and learning strategies for middle and high school students. Dubuque, IA: Kendall/Hunt Publishing Co.

Levine, P., & Lopez, M. (2002). *Youth voter turnout has declined, by any measure*. Retrieved November 2004 from http://www.civicyouth.org/research/products/Measuring_Youth_Voter_Turnout.pdf

Levine, P., & Lopez, M. (2004). *Themes emphasized in social studies and civics classes: New evidence*. Retrieved November 2004 from http://www.civicyouth.org/PopUps/FactSheets/FS_Themes_Emphasized_SocStudies_Civics.pdf

Lightfoot, J., (n.d.). Outline of Sam Wineburg's "On the reading of historical texts." Retrieved January 2005 from http://home.earthlink.net/~judylightfoot/Wineburg.html.

Limbach, B., & Waugh, W. (2005). Questioning the lecture format. *Thought & Action, XXI,* 47–54. Washington, DC: National Education Association.

Lipka, R. (1997). Enhancing self-concept/self-esteem in young adolescents. In J. Irvin (Ed.), *What current research says to the middle level practitioner* (pp. 31–40).

Columbus, OH: National Middle School Association.

Los Angeles Unified School District. (1992). *Educating for diversity: A framework for multicultural and human relations education.* Los Angeles: Author.

Lutkus, A. D., Weiss, A. R., Campbell, J. R., Mazzeo, J., & Lazer, S. (1999, November). *NAEP 1998 civics report card for the nation.* Retrieved November 2004 from http://nces.ed.gov/nationsreportcard/pubs/main1998/2000457.asp

Marzano, R., & Pickering, D. (2005). *Building academic vocabulary: Teacher's manual.* Alexandria, VA: Association for Supervision and Curriculum Development.

Marzano, R., Pickering, D., & Pollock, J. (2001). *Classroom instruction that works.* Alexandria, VA: Association for Supervision and Curriculum Development.

McCarthy, C. (1992, September). Why we must teach peace. *Educational Leadership, 50*(1), 5–9.

McKeown, M. G. (1993). Creating effective definitions for young word learners. *Reading Research Quarterly, 28*(1), 16–31.

Meier, D. (2002). *The power of their ideas: Lessons for America from a small school in Harlem.* Boston: Beacon Press.

Milgram, R. (1992). A portrait of diversity: The middle level student. In J. Irvin (Ed.), *Transforming middle level education* (pp. 16–27). Boston, MA: Allyn & Bacon.

MUN-USA. (2005). Model U.N. facts and questions. Downloaded February 11, 2005, from http://www.unausa.org

Nagy, W. (1988). *Teaching vocabulary to improve reading comprehension.* Newark, DE: International Reading Association.

Nagy, W., Anderson, R. C., & Herman, R. (1987). Learning word meanings from context during normal reading. *American Educational Research Journal, 24,* 237–270.

Nagy, W. E., Diakidoy, I. N., & Anderson, R. C. (1993). The acquisition of morphology: Learning the contribution of suffixes to the meanings of derivatives. *Journal of Reading Behavior, 25*(2), 155–170.

National Assessment of Educational Progress (NAEP). (1996). *Reading report card: Findings for the nation and states.* Washington, DC: U.S. Department of Education, Office of Educational Research and Improvement.

National Council for the Social Studies. (1997). *Fostering civic virtue: Character education in the social studies.* Retrieved December 2004 from http://www.socialstudies.org/positions/character/

National Council for the Social Studies. (2004). About NCSS. Retrieved September 17, 2004, from http://www.socialstudies.org/about

National Council for the Social Studies. (2005). *A vision of powerful teaching and learning in the social studies: Building social understanding and civic efficacy.* Retrieved December 2004, from http://www.socialstudies.org/positions/powerful/

Ogle, D. (1989). The Know, Want to Know, Learn Strategy. In K. D. Muth (Ed.), *Children's comprehension of text: Research into practice* (pp. 205–223). Newark, DE: International Reading Association.

Ogle, D., & Blachowicz, C. (2002). Helping students comprehend informational text. In M. Pressley & C. Block (Eds.), *Comprehension instruction: Research-based practices* (pp. 259–274). New York: Guilford Press.

Patberg, J. P., Graves, M. F., & Stibbe, M. A. (1984). Effects of active teaching and practice in facilitating students' use of context clues. In *Changing perspectives on research in reading language processing and instruction. Thirty-third yearbook of the National Reading Conference* (Vol. 33, pp. 146–151). Rochester, NY: National Reading Conference.

Patrick, H., Hicks, L., & Ryan, A. (1997). Relations of perceived social efficacy and social goal pursuit to self-efficacy for academic work. *Journal of Early Adolescence, 17*(2) 109–128.

Quindlen, T. (Ed.). (2004). *ASCD Education Update.* Alexandria, VA: Association for Supervision and Curriculum Development.

RAND Reading Study Group. (2003). *Reading for understanding: Toward an R & D program in reading comprehension.* Santa Monica, CA: RAND.

Robb, L., Klemp, R., & Schwartz, W. (2002). *Reader's handbook: A student guide for reading and learning.* Wilmington, MA: Great Source.

Rodriguez, L. (2004). A message from the vice president. *The Delegate.* Retrieved from http://www.unausa.org

Routliffe, K. (2005, January 20). Senior studies: Program invites students to help others in the world. *Evanston* [IL] *Review.*

Sautter, C. (1995). Standing up to violence. *Kappan, 76*(5), 1–12.

Schine, J. (1997). Service learning and young adolescent development: A good fit. In J. Irvin (Ed.), *What current research says to the middle level practitioner* (pp. 257–264). Columbus, OH: National Middle School Association.

Schwartz, R.M., & Raphael, T.E. (1985). Concept of definition: A key to improving students' vocabulary. *The Reading Teacher, 39*(2), 198–205.

Shapiro, S., & Klemp, R. (1996). The interdisciplinary team organization: Promoting teacher efficacy and collaboration. *Michigan Middle School Journal, 20*(2), 26–32.

Sinatra, R., & Dowd, C. (1999). Using syntactic and semantic clues to learn vocabulary. *Journal of Reading, 35*(3), 224–229.

Smith, F. (1994). *Understanding reading: A psycholinguistic analysis of reading and learning to read* (5th ed.). Hillsdale, NJ: Erlbaum.

Sousa, D. (2001). *How the brain learns.* Thousand Oaks, CA: Corwin Press.

Sprenger, M. (1999). *Learning and memory: The brain in action.* Alexandria, VA: Association for Supervision and Curriculum Development.

Stahl, S. (1986). Three principles of effective vocabulary instruction. *Journal of Reading, 29,* 662–671.

Stahl, S. (1999). *Vocabulary development.* Cambridge, MA: Brookline Books.

Stahl, S., & Fairbanks, M. (1986). The effects of vocabulary instruction: A model-based meta-analysis. *Review of Educational Research, 56,* 72–110.

Taylor, B.M., Frye, B.J., & Maruyama, G.M. (1990). Time spent reading and reading growth. *American Educational Research Journal, 27,* 351–362.

Toms-Bronowski, S. (1983). An investigation of the effectiveness of selected vocabulary teaching strategies with intermediate grade level students. Doctoral dissertation, University of Wisconsin, Madison. *Dissertation Abstracts International, 44,* 1405A. (University Microfilms, No. 83-16, 238).

Torney-Purta, J., & Barber, C.H. (2004). *Strengths and weaknesses in U.S. students' knowledge and skills: Analysis from the IEA Civic Education Study.* Retrieved January 2005 from http://www.civicyouth.org/PopUps/FactSheets/FS_CivicKnowledge.pdf

Torney-Purta, J., Lehmann, R., Oswald, H., & Schulz, W. (2001). *Citizenship and education in twenty-eight countries: Civic knowledge and engagement at age fourteen.* Retrieved January 2005 from http://www2.hu-berlin.de/empir_bf/Exe_Sum_embargoed.pdf

Vacca, R., & Vacca, J. (1999). *Content area reading: Literacy and learning across the curriculum* (6th ed.). New York: Longman.

Walker, H.M., Ramsey, E., & Gresham, F.M. (2003). Early intervention can reduce antisocial behavior—and win back teaching time. *American Educator,* Winter 2003/2004.

Webster's Ninth New Collegiate Dictionary. (1983). Springfield, MA: Merriam-Webster.

White, T.G., Sowell, J., & Yanagihara, A. (1989). Teaching elementary students to use word-part clues. *The Reading Teacher, 42,* 302–309.

Wiggins, G., & McTighe, J. (2005). *Understanding by design* (2nd ed.). Alexandria, VA: Association for Supervision and Curriculum Development.

Wineburg, S. (2001). *Historical thinking and other unnatural acts.* Philadelphia: Temple University Press.

Wineburg, S., & Martin, D. (2004, September). Reading and rewriting history. *Educational Leadership, 62*(1), 42–45.

Woiwode, L. (1992). Television: The Cyclops that eats books. *Imprimis, 21*(2), 1.

Wynn, M. (1993). Proprietary vocabulary acquisition: A creative, thematic adventure. *Reading Horizons, 33*(5), 389–400.

Wysocki, B.L. (1999). Evaluating students in a course on social advocacy. *Social Education, 63*(6), 346–350.

Yell, M.M., & Scheurman, G. (2004). A link to the past: Engaging students in the study of history. *NCSS Bulletin, 102.* Silver Spring, MD: National Council for the Social Studies.

Index

Figures are indicated with an italicized *f* following the page number.

About the Authors

Donna Ogle is Professor of Reading and Language at National-Louis University (NLU) in Chicago, Illinois. She is involved in research and staff development projects in the U.S. and abroad, in Asia, South America, and Eastern Europe. She is currently directing two middle school literacy projects, Project ALL—Advancing Literacy for Learning and the Transitional Adolescent Literacy Project in Chicago Public Schools. Donna has served as a consultant to the NLU's Adventures of the American Mind Project, the Teaching American History grant (Creating A Community of Scholars) and Picturing Chicago, an NEH funded grant. She served as president of the International Reading Association 2001–2002, and as executive officer from 1999–2001. She is the author of several books and many professional articles, chapters, and student materials. She is perhaps best known as developer of the K-W-L learning strategy.

Ron Klemp has been with the LA Unified School district since 1973. He taught reading, English, and social studies in the inner city of Los Angeles at a junior high and a high school. He was a dean of discipline for 10 years at two middle schools and was a facilitator at the district's Secondary Northridge Practitioner Center, a professional development program for new and continuing service teachers. He has presented cooperative literacy in several states at local and national conferences. He has taught at California State University, Northridge, since 1986 and also at Cal Lutheran University, and was an associate professor at

National University. He served two terms as a member of the National Middle School Association Research Committee, and has published in the *Middle School Journal, The Reading Teacher,* and various state middle school journals. He created the Middle School Peace Institutes in Los Angeles, California, and in Jackson, Mississippi. Recently he has contributed to two books on reading for secondary students. Ron can be reached at Ron.Klemp@lausd.net.

Bill McBride is a well-known national speaker, educator, and author. A former middle and high school reading specialist, English teacher, and social studies teacher, Bill presently trains teachers both nationally and internationally in content area reading methodologies. His workshops are known for both their humor and their practical application to the classroom. He holds a Masters of Education in reading and a Doctor of Education in Curriculum and Instruction from the University of North Carolina at Chapel Hill. Bill has contributed to the development of a number of school textbook series in language arts, social studies, science, and vocabulary development. He is also known for his heartwarming novel *Entertaining an Elephant.* Already in its fourteenth printing and used by school districts across the nation, the book tells the moving story of a burned-out teacher who becomes re-inspired with both his profession and his life.